THE FIRST
INFORMATION WAR

*The story of communications, computers
and intelligence systems in the Persian Gulf War*

ALAN D. CAMPEN
Contributing Editor

AFCEA International Press
Fairfax, Virginia

AFCEA International Press is the book publishing arm of AFCEA, publisher of *SIGNAL* Magazine. Acquisition and General Editorship of AIP books are under the direction of Colonel Alan D. Campen, USAF, (Ret.)

Book and jacket design by Donna Seward.

October 1992

Published by AFCEA International Press (AIP)
A Division of AFCEA Publications Department
4400 Fair Lakes Court
Fairfax, Virginia 22033-3899 USA
(703) 631-6190 or (800) 336-4583 ext. 6190

Library of Congress Cataloging-in-Publication Data

The First Information War: the story of communications, computers, and intelligence systems in the Persian Gulf War/Alan D. Campen, contributing editor.
     p. 220 cm.
     Some articles reprinted from *Signal* Magazine, official journal of the Armed Forces Communications and Electronics Association.
     "October 1992"--CIP verso t.p.
     Includes bibliographical references and index.
     ISBN 0-916159-24-8
     1. Command and control systems. 2.Military telecommunications.
     3. Military intelligence. 4. Persian Gulf War. 1991-
     -communications. I. Campen, Alan D. II Signal magazine.
     IN PROCESS
355'. 0028'5--dc20   92-33100
                                                    CIP

This book is dedicated to the men and women who built the information systems that made it possible.

CONTENTS

PREFACE

William Safire says that the *preface* to a book once was called the *apology*, wherein the author apologized for "writing the work, or for being alive." This editor makes no apology, but—as the title to the book avers—does admit to fervent biases as to what brought about victory in the Persian Gulf and that:

• this war differed fundamentally from any previous conflict;

• the outcome turned as much on superior management of *knowledge* as it did upon performances of people or weapons;

• history would overlook, misunderstand, misrepresent or deprecate the key role played by information systems and the people who built them;

• these invaluable assets would be disbanded and a precious resource lost because they were not understood; and

• if soundly grasped and properly assimilated, the principles of information warfare will lead to U.S. military forces that are not only much leaner and cheaper to field, but still capable of effective support to the nation's goals and objectives.

Our search for "ground truth" began and ended with what the Department of Defense reported to Congress about itself,[1] with other government records and with what was written by the press. Data collection had the full and unrestricted support of military and civilian officials, yet the results were disappointing.

The history of Desert Shield/Desert Storm legitimately heaps accolades on such vital matters as unity of command, highly motivated troops and stunning performance of weapons, but it is almost silent on the underlying structure of information systems without which Desert Storm could not and would not have been waged as it was: the air campaign coming most quickly to mind.

Western society and its military components have come to regard information as a utility: ubiquitous, commonly shared, commonly financed, uncommonly reliable and always available—or almost always. Forgotten are those infrequent but terrifying moments when global finance or air traffic control networks are halted by momentary lapses in computer or human behavior.

The shibboleth "Train as we fight and fight as we train" occasionally rings hollow: the deleterious effects of battle on information systems are too seldom practiced, simply because disruption to the rehearsal is too severe. The public history of this war tends to treat information systems in the same way—as a given.

Accordingly, the main thrust of our inquiry came to concentrate on what the people themselves—those who successfully overcame the obstacles—said and wrote about what they did and how they did it, and an inquiry that began with the focus on organization and doctrine ended as a chronicle of "catch-up," of Yankee ingenuity and of extraordinary improvisation by the unheralded.

Early in my military career I was counseled that clarity of vision and depth of understanding improved with the passage of time and as the square of the distance from the Pentagon. Eighteen months of sifting through the aftermath of the Persian Gulf War did nothing to weaken those postulates.

However, the delay was fortuitous, as both euphoria and gloom about war fade over time. We trust this delay yields a more accurate, balanced, reasoned and dispassionate view of certain events and entreats others to contribute.

Deep gratitude goes to the many officials—military, civil servants, contractors, consultants—who wrote, researched or were interviewed for this book. The defense establishment has more pressing things on the mind these troubling days.

Having just won a major victory, the U.S. military is now scrambling to preserve the resources needed should anyone ask them to do it again. The patience and dedication of those many individuals made a difficult task possible and often pleasurable.

The essays written by the editor were examined for technical accuracy by military services and agencies and some for compliance with military security policy. However, opinions or views are those of the editor or authors and not, necessarily, those of the Department of Defense.

---

[1] Conduct of the Persian Gulf Conflict, pursuant to Title V Persian Gulf Conflict Supplemental Authorization and Personnel Benefits Act of 1991 (Public Law 102-25).

INTRODUCTION

The United States unveiled a radically new form of warfare in the Persian Gulf in 1991. By exploiting *knowledge*, it devastated Iraq's formidable military machine, astonished the world, confounded defense critics, surprised itself and quite possibly "changed the standards for performance of U.S. forces in armed conflict."[1]

By leveraging *information*, U.S. and allied forces brought to warfare a degree of flexibility, synchronization, speed and precision heretofore unknown. More to the point, Desert Storm shows that, by leveraging information, a much smaller and less expensive military force can continue to underpin U.S. foreign policy in an unpredictable and disorderly new world.

> *When large bodies of armed men are assembled and expected to act in concert, the part played by communications cannot be overestimated.* [2]

What are we to make of the role of information in Desert Storm? Will it be a harbinger; one of those singularly rare defining moments in military history that shapes force structure and doctrine? Or, will it be dismissed as an aberration—the product of an improbable scenario and unworthy of serious study?

The answer heavily depends on how well those whose actions determine the size and shape military forces can grasp and assimilate the *essence* of information war: that is, the systems, the people, the procedures and management structures that made it work to near perfection, and without which the winning strategy might not have worked at all.

The U.S. Army's Chief of Staff called Desert Shield/Storm the "knowledge war," and its veterans are now struggling to sift useful lessons from an extraordinary scenario that exposed little of their machinery to normal war-time stresses. Unfortunately,

> *It was a war of knowledge.*

these analysts also labor from an unsteady and unsure baseline of documentation. Much of the official documentation of Desert Storm will not be helpful in understanding information warfare.

True, the Defense Department is awash in lessons learned and "after-action" reports. However, while reporting of the war was surprisingly candid, much was long on hyperbole, too often tailored to buttress arguments against declining defense budgets and—when it comes to grasping the vital role played by information systems—too often lacking in comprehension and insight.[3]

Martin Van Creveld anticipated how difficult it is to understand the military communications infrastructure when he wrote, "Few people pay any attention to long-distance telephone calls unless they are exceptionally difficult (or easy) to make. That vast organizations...are necessary to make the call possible at all is something of which most of us are only dimly aware."[4]

Fails to convey enormity of communications task and the competence with which it was fulfilled. [5]

It need not denigrate the remarkable achievements of superbly trained and motivated personnel, nor the spectacular performance of their exotic weaponry, to observe that these troops and their machines were coupled together through—and whose efforts might have been fatally hampered without—the constant flow of timely and precise battle information. However, what it took to assure that orderly flow of information is a story that was lost as after-action reports crept upward through and were filtered and tailored within the chain of command.

Justifiable Pride and Useful Modesty

"Getting the right balance between justifiable pride and useful modesty..." will be difficult, wrote Jim Hoagland in the *Washington Post*. "There is much to take pride in; there is much to be modest about in this war's conduct and aftermath," he said.

Just enough and just in time!

The performance of information systems also provides ample grounds for such mixed emotions: pride in what was achieved; modesty because we arrived so poorly prepared to fight and took so long to overcome foreseeable problems; and, finally, concerns that the U.S. military might be unable to marshall the tools and talent to arrive any better prepared on some future battlefield.

The Information Differential

Because of the strategies of deception, maneuver and speed employed by coalition forces in Desert Storm, *knowledge* came to rival weapons and tactics in importance, giving credence to the notion that an enemy might be brought to its knees principally through destruction and disruption of the means for command and control.

Some military analysts have sifted the desert sands and concluded the time has come for the military to anoint command, control, communications, computers and intelligence (C[4]I) as a formal "warfare area," a change in course already adopted, in part, by the U.S. Navy.[6]

Superior knowledge has always been an important—often decisive—factor in combat, but battles were seldom delayed and almost never halted because of severed communications. Indeed, an astute commander assumed that his communications would be disrupted, because they almost always were.

As airman and author James P. Coyne notes in his book on airpower in the Gulf: "Before the age of electronics and aerospace technology, command and control—in the modern sense of the term—was a comparatively minor element in warfare."[7]

Battles were fought, albeit inefficiently and often ineffectively, independent of the health of supporting communications. Commanders no longer can afford to be cavalier about the state of their information systems.

Desert Storm was different: knowledge—and its denial to an enemy—became an indispensable factor. Air Force official Martin Faga succinctly put it: "We could see, hear and talk all through the war. After a few hours, he could not." Using advanced technologies, coalition forces concentrated firepower to create what Joint Warfare Publication 1 calls an "information differential."[8] Then, with devastating effectiveness, they exploited that differential, first to fix and then, in a matter of days, to flatten a formidable and battle-tested military power.

> *We could see, hear and talk all through the war. After a few hours, he could not.*

It was a war where an ounce of silicon in a computer may have had more effect than a ton of depleted uranium: a provoking notion that, if true, should factor heavily in debates about how to downsize U.S. military forces and the priority to be given the role of information systems.

The strategies and tactics used with such sensational effectiveness in Desert Storm worked well because they were conducted in what Robert Hermann once called a "free-signaling environment." What the outcome might have been had the ether been less than benign, should be a matter for serious inquiry; certainly before new doctrine that rests upon the assumption of bountiful communications is hammered into place.

Understanding Information War

It is simply not possible to wage information warfare without assured dominance in the electromagnetic spectrum. The Air Force should understand this better than any: The analogy is the same as that for air supremacy. Yet, beyond a small cadre of practitioners of the arcane art of electronics, who else comprehends the elements of information warfare, their sources and the talents required to weave and maintain the intricate fabrics that make up command and control systems?

The key roles played by exotic weapons and skilled, superbly trained and motivated people were revealed through television, widely reported in the media and thoroughly documented in after-action reports. Implicit but unseen in those reports are the information systems—networks of computers and communications that synchronized the awesome air campaign and that turned dumb bombs into sure-kill weapons. Without those systems, combat forces could never have been applied so skillfully and effectively. Without those systems, the outcome of the war might have been tragically different.

> *An ounce of silicon may have been worth more than a ton of depleted uranium.*

The weapons and the tactics by which they were so skillfully employed are the product of years of careful research, excruciating testing and evaluation, realistic unit training, simulations and endless rehearsals—many just hours before Desert Shield became Desert Storm.

Not so the information systems. As one observer noted, "much of what they did from August through February had not even been dreamed of in July."[9]

Yankee Ingenuity

Many of the most critical information systems used to distribute target and battle information during Desert Storm did not exist on the day that Iraq invaded Kuwait. Instead, they were improvised, on the spot, by technicians who, upon discovering that communications and computer equipment would be late in arriving and lacked range, capacity and connectivity to meet operational needs, contrived networks by unorthodox and unauthorized use of agglomerations of military and civilian *informationware*.

Much of what they did from August through February had not even been dreamed of in July.

Further, virtually all of the long-haul telecommunications assets of the free world were brought together under the cloak of the United Nations and dedicated to this one task. Yet, even when functioning at design speeds in an undisturbed environment, some systems trailed a giant step behind customer demands. How well those systems—and the strategies and tactics they supported so effectively—would have fared under stress of enemy attack is arguable, unknown, probably unknowable and therefore a source for concern.

The essays in this book are written by people who either labored in the war zone, provided supervision and support from the United States, or had unfettered access to the information. Hopefully they will provide thoughtful and useful insights into the extraordinary improvisation needed to provide information systems that were "just enough and just in time."

Summary of Essays

DESERT STORM COMMUNICATIONS.

Ingenuity, innovation and improvisation. That theme weaves through every essay in this book. But, as "Desert Storm Communications" emphasizes (p. 1), technical foundations for these spectacular accomplishments were laid years before. Herculean efforts high up in DOD—and also in Congress—imposed standards and criteria for interoperable communications upon an Army, a Navy and an Air Force that clearly had something other than exigencies of joint warfare on their minds.

Innovative modifications or upgrades made interfaces possible.

The lead essay is a concise overview of the largest joint military communications structure ever built; a task accomplished by highly trained and motivated people in record time and one that produced systems that operated at a phenomenal 98 percent availability rate.

COMMUNICATIONS—INTEGRATED WARFARE.

Before coalition forces could fight together, they first had to talk together, and that was not easily done. "Communications Support For The High Technology Battlefield" (p. 7) describes how teams from military, contractor and civil agencies collaborated under CENTCOM guidance and with technical direction from the Defense Information Systems Agency, built a global, *integrated* communications network out of components not originally intended for that purpose. This article (along with charts) describes the voice, message and data switching systems; satellite networks; the planning, engineering, contracting and installation processes; the technical incompatibilites that were overcome; and the management structures that evolved to run the many networks.

COMMUNICATIONS—AIR WAR.

Combat forces arriving in Saudi Arabia in early November 1990 had every reason to believe that Saddam Hussein was poised to roll into that poorly defended kingdom. The first U.S. ground elements that arrived in the Gulf characterized themselves as little more than "speed bumps" in the path of one of the world's largest tank armies. So, all eyes turned to air power to blunt and delay Iraqi armor until reinforcements arrived.

We've overburdened satellites...we are demanding too much from limited assets. [10]

Tactical fighter aircraft arrived ready for combat on November 9, 1990, but the "quick reaction" communications packages they brought were intended only to plug into some existing communications infrastructure. There was no such structure, nor was there airlift to bring forward the bulky microwave, tropospheric scatter and message/voice switches the U.S. Air Force desperately needed to weave scattered fighter units and a control and airspace management system into a cohesive force.

How this challenge was overcome and the lessons learned by the Air Force are developed from interviews with and data provided by the Communications and Computer Division of the Ninth Air Force (the air component arm of the U.S. Central Command and the single airspace authority in the war) and is presented in "Information Systems and Air Warfare" (p. 23). Charts and diagrams show how tactical satellite terminals were used for theater-level trunking and the extensive voice and message switching networks that were improvised.

AIR WARFARE—FORCE MANAGEMENT.

The U.S. Air Force flew to the Persian Gulf eager to prove a deeply held belief that airpower could be a decisive factor in the war, and they were granted what airmen have heretofore been denied—single managership for all air assets in the theater of operation. They almost got more than they bargained for. The mission dropped on their platter by General Schwarzkopf put severe strains on the automated system to plan and execute their concept.

The ATO transmission process was slow and cumbersome because of inadequate interoperability. [11]

In fairness, tactical air forces did have a system—called Computer-Assisted Force Management—but it was undersized for an air operation of this magnitude, and it could not easily connect into the automated communications systems of air elements of the Navy, Army, Marines or allied air forces.

Fortunately, as the essay titled "CAFMS Goes To War" (p. 37) shows, a talented group of technicians were able to work out solutions in the field to most (not all) of the problems. As the authors say, these technicians produced just enough and just in time and, more importantly, learned what is needed to produce an information system for control of joint and coalition warfare.[12]

ELECTRONIC WARFARE.

The targets of the opening shots in Desert Storm were two Iraqi radars located just inside Iraq's border with Saudi Arabia. Hit from Army helicopters firing Hellfire missiles, these stations went silent. Moments later, a stealthy F-117 launched a 2,000 pound laser guided bomb on an interceptor control station. Those two attacks opened a door in an electronic wall through which 668 aircraft were to streak into Iraq.[13]

Electronic warfare has been a necessary and oft-times effective component of air war since World War II. But in Desert Storm, only the stealth fighter ventured into enemy airspace unaccompanied by a swarm of supporting airplanes: some launching decoys to trigger enemy radar into action; some carrying anti-radiation missiles that instantly homed in as those radars came up. Stand-off jammers were out of range of enemy weapons but close enough to blank out enemy radios. It was a devastating combination of hard and soft kill, and it wrote a new chapter in the saga of warfare.

Jamming support was normally a "go/no go" criterion for a strike. [14]

Concurrent SEAD (suppression of enemy air defense) is what U.S. Navy Captain James M. Burin calls it in his story of electronic warfare, "The Electronic Sanctuary" (p. 47). In it he describes how *hard* and *soft* combined to strike an Iraqi airfield.

INTELLIGENCE—COMMUNICATIONS SUPPORT.

Military intelligence received mixed reviews from operational commanders, and the sharpest criticism concerned inability to get current photographs into the hands of targeteers in time to be of use. That turned out to be largely a problem with communications systems. They lacked the capacity to handle data-intensive photographs; they were technically incompatible with each other and could not exchange data; or they lacked the connectivity to lower level combat units (divisions and below, airfields and ships afloat). Those problems are nothing new—the intelligence and communications communities have been squabbling over inadequate support for high data rates for years—and they will not be easily solved. The essay titled "Communications Support To Intelligence" (p. 51) delves into the problems, issues and solutions to this serious deficiency.

Dissemination was probably at the heart of our intelligence problem. [15]

INTELLIGENCE—THEATER LEVEL.

Cameras in military satellites can photograph objects as small as a foot in diameter and almost anywhere on the surface of the earth or sea. That is a remarkable achievement and one that proved useful in peering over the Iron Curtain.

However, these spy satellites usually put the images under the skilled eyes of photo interpreters in Washington who had to try to make sense of what one critic calls "a view of the battlefield seen through a straw." Further, this vital intelligence cycle does not end until reports are delivered to a combat commander or his fire support control center, at or below a division. That last step is not easily done. [16]

The author of "Extending Real-Time Intelligence to Theater Level" (p. 61) writes that "the list of intelligence lessons learned from Desert Storm already is replete with the cries of commanders for additional battlefield imagery that can be distributed in a timely

> *Tactical commanders were frustrated because needs exceeded organic capability.* [17]

manner." This essay—by the then-director of the Defense Intelligence Agency—describes what was done to get national-level intelligence to the battlefield.

ELECTRONIC RECONNAISSANCE.

The intelligence community strives mightily to screen its sources and methods and those who labor in its behalf often go unsung. Desert Shield/Desert Storm is no exception.

Flying within the 600+ strike package that hit Iraq on January 17, 1991, was "a big RC-135 Rivet Joint aircraft [that] eavesdropped electronically, pinpointing any Iraqi communicators or radar operators who were transmitting."[18]

"Ears Of The Storm" (p. 65) comes as close as current security policies permit to telling the story that may never fully be known: the tale of airmen and women who fly into the teeth of enemy air defense systems during peace and war, forcing radars to come to a posture that reveals technical and operational characteristics, that then are cataloged in an "electronic order of battle."

INTELLIGENCE SUPPORT—ARMY.

The U.S. Army—as did most other intelligence organizations—built its collection and reporting systems separately and from the bottom-up: and for good reasons.

The most useful intelligence in past wars was collected by troops in contact and passed rearward and upward.

But that was before cameras, radars and radio receivers were hung onto satellites and high-fliers, where they could reach much farther into the battlefield than could those carried by combat forces. Technology, high-speed and maneuver warfare turned the old paradigm on its head. Not many intelligence systems worked the way they needed to in the Gulf War, mainly because what had been collected and assessed could

> *We've created some real expectations among young officers about the intelligence they're going to receive.* [19]

not always be delivered to fire support centers in time to be of use.

"Responsive Communications Key To Army Intelligence" (p. 71) does not dwell in great depth on problems from Desert Shield/Storm; however, these can readily be inferred from an essay that goes into considerable detail on U.S. Army intelligence community plans and programs to build a system that will integrate intelligence from top-to-bottom and from national-to-maneuver brigade.

BATTLEFIELD TEMPLATES.

A paradox of modern battlefield technology is that an intelligence analyst in Washington, D.C. , often knows better than the infantryman what lies beyond the next hill. The challenge is to fuse that knowledge with data collected from other sources, preserve security and still get the product into the hands of the soldier before he must solve the mystery himself—the hard way.

Templates are drawings that show the disposition of enemy forces and are invaluable to those who plan attacks—even down to platoon level. Their value increases with accuracy and with timeliness. Accuracy improves as each intelligence analyst adds his piece to the puzzle: time is shortened if all analysts can work on the same template at the same time, on a virtual network. The story of how the Army accomplished this is told in "Electronic Templates" (p. 75).

INTELLIGENCE SUPPORT—AIR FORCES.

Execution of joint warfare demands products that integrate information from all sources. But the U.S. Air Force arrived in Saudi Arabia with a collection of what it calls "stovepipe systems," that is, vertical systems that collect, process and analyze and disseminate one category of intelligence without integrating other types of intelligence into the final product. This left fusing to the customers—something they had neither the skills nor time to do. As the author of "Desert War: Crucible For Intelligence Systems" (p. 81) says, the intelligence community had difficulty providing an integrated, all-source product tailored to users' needs and then finding a robust communications network to make timely deliveries of imagery.

> *The insatiable appetite for imagery and imagery-derived products could not be met.*[20]

This essay is the frank, blunt story of actions taken by the U.S. Air Force to overcome lack of an intelligence architecture in the combat theater and steps planned for the future to provide a "one-button" source through which airmen can pull the information they need from a common data base.

THE MEDIA AND WARFARE.

When the warriors in Riyadh had launched phase one of the air war at 3 a.m. on January 17, 1991, Air Force Major Rogers was sent to monitor ABC and Cable News Network, which were broadcasting live from Baghdad. CNN went off the air at the very moment that the war plan called for a bomb from an F-117 stealth fighter to penetrate the city's main telecommunications center. "The first bomb-damage assessment of the war had been delivered by network television."[21]

> *TV works past censorship—the genie cannot be put back in the bottle.*[22]

Desert Storm was and future wars will be fought in the unforgiving glare of public television. What a military commander does may be aimed as much at influencing public opinion as it is at countering the enemy. Television will be the weapon of choice in psychological warfare.

The real "media" story of Desert Storm is the impact of direct and undisciplined television coverage and the newfound access to satellite photography that surely will be available to the "CNNs" of the next war. The Defense Department and the media have negotiated new rules of engagement that govern in a battle zone, but those accords are silent on instantaneous reporting over television.

"Information, Truth and War" (p. 87) examines the role of the media in this and past wars and asks how the Fourth Estate will handle the unprecedented powers to influence events that have been thrust into their uncertain hands by space-based communications and photographic technology.

COMMUNICATIONS WITH RAPID MOVERS.

The 141st Signal Battalion faced a unique challenge in providing multi-channel communications to the 1st Armored Division. Communications doctrine could not keep pace with the speed and intensity of Old Iron sides' race of 144 kilometers in 18 hours to hit the flank of the elite Iraqi Republican Guards.

So, says the author of "Communicating on the Move" (p. 93), the battalion threw away the book on conventional signal doctrine and improvised a network completely different from its wartime signal mission: one that—"despite dust, smoke and downpours"—provided operational circuits to all maneuver commanders.

This essay follows the network configurations as they changed shape in rehearsal and on each day from February 24 through 28, 1991.

COMMUNICATIONS FOR MANEUVER WARFARE.

When the 2d Brigade, 1st Cavalry Division deployed to Saudi Arabia, it quickly realized that the doctrine and force structure tailored for a European scenario had to change to fit the expanse of desert terrain. How those changes were made is the subject of "C^2 In a Heavy Brigade" (p. 101).

The unit contrived, tested and proved the concept of a *brigade wedge* as the means to control from brigade to platoon while maneuvering a battle task force over long distances in desert terrain. Flexibility and effectiveness were limited by the command post vehicle, which could not keep pace. New command and control schemes had to be improvised because the command posts could not keep up with a force that moved 60 kilometers in 4 hours.

No commander is less fortunate then he who operates with a telegraph wire stuck into his back.[23]

The names of communications and control systems such as SINCGARS, remote access units, MSE and MCS take on new meaning when their effect on operations is explained by the brigade commander and his S3. The article explains how the concepts were developed in exercises in December, tested in the long flanking movement to the west and proved in attacks up the Wadi AL Batin and into Iraq in February 1991.

PACKET SWITCHED NETWORKS.

The most glaring deficiency in tactical communications was its inability to initially handle data communications for the myriad of users who brought their PC-based management systems to war. Tactical communications were geared to and designed for wars where troops communicated over telephones, exchanged written messages through a central communications center or dispatched couriers. "Rapid Preparation and Distribution of Battlefield Information" (p. 109) tells how a packet switched network was constructed for ARCENT using standard commercial local area networks (LAN) and connected through tactical transmission systems never designed for such purposes.

SPACE WARFARE.

Over 60 Western military satellites and more from the commercial sector were directly involved in the Persian Gulf War, connecting over 400,000 troops, aiding weather forecasters, providing detailed images of Iraqi targets, passing Scud launch warnings, providing location accuracies in dozens of feet to pilots, truck drivers and special forces, and, for the first time ever, carrying the war—instantly, live and in color—to over 100 nations. "The First Space War" (p. 121) contains a listing of all surveillance satellites and tells how the space resources of many nations contributed to the war effort.

SATELLITE COMMUNICATIONS.

The war in the Persian Gulf could never have been prosecuted as it was—and the highly integrated and carefully synchronized tactics might not have been considered seriously—had there not been high confidence that space-based sensors, cameras, radars and communications repeaters would give the coalition a decisive edge. War planners also implicitly assumed that Iraq possessed neither the ability nor the resolve to interfere with the functioning of any of those satellites. Their low-risk gamble paid off, but, as one expert was to say: "We were lucky this time."

Satellites lifted to track Soviet ICBMs provided target data to tank commanders and pilots.[24]

As with most other information systems in the Gulf War, satellites too were used in strange ways, possible only because of sound technical and management decisions made two decades ago and because a corps of experts was available to make the necessary changes, on-the-fly, and to fix things that failed at the worst possible moment.

"Silent Space Warriors" (p. 135) is the story of communications satellite networks being reworked to tie together not only far-flung nodes, but also people only a few kilometers apart. It is the story of soldiers who mounted fixed earth stations onto flat-bed trailers and chased tanks across the desert and of technicians who knew how to reactivate an aging satellite and move it half way around the world in time to join the battle.

It is also the story of international cooperation and of joint standards that permitted commercial, U.S. and foreign military communications satellites to meet and exchange signals; to put together the largest network of communications satellites in history.

INTEGRATED SWITCHING.

Tactical communicators arrive in a combat zone searching for and expecting to quickly find the plug into the vast, global strategic networks that extend their circuits back to home and the vital support that flows from the United States. They found no such plug in Saudi Arabia. Instead, they had to reach back to the United States over satellite channels, requiring tactical and strategic switching to interoperate in ways never planned.

An integrated system needs a single manager who sees all elements.

"Integrating Tactical and Strategic Switching" (p. 143) is the story of the labors of the Defense Information Systems Agency (then called DCA) to fabricate a network from tactical, strategic and commercial switched systems arrayed around the world. Working with military engineers, contractors and commercial carriers, they struggled to sort out technical incompatibilities that interrupted the smooth flow of data across many interfaces.

MARINE DATA SYSTEMS.

The U.S. Marine Corps had its data systems well in hand when the Marines arrived in the Persian Gulf. As the author says in "Established Architecture Keys Marine Data" (p. 149), "They were able to plug into a global system and access maintenance and supply information directly from the front lines." The Marines had built a global information network providing message services, E-mail and data file transfer. Even so, the scope of Gulf operations forced them to do what once had been unthinkable— put an administrative computer support van element into a tactical environment—from drawing board in August to full operation in Jubail on October 5.

SPECTRUM MANAGEMENT.

The tools employed in waging information warfare demand a well-ordered electromagnetic (radio frequency) spectrum, but these tools fall into disrepair between wars. Desert Shield was no exception. The tools and talent for efficient and effective spectrum management were not in place in August 1990. How serious conflicts were avoided over use of the ether is described in "Spectrum Management" (p. 155).

Frequency management challenges were enormous.[24]

JOINT C-E OPERATING INSTRUCTIONS.

A key tenet of information warfare is the ability to manage radio callsigns and frequencies in a way that confuses the enemy but not our own forces. Each military service has its own means to do this and did so in contingencies such as Just Cause. But, in the joint environment, all must rely on centrally prepared Joint Communications-Electronics Operating Instructions, or JCEOI. The JCEOI is not unlike the telephone book: bulky, when large numbers of forces are involved; hard to keep current when the forces structure keeps changing—as it did in Desert Shield; but devastating to a military operation if one is compromised. The Joint Staff turned to the National Security Agency to produce the JCEOI for the Persian Gulf—no other agency had the computing and printing plant power to turn out a publication that exceeded 600,000 in number before it was over. The collaboration among the Joint Staff, the military services and NSA is described in *The Joint CEOI* (p. 161).

JOINT STARS GOES TO WAR.

Joint STARS—the flying, deep probing, all weather radar plane, was a promising program in late stages of development testing when war broke out in the Persian Gulf. A series of demonstration flights in Europe had convinced senior commanders that this was just what was needed to counter the formidable Iraqi tank army. The Air Force was understandably reluctant to send its only two prototypes to war, but CINCCENT prevailed. A hastily formed unit made up of airmen, soldiers and civilians pushed two E-8A aircraft into service in days after arrival in Saudi Arabia, and the rest is history. Originally deployed as a surveillance platform— engineered to peer hundreds of miles deep and to detect movements of large enemy concentrations—J-STARS, in days, showed its potential to see small targets and to serve as a weapons control platform as well. The story is told in "Joint STARS in Desert Storm" (p.167).

Aircraft consistently ran out of ammunition before they ran low on fuel.

IRAQI COMMAND AND CONTROL.

Measured by any standard, Iraq had fielded a huge and modern military force: one to be seriously reckoned with in planning the attack of coalition forces.

For one, it emulated both the shape and style of the Soviet Union—its prime mentor—and that very Soviet model had been the impetus for U.S. and NATO weapons development for more than 40 years. Moreover, it had armed itself with some of the best weapons from the United States, France and the United Kingdom. How then was this formidable force so easily and quickly subdued?

Entirely inadequate for the type of war waged against them.

"Iraqi Command and Control: The Information Differential" (p. 171) looks at that issue from a U.S. and Soviet perspective and finds consensus among disparate experts: *we will never know how well Iraq's military might have done because the initial attacks took down its control network and, with it, any hope for Iraq to know what had happened, what was about to happen and what it might do about it.* The coalition forces had taken a page from Soviet military doctrine, created a "differential in information" and won what can fairly be called *The First Information War*.

Endnotes

[1] *Airpower in the Gulf*, The Air Force Association, 1992.

[2] Van Creveld, Martin, *Technology and War*, The Free Press, 1989.

[3] A reader of the *Conduct of the Persian War, Final Report to Congress*, April 1992, might well conclude that information in that war was a critical issue only to the loser: a source of weakness, of vulnerability, but not of strength. When mention is made of information systems, it is usually to remark not on how those systems enabled what was done to be done, but, instead, upon the limitations that technical deficiencies placed upon commanders. The

report by the House Armed Services Committee, "Defense For A New Era, Lessons of the Persian Gulf War," March 20, 1992, is only marginally more helpful, noting that "...acquiring support [information?] systems consistent with high-tech weapons may be more important than buying the next generation plane or tank."

4 Van Creveld, Martin, *Command in War*, Harvard University Press, 1985.

5 Anson, Sir Peter, "The First Space War."

6 See "C⁴I: The New Linchpin," by Robert David Steele, U. S. Naval Institute *Proceedings*, July 1992. Actually, the Soviet Union moved to formalize targeting of command and control almost two decades ago when it adopted Radio-Electronic Combat (REC) as a formal doctrine and created forces to execute the concept of physical and electronic attacks on enemy command and control systems. The U.S. Navy is already moving in this direction and has formalized "Space and Electronic Warfare (SAW) as a naval warfare area. (See the article "The Electronic Sanctuary" by Captain Burin in this book.)

7 *Airpower in the Gulf*, ibid.

8 "The joint campaign should fully exploit the information differential, that is, the superior access to and ability to effectively employ information on the strategic, operational and tactical situation which advanced U.S. technologies provide our forces."

9 Paraphrased from comments by Larry Lynn, Atlantic Aerospace Research, Inc., from lecture at AFCEA International convention, June 24, 1992.

10 Boomer, Walter E., Lt. Gen., USMC, from interview in *Armed Forces Journal International*, August 1992.

11 *Conduct of the Persian Gulf War, Final Report to Congress,* April 1992.

12 It is not surprising that, given the extraordinary difficulty of connecting into and utilizing data from the Air Force's ATO, some in the Navy have another view. Those who would know more about the difficulties of meshing the vastly different U.S. Air Force and U.S. Navy concepts of air warfare are referred to "Exocets, Air Traffic, & the Air Tasking Order," *Proceedings*, August 1992.

13 *Airpower in the Gulf*, ibid.

14 Burin, James M., Capt. USN, "The Electronic Sanctuary."

15 Boomer, ibid.

16 "The available circuits simply were not able to handle the magnitude of [image] data." *Conduct of the Persian Gulf War*, ibid.

17 *Conduct of the Persian Gulf War*, ibid.

18 *Conduct of the Persian Gulf War*, ibid.

19 Boomer, ibid.

20 *Conduct of the Persian Gulf War*, ibid.

21 *Airpower in the Gulf*, ibid.

22 Whiting, John R., "War-Live," *Proceedings*, August 1991.

23 Moltke, General H. von, Sr., quoted in *Command in War*, ibid.

24 May, Ernest, "Intelligence Backing into the Future," *Foreign Affairs Summer 1992.*

DESERT STORM COMMUNICATIONS

Joseph S. Toma

In the year since Operation Desert Storm we have seen many "lessons learned" reports. Government agencies, industry, universities, and think tanks have all reached their own conclusions about what the experience means to them. Try as they did, even critics had difficulty in identifying what went wrong in the operation. That's because it was remarkably successful.

The communications community was challenged in many ways during the buildup and the war, but the community—government and industry—met successfully each challenge. We continue to analyze and write about the operation so that its lessons can be imparted to those who have a stake in maintaining and improving our capabilities.

Dramatic events that took place in the Persian Gulf region began in August 1990 when Iraq invaded Kuwait. Over several months, more than 540,000 United States military personnel deployed to the region; fought and won a war against Iraq; and returned to the United States, Europe, and the Pacific.

In July 1991, the Senate Armed Services Committee (SASC) expressed its views on the reasons for the superb performance by our military forces at all levels. The SASC found that several factors contributed to the victory: the high quality of U.S. military commanders and their personnel; tough, realistic training; streamlined joint command relationships; and sophisticated technology.

The sophisticated technology included some of the best communication equipment ever provided to U.S. forces. The communication network that supported Operation Desert Storm was the largest joint theater system ever established. It was built in record time and maintained a phenomenal 98 percent availability rate. At the height of the operation, the system supported 700,000 telephone calls and 152,000 messages per day. More than 30,000 radio frequencies were managed to provide necessary connectivity and to ensure minimum interference.

This immense network relied on circuit and message switches that had been developed under the joint TRI-TAC program. The automatic circuit switch (TTC-39A) and automatic message switch (TYC-39) were used to link long-haul communications with tactical, service-unique systems. Some of these same switches provided the interface between analog and digital systems in theater. The interoperability of these systems was the result of coordinated planning, designing, and testing begun long before Desert Storm, although additional modifications were made there under stressed conditions. From a joint perspective, the success of Desert Storm command, control, communications, and computer (C^4) systems operations was more than an engineering achievement, it was also the result of legislative, doctrinal, and training accomplishments.

Role of Communication Satellites

Satellites were the single most important factor that enabled U.S. land-based forces to transition quickly and smoothly from almost nothing to an extensive tactical communications network in the area of operations. For about 40 years, there had been a U.S. naval presence in the Persian Gulf. It began in 1949 with the establishment of the Mideast Force whose home port was the British naval base at Jufair, Bahrain. Communications from ashore to U.S. forces afloat were provided over a variety of transmission systems for fleet broadcast, teletype circuits, on-call circuits, high-speed message and data systems, as well as a variety of voice circuits.

At sea, the afloat command and control system is an aggregate of components that receives input both from within and outside the battle group. Space systems have become an integral part of battle force resources. UHF communications satellites, such as FLEETSAT, are used during normal operations as well as combat operations.

Until recently, the Persian Gulf region was almost devoid of United States global communication other than for fleet operations. The Defense Communications System (DCS) essentially stopped at Turkey in the west and at the Philippine Islands in the east. The commercial communications available in nations of the region were very limited, and military systems were just beginning to come on-line.

Two Defense Satellite Communications System (DSCS) spacecraft were available for the initial buildup: an Indian Ocean DSCS-II satellite netted into Landstuhl, Germany, and an Eastern Atlantic DSCS-III satellite netted into Croughton, England, and Fort Meade, Maryland. The size and speed of early force deployment quickly pushed these systems to their limits. In one month, the population of SHF earth terminals had increased from four to 49 in the area of operations.

By the end of October 1990, the basic command and control structure was in place. Additional communications capacity and European gateways were added to support the larger force structure that was directed. Increased connectivity into Europe was needed to tie the VII Corps to its sustaining base in Germany.

Before the air attacks began in January 1991, additional capacity had been added on DSCS, NATO satellites provided some added support, and 11 T-1 trunks were leased. Approximately 75 percent of the communications load was on DSCS, 5 percent on NATO satellites, and 20 percent on commercial satellites. There were then 127 ground mobile force and DSCS heavy terminals and 14 commercial terminals in use with the land-based forces.

Switched Networks and Terrestrial Systems

By the end of the first week of the deployments to the Persian Gulf in August 1990, communications had been established to Riyadh, Dhahran, and Al Jubayl in Saudi Arabia, and Thumrait, Oman, via a dozen ground mobile forces satellites communications terminals. Communications equipment and people continued to get priority airlift side-by-side with combat forces. Switched networks and terrestrial communications links were built to augment and replace point-to-point satellite communications being used for both intra- and inter-theater communications. By February 1991, 35 tropospheric scatter and microwave links (eight of them commercial leased) had been installed. There were 20 TRI-TAC message switches and 60 TRI-TAC voice switches in theater.

The switched networks with satellite and terrestrial links provided more than 300 Defense Switched Network (DSN) voice trunks, 26 Automatic Digital Network (AUTODIN) message circuits and numerous dedicated and data circuits. From the CONUS through DSN gateways, a Mobile Subscriber Equipment (MSE) equipped company on the move could be reached by direct dialing through TRI-TAC switches in the theater.

Packet-Switched Networks and Computers

Desert Storm-Desert Shield was the first major sustained military operation in the microprocessor era. USCENTCOM Headquarters and those of most components were supported by interconnected local area networks and computer resources both in theater and in the CONUS. Packet-switched networks supported the efficient exchange of data base information, messages, and teleconferencing. Deployment of Defense Data Network (DDN) Secure Network (DSNET) nodes and concentrator systems at lower echelons provided relief to the circuit-switched systems designed for voice telephone calls.

Reliance on computers grew as the operation continued. People who used computers in garrison took them along into the field. Thousands of computer terminals were used, most of them off-the-shelf PCs. They held up well in the desert environment, with sensible user maintenance.

Automation systems for operations, logistics and maintenance, administration, and personnel, were deployed in a variety of configurations. Some were stand alone, or connected locally; some connected individually to CONUS main frames and some connected to deployed main frames. Concentrators were used to make more efficient use of circuits. In some cases, floppy disks were hand carried from one echelon to another.

The Joint Staff, Service, CINC, and agency commands were in an intercomputer network that supported the joint mission of planning and executing the deployment, mobilization, employment, and sustainment of forces and equipment for the operation. The Joint Operational Planning and Execution System (JOPES) software is being developed in increments and runs on Honeywell main frame computers. DSNET 2, a Top Secret, secure, packet-switched network provides connectivity between sites. JOPES employs software applications that included procedures, reports, formats, and functional tools to plan joint operations.

The Dynamic Analysis Replanning Tool (DART) is an analytical tool developed outside of the JOPES system standards. The software is written in a different computer language than JOPES (C vice Ada) and operates on a Sun work station with a different data base design. DART, however, provided unique analytic capabilities not available in JOPES. It had the ability to resequence or modify the order of deployment rapidly in operational plans and permitted rapid transportation feasibility estimates.

JOPES was used early in the Desert Shield-Desert Storm deployment, and DART was effectively employed in the Phase II deployment from Europe to the Persian Gulf. Current plans are to interface the DART planning tool with JOPES so that transactions from planning and analysis in DART can be used to modify existing plans more rapidly.

Control of Air Operations

All of the services operated aircraft and fielded air defense systems in the Persian Gulf region. Desert Storm presented a challenge to put together a system where the aircraft of different services and nations could fly to and from their target assignments and not conflict with each other. The scheduling of air tasking was one side of the problem, and the real time command and control of these assets once airborne was the other. This was accomplished using various command and control platforms connected by a system begun 25 years ago called Tactical Digital Information Link (TADIL).

AWACS, E-2C, Aegis, Hawk, Patriot, and ground-based surveillance radars tracked and deconflicted the numerous air contacts, thus providing identification of friend or foe and ensuring against fratricide. All airborne contacts were tracked and passed to weapons platforms when required. The U.S. Army added a 386 microcomputer to its Patriot system a few years ago, which made it possible to include Patriot in the nets. Two Joint Surveillance and Target Attack Radar Systems (JSTARS) aircraft were put in operation in Desert Storm. Through use of the Airborne Interface System (AIS) buffer, JSTARS information also was linked by TADIL into the Air Operations Network.

Thus, several generations of technologies were made interoperable for airspace control. The result was a complex integrated system that supported up to 3,000 combined air sorties per day and controlled more than 25 air defense sites and six carrier battle group air defense platforms.

Air operations were scheduled by a single joint air tasking order (ATO), developed by the Joint Forces Air Component Commander (JFACC). The ATO was used to deconflict tasking, avoid designated firing areas and assign aircraft and ordinance for specific missions. It varied between an average of 200 pages to a high of 800 pages, detailing as many as 3,000 sorties. It was distributed daily to all the allied air units in the Area of Operations and Turkey, as well as air defense units, AWACS, and battle groups at sea. Creating the ATO every day would have been impossible without the Air Force Computer-Assisted Force Management System (CAFMS), consisting of minicomputers linked together and tying the tactical air control center to Army, Air Force, and Marine units. Since allied air forces were collocated with U.S. air forces, CAFMS could reach all the ground based air wings. There was some difficulty in getting the ATO to the carrier-based air wings, and air couriers had to be used to ferry floppy disks. The U.S. Navy has since been modifying carrier communications so that wideband links can be used for ATO and other high-speed data transfers.

The overall success of Desert Storm air operations validated the JFACC concept and demonstrated how effectively a multinational/multiservice force can execute air operations in support of a theater campaign plan. Efforts are underway to improve joint doctrine that institutionalizes the JFACC concept.

Technology and Doctrine

A major factor contributing to the coalition victory in Operation Desert Storm was that our commanders had a picture of the battlefield, and the enemy did not. That was made possible through our communications. The enemy was denied his. The public can readily identify the forces and weapons used in the war, such as the VII and XVIII Corps, M1A1s, F-14s, F-15s, F-16s, F-117 and Patriots. It knows when and where they were used. However, the communications, sensors, and computer systems that allowed the impressive array of sophisticated weaponry to be employed with such precision and impact are much less understood.

Technology and doctrine for C^4 systems have been evolving since the 1960s. This is the first conflict of such size and complexity in which C^4 systems technology made a big difference. The difference is not just in conducting operations more effectively. Communications and computing capabilities made it possible to do things very innovatively. For example, resources 7,000 miles away from the battlefield were used to assist the commanders and staffs. Technology was adapted quickly to meet operational needs. The technology and the people were flexible enough to react to changing requirements of the situation.

It seems that there are some lessons that can be drawn that have wider public sector application. What was accomplished was possible partly because of investment in organization and standards implemented far in advance of the crisis; partly because of investment in education, training, and doctrine development, and partly because of sustained support for technology and innovation.

Edited and updated from an article that originally appeared in the January 1992 issue of *IEEE Communications Magazine*.

COMMUNICATIONS SUPPORT FOR THE HIGH TECHNOLOGY BATTLEFIELD

Larry K. Wentz

Just enough, just in time, and good old Yankee ingenuity is a correct but incomplete and imperfect description of the heroic activities that provided coalition forces in the Persian Gulf with the largest integrated strategic-tactical communications network ever built. Add teamwork by dedicated and well trained people, innovation, and some plain old good luck, and one begins to get a sense of the incredible activities that came together to produce the information system that allowed Operation Desert Storm to happen in the manner that it did.

The rapid pace of the build-up during Desert Shield and the continuous movement of forces during Desert Storm heaped a formidable task on communicators, mainly because they lacked a comprehensive joint architecture to guide development of an integrated network and helped forestall or at least resolve the many interoperability issues that tend to arise when dissimilar equipments are hurredly pieced together.

Add to this formula the numerous and unprecedented political, operational, and security uncertainties that had to be first resolved in real-time before technical solutions could be applied.

Before coalition forces could fight together, they first had to talk together, but there were major communications interoperability problems among the nations, and the United States itself fielded several generations of analog and digital tactical communications equipment, further compounding an already complex systems integration task.

Despite these difficulties, a flexible and responsive network was built in record time; and it worked!

In addition, some valuable lessons were learned about managing a global, space-based, joint, integrated communications network when forces are employed under the guidelines of the Goldwater-Nichols Act.

Background

The invasion of Kuwait by Iraqi forces achieved tactical surprise and revealed significant voids in the data needed to prosecute a response by the United States. For example, the Defense Information Systems Agency (DISA, formerly DCA) maintains an inventory of communications resources in areas of the world of potential interest to the United States, but that portion covering the Persian Gulf area was incomplete and virtually useless during the early, frantic build-up of forces.

Although the U.S. Central Command (CENTCOM) had just conducted an exercise in July 1990 that projected an Iraqi invasion of Kuwait, the supporting annexes of the operation plan that detail who and what goes where and when had not yet been developed and, in any event, could never have foreseen the massive international build-up of forces about to cascade into Saudi Arabia. As a result, the Communications Annex to the operations plan was developed in reaction to, not in anticipation of, the forces as they arrived on the scene.

Everything that could be used was used. Operation Desert Shield brought about the assemblage of a mix of commercial and long-haul strategic and tactical military communications, but without the benefit of blueprints for their technical integration. The enormity and complexity of this accomplishment is not well enough recognized outside of the small community of experts who brought it off.

The challenges confronting the CENTCOM J-6 at the outset of this operation were formidable. There was no plan, and the foundation for building such a plan was shifting daily as perceptions of military need changed. The threat of invasion of Saudi Arabia was obvious, so the highest priority was to get combat forces—the "shooters"—on the ground quickly. Communications support for the early arriving forces was limited to tactical satellite terminals and whatever else the troops could carry into the theater on their backs—airlift was inadequate for the heavy and bulky terrestrial communications systems that normally provide theater-level backbone communications.

On August 8, 1990, the Central Command deployed the first contingent of communications equipment and personnel from the Joint Communications Support Element.[1] The XVIII Airborne Corps, 1st Marine Expeditionary Force, and the Ninth Air Force also deployed during the initial phase of Desert Shield, adding their resources of light-weight satellite equipment. The communications capabilities deployed during this phase were used to support command and control connectivity among the Commander-in-Chief in Riyadh, his component commands, and the National Command Authorities in Washington. It was "just enough and just in time."

The early communications capabilities consisted of UHF and SHF satellite communications, some high frequency radio, secure voice, facsimile and limited access to the Defense Switched Network (voice), the Automatic Digital Network (message), and to the World-wide Military Command and Control System (WWMCCS).

Despite a lack of doctrinal guidance or warplan requirements for data services to and within the theater, on August 27 the U.S. Army Information Systems Command extended its Internet services through a theater gateway, providing early support for E-mail, file transfer, and remote log-in services. The intelligence community also provided early secure data network services through extension to the theater of the CENTCOM/SOCOM Rear Garrison automated intelligence local area network at MacDill Air Force Base in Florida. Bridges were employed to interconnect the LANs, and connectivity was provided through a commercial satellite link.

With the President's order to deploy the VII Corps from Germany, the military strategy shifted to the offense which, in turn, laid a new set of unplanned operational needs on the burgeoning communications network.

Network planning, implementation, and management of all phases of this operation involved the CINC, the JCS, the military services, DISA, and other DoD agencies, and required significant collaboration and strong leadership. Early in the operation, the CENTCOM J-6 assumed control for all long-haul communications into and within the AOR. While initially contested, this high degree of centralized control proved essential in ensuring that the limited communications resources were equitably shared and applied to the CINC's priorities.

The initial communications problem dealt with the apportionment of organic tactical assets carried into the theater by the Army, Marine Corps and Air Force. This equipment was intended to interconnect the component headquarters with their subordinate combat forces and to provide them with access to the common-user voice and message networks. Instead, many of these organic resources had to be diverted to establish the in-theater joint common-user backbone network and to provide other units with access to long-haul networks.

As air and surface transports brought more communications equipment into the theater, the J-6 was able to release the tactical equipment to the original users and purposes and to use the new equipment to flesh out and strengthen the growing common-user theater trunking system to the point where it could support the coming offensive operations. This joint network grew to over 2,500 circuits.

The joint network planning, implementation, and management was not without its problems. Nothing of this scope and complexity had ever before been attempted. There were the expected "getting started" and "who's in charge" questions, as well as doctrinal, procedural, and technical issues to be resolved.

An immediate and potentially disruptive question concerned the place and means to interface and interconnect theater communications to strategic gateways. With communications doctrine assuming a strategic gateway in the theater, provided by the Defense Communications System (DCS)[2], tactical and theater-level systems should have only had a relatively short hop to access worldwide connectivity. However, in the Persian Gulf, there was no gateway to provide such connectivity, and CENTCOM J-6 made an early decision to extend theater connectivity to CONUS, Europe and the Pacific rather than to formally establish a DCS gateway in theater. As a result, during the initial phases of establishing long-haul communications connectivity, many users attempted to seek out their own path back to the United States, and this resulted in a hybrid network that was neither strategic nor tactical.

The ad hoc establishment of an integrated strategic-tactical network without the benefit of systematic, top-down, network dimensioning and end-to-end engineering, created concern for some system planners and managers about the ability of the resulting operational network to meet the expected end-to-end performance needs of the many users.

Difficulties notwithstanding, by January 1991 a network consisting of 118 ground mobile force tactical satellite terminals, 12 commercial satellite terminals, 61 tactical circuit switches, and 20 tactical message switches had been installed and integrated into the worldwide network through roughly 329 voice and 30 message circuits.

As a result of this integrated network, the traditional management boundaries between the so-called strategic (or DCS) and tactical systems disappeared. As the number of interconnections proliferated, the network routing became much more integrated—"seamless" is the term currently favored. What evolved was a system that contained all of the management elements that, in another place and another time, would have been called the Defense Communications System. (See Figure 1)

The relative ease with which these many dissimilar systems were connected can be credited largely to joint communications programs such as the Tri-Service Tactical Communications (TRI-TAC), joint technical design standards, and NATO programs for interoperability of tactical communications. It was because of these efforts that connections were made—not without growing pains—to the British PTARMIGAN and French RITA systems.

In addition, a mixture of dedicated voice, data, and imagery connectivity was also provided. Data network access consisted of multiple MILNET and DSNET3 (Top Secret/SCI) gateways and a DSNET 1 (Secret) packet switch node. DSNET 2 (Top Secret) connectivity was provided through theater user terminal access to WWMCCS computers in the United States.

In September 1990, plans were formulated for a "DCS-like" theater infrastructure, referred to at the time as the Regional Communications Architecture, but later called the Southwest Asia Telecommunications System (SATS). Figure 2 shows the (SATS) configuration that is now under consideration to support post-conflict U.S. presence in the Gulf area.

Role of SATCOM

Operation Desert Shield/Storm must surely end any speculation about the criticality of satellite communications in a highly mobile war. The "just enough and just in time" support was possible because the military satellite infrastructure was already in place—it had only to be shifted in orbit and its antennas refocused. These scarce military satellite assets were allocated and reallocated when required, and expedient solutions were worked to meet the needs of CENTCOM and the coalition forces.

Satellite communications of all types were vital in supporting beyond line-of-sight requirements—some as short as a few miles—because there were no alternative means to extend range. DoD DSCS and UHF tactical satellites were the mainstays and were used by all military components. The scale of effort pushed these systems to their limit and caused some problems, especially in self-interference on some UHF links.

Every UHF platform (i.e., LEASAT, FLEETSAT, GAPFILLER, LES-9) was used to its maximum potential, with several initiatives being taken to regulate traffic,

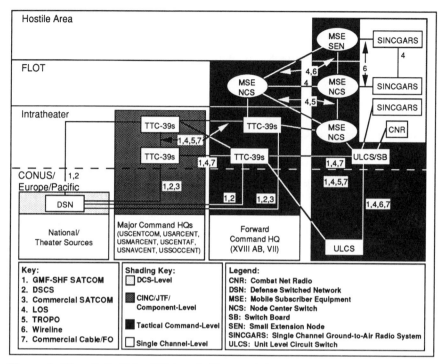

Figure 1. Circuit-Switched Network Connectivity.

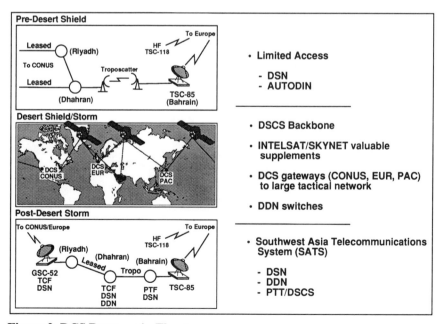

Figure 2. DCS Presence in Theater

increase capacity and optimize utilization. Several user communities were required not only to use the same transponder, but often the same frequency, and this caused interference problems. User-controlled discipline of emitted power setup was also a problem. As a result, performance at times was very unsatisfactory. Dedicated command networks with limited subscribers and strict transmitter discipline fared much better.

The Navy, having no alternative but HF radio, was the primary user of UHF TACSAT. The scale of fleet operations (6 battle groups, 3 amphibious groups, and 3 task force command centers) obliged the Navy to take several measures to increase the effective use of TACSAT resources and multiply the number of networks. The normal number of Common User Digital Information Exchange System (CUDIX) and Fleet Broadcast networks was almost tripled.

The availability of SHF capacity in the DSCS constellation covering the area of operation had to be expanded. Various innovative approaches to achieve augmentation were applied (see Figure 3). A reserve DSCS spacecraft was moved to provide needed augmentation.[3]

The availability of SKYNET and a prior agreement with the United Kingdom on cooperation, permitted creative use of this spacecraft.[4]

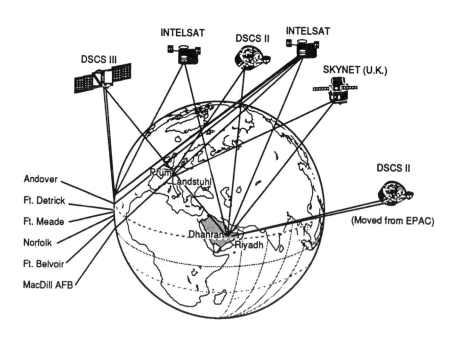

Figure 3. Desert Storm Satellite Connectivity (January 17, 1991)

An experimental EHF SATCOM link was even brought into play for direct, secure communications between CINCCENT and the Chairman, JCS.

Commercial satellites provided valuable complementary capacity. The initial complement of commercial satellite circuits, established in August and September 1990, linked CENTCOM Forward in Riyadh with its home base in Florida and also provided the XVIII Airborne Corps with its only connectivity to Fort Bragg, North Carolina.

There was significant expansion of the commercial networks in the following months, including additional leased commercial terminals deployed to other locations in Saudi Arabia. These terminals provided T1 capacity through INTELSAT. This enabled DISA, CENTCOM, and the components to extend AUTOVON trunks, AUTODIN circuits, and dedicated voice and data circuits from the United States to multiple locations in the theater. These commercial T1 trunks allowed the components to release tactical satellite terminals back to direct support of the forthcoming combat operations. Commercial satellite connectivity also provided the VII Corps with circuits to their support bases in Germany.

INTELSAT provided about half of the out-of-theater SHF capacity and some 20% of the total SHF capacity. The Army used its C- and Ku-band earth terminals from their TROJAN system to exploit INTELSAT for intra-theater links to VII Corps and the 1st Infantry Division.

INMARSAT supported major naval task forces, sealift, and some ground unit commanders. In particular, it supported extensive unclassified and some classified traffic (secured with STU-III) for the Military Sealift Command, and provided connectivity to allied Navy and merchant ships.

However, TACSAT capacity was in such short supply that INMARSAT terminals also supported sealift and battle group commanders. It is believed that, worldwide, the Navy had INMARSAT on some 200 platforms (mostly sealift) with more planned, especially for combatant ships. The XVIII Airborne Corps also leased INMARSAT service for 18 terminals.

Voice Switched Network

The Defense Switched Network (DSN) provides the worldwide, long haul, common-user voice services for DoD. Initial connectivity to DSN had to be extended to remote switching centers over the GMF satellite network. The handful of voice circuits that represented the initial capability grew into a robust network of over 300 trunks connecting 25 tactical circuit switches (TTC-39s) in the theater to 4 DSN gateway switches in the United States, 3 in Europe and 1 in the Pacific. (See Figure 4). This evolved into a highly integrated strategic-tactical circuit switched network that supported clear and secure voice, data and facsimile services. The average intra-theater grade-of-service varied widely from poor (60% probability of blocking) to good (less than 15%).

Limited interswitch trunking contributed to the poor performance, but the unexpected use of modem-connected personal computers and facsimile machines extended the average call holding time and made the problem even worse.[5]

There were only a limited number of analog access ports equipped on the TTC-39 circuit switches deployed. This too served to frustrate users who were attempting

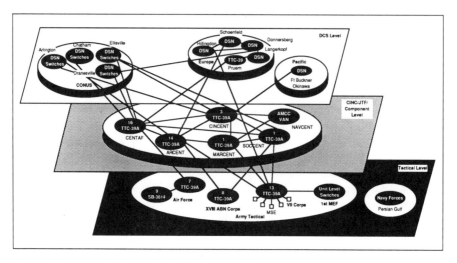

Figure 4. Levels of Circuit Switch Connectivity

to use these circuit switches, not for phone calls, but for their STU-IIIs, personal computers and facsimile machines that required the user of the analog ports to access the network. A routine practice at home became an expected but limited capability available in the combat zone. This use of the circuit switched networks was unpredicted when designs were laid down for the TRI-TAC switches in the early 1970s, and the heavier traffic demands (call attempts, holding times, communities of interest, etc.) were more than the integrated network had been engineered to provide.

Further, as has already been noted, interswitch trunking was limited by the availability of tactical communications assets that had been released for this unplanned mission. Also, the somewhat unruly mix of analog and digital circuits required many analog-to-digital conversions that yielded poor circuit and end-to-end performance; a phenomena inexplicable to many users conditioned by excellent service from commercial communications back home.

Engineering, implementing, and managing such a complex network was a challenging and unprecedented task. For example, the Army deployed three different generations of tactical communication systems; the all-digital Mobile Subscriber Equipment (MSE), the TRI-TAC system with both analog and digital capability and the Improved Army Tactical Communications Systems (IATACS)—an older analog system. TRI-TAC interoperated with either MSE or IATACS, but MSE and IATACS would not interoperate with each other. Hence, TRI-TAC had to serve as an interoperability bridge between the two systems.

Network interface problems were encountered between the TTC-39 tactical switch in Riyadh and the commercial #5 ESS gateway switch in Dranesville, Virginia. It took a team of government engineers, working with their commercial partners in AT&T and GTE, almost three months to isolate and resolve an incompatible interswitch signalling problem.[6]

Switch interface problems were also experienced between the Marine Corps Unit Level Circuit Switch (ULCS) and the TTC-39A, requiring a software modification.

U.S. liaison teams were employed with all major coalition forces to facilitate communications interoperability, and the NATO STANAG 5040 interface provided network interoperability between TRI-TAC and the UK Ptarmigan and French RITA tactical switches.

Message Switched Network

Early deploying forces were serviced by message centers in Riyadh and Dhahran that were connected into AUTODIN by 300 baud circuits. Although CENTCOM quickly upgraded those circuits to 1200 baud, it was not until the TYC-39 tactical message switches began to arrive in theater that a true message network started to emerge.

The message traffic loading grew rapidly during the fall as the forces deployed. Processing of this traffic was limited to low speed circuits over satellite links. Precedence and message length abuse (average message size grew by 50%) further compounded the message delivery capability of the network. The integrated network is shown in Figure 5. It consisted of 26 trunks connecting 20 tactical switches in the theater to 3 AUTODIN switching centers in the United States, one in Europe, and one in the Pacific. The network eventually supported 286 message centers.[7]

The average message delivery time during the Desert Storm phase of the operation was 23 minutes.

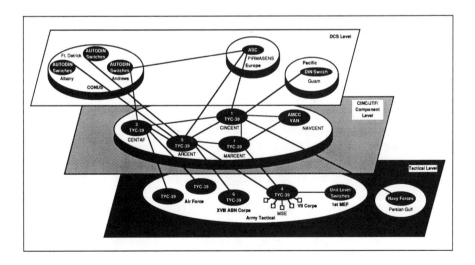

Figure 5. Levels of Message Switch Connectivity

Data Switching Networks

The Defense Data Network (DDN) got its first taste of combat support operations in the Persian Gulf. All four DDN networks were eventually used heavily. MILNET was used for unclassified common user service; DSNET1 was used for Secret level common-user traffic; DSNET2 was used for Top Secret and the WWMCCS community; and DSNET3 was used for Top Secret/SCI intelligence support.

The tactical use of personal computers to communicate with other PCs and hosts proved indispensable in many applications. However, the lack of a pre-planned common-user data network architecture for the tactical infrastructure required "homegrown" solutions that demonstrated ingenuity but lacked a network perspective. Additionally, commercial PCs using protocols such as KERMIT had some difficulty operating over 16 kbps, high error rate tactical links. As the demand for data communications increased, the Army took the lead in establishing a data networking capability in the theater. The Army Information Systems Command installed the first CISCO™ gateway to MILNET on August 27, and this network grew to 5 gateways, 12 hosts, and 7 terminal servers, with service into 5 different MILNET packet switched nodes. By the end of Desert Storm, the data system was delivering over one million packets daily between DDN and the Army gateways.[8]

A number of problems were encountered in establishing this network. For example, the noisy tactical circuits required modification of TCP timeout parameters in host computers. The DDN core gateways (Mailbridges) were overloaded and were transmitting corrupted EGP routing information to the Army gateways. Static routing tables were down-loaded to the gateways, and DISA implemented a patch to fix the EGP. The complex collection of routers, bridges, packet switches and satellite circuits required constant network management attention from a centralized location. The need to manage a global data network by a single control authority was a key finding by both Army and DISA in after-action reports.

Security was also a serious concern, and special actions such as forbidding anonymous log-ons, multiple passwords and tightly controlled manning of host and gateways were used as typical access control measures.

A van-mounted DSNET1 node was assembled by the Army and DISA at the Tobyhanna Army depot. The node became operational on January 23, 1991 and was serving classified users by early February, well before the ground attack commenced. The node was connected by two circuits to the DSNET1 network. Monitoring and control of the theater DSNET1 node was done by the DISA-Europe Area Control Center near Stuttgart, Germany. The full potential of this system was never tested because hostilities ended quickly after its arrival.

Access to DSNET2 and WWMCCS was provided through remote 9.6 kbps satellite access to WWMCCS host computers in the United States. Likewise, access to DSNET3 was accomplished by initially extending CENTCOM's Garrison LAN via bridges from Florida over a commercial satellite link. Later, theater gateways to DSNET3 were implemented.

Network Planning, Management and Control

Desert Storm demonstrated the urgent need to perform centralized network planning and management. The complexity of the integrated network, coupled with a multitude of organizations involved, created a very difficult situation for accomplishing joint end-to-end engineering and control of the operational network. The process was largely manual, cumbersome, and sometimes unresponsive. Automation and standards are badly needed.

The processing of Telecommunications Service Requests (TSR) met with numerous difficulties, but work-arounds and highly skilled, dedicated personnel made the process work. Problems arose early when, in the heat and pressure of initial deployment, many verbal requests were received that were duplicative and often contradictory. These requests made it more difficult to maintain databases of circuits and trunks.

Many of the in-theater personnel were unfamiliar with preparing TSRs and therefore made mistakes. Difficult or unusual circuit engineering requests involving commercial-to-tactical interfaces also contained errors that resulted in unsatisfactory and delayed implementation. Requests also came in piecemeal and with high priority. This did not always allow for efficient handling for expeditious and cost-effective implementation. When TSRs were accepted by telephone, considerable lag occurred before sufficient information was entered into databases and circuit records to ensure an accurate picture of the implemented connectivity.

Inspired by the urgency of the impending military operations, a number of users attempted to directly contract for commercial communications services, sometimes soliciting carriers without proper credentials or who did not have the required licenses to operate in Saudi Arabia. In those instances DECCO had to intervene in the contract action. DECCO maintains a list of qualified contractors for commercial services, but in the early phases of the operation it was not always consulted by those attempting to obtain such services.

DECCO awarded over 700 circuit contracts in support of Desert Shield/Storm. The Inquiry/Quote/Order procedure was used extensively to place contracts competitively, yet quickly. In most cases contracts were awarded within two hours of definition. Contracts awarded contained clauses to deal with commencement of hostilities, providing either for continuation of contract services or agreement by the contractor to train military personnel.

By November 1990, the provisioning process was under control and performed well during Desert Storm. The process improved as the users became better acquainted with the procedures and when Telecommunications Control Offices were established in the theater.

The TSR process is necessary to ensure accurate specification of the numerous interfaces and equipment needed to implement a circuit. As noted, procedures existed to expedite the process. However, due to the scope and scale of this contingency, the paperwork process was inadequate. Thus, while most of the circuits were implemented in a timely way, entry and distribution of the technical data were not sufficient to provide for efficient trouble-isolation and configuration management, especially across network management and operations/maintenance organizational boundaries. Also, some of the complex circuits such as those for data services were improperly specified and engineered, requiring extensive effort to correct at the time of implementation.

The worldwide network implemented to support Desert Storm involved almost every type of commercial, strategic, and tactical telecommunication equipment in the inventory. At present, network management is largely a manual process. Also, unlike established theaters of operation, such as Europe and the Pacific, DISA did not have a previously established infrastructure in the SouthWest Asia theater to support the management process. Hence, the usual procedure of defining strict network boundaries with limited interfaces and configuration visibility between them was found to be inadequate due to the number and variety of networks and interconnections.

Engineering a system to optimize network performance in both benign and stressed environments requires an integrated approach. The solutions for routing plans, trunk cross-sections, and topology need to be properly balanced. The CENTCOM J-6 held numerous meetings to ensure coordination in network planning. Furthermore, personnel trained in such procedures and who had participated in joint exercises were placed on his team from DISA and related Service organizations. The sharing of configuration files between component commands and DISA allowed some "what if" analysis to be performed to assess network performance and restoration configurations that might result from a physical attack on the network.

Enhanced network planning and management tools and procedures would have provided the system manager an ability to engineer a much better level of performance and exploit the redundancy of the network to support contingencies. Low levels of jamming or a Scud hit on a communications node could have seriously degraded network performance, and tools for rapid reconfiguration and reconstitution were lacking.

In general, management of the operational AUTODIN networks and SATCOM networks worked well and as they were designed to do. Management of voice networks was less successful, requiring more workarounds. The data networks were the newest element in the inventory and required much improvisation.

In summary, network management and control was a sub-optimized, manual process, and much of it was improvised on the spot and under enormous pressure for instant results. Furthermore, any system disruptions were self-induced—there was no jamming or physical destruction of communications nodes. Had that occurred, the lack of automated planning and engineering tools would have severely hampered responses. However, the process worked well due to the many agencies and people that cooperated to make it all come together.

Interoperability With Coalition Forces

Interoperability with and among coalition forces was accomplished through the NATO version of the STU-II (and the STU-IIIA, which is interoperable with the STU-II), sharing of national and commercial satellite resources, and the exchange of liaison teams.

The loan of five tactical satellite terminals from Air Force and JCSE assets to the United Kingdom helped fill shortages in long-haul communications.

The Army formed six liaison teams to provide face-to-face coordination between the ARCENT staff and the senior headquarters of the coalition forces. The

Marines also provided their ANGLICO teams to attached Army units and to Pan Arab forces.

Army liaison teams consisted of 50 to 100 personnel. Military Intelligence and Special Operations Forces provided personnel with requisite language skills. The liaison teams were equipped with a wide range of communications equipment that they collocated with the supported unit. Equipment included field telephones, STU-IIIs, teletypewriters, facsimiles, and computers.

Transmission equipment included connections with host nation communications; AN/PSC-3 and the AN/TSC-85A or AN/TSC-93 satellite terminals; AN/GRC-193, AN/GRC-122 or AN/GRC-142 high frequency radios; landlines for stationary operations; and the AN/VRC-46 for mobile needs.

Team members reported that SATCOM was the primary transmission means and that use of HF radio was avoided for fear that signatures might compromise operations. Radio teletype equipment was carried for backup, but was not needed. Encrypted facsimile was the most used terminal equipment. Computers served primarily for word processing and other administrative purposes.

The liaison teams proved extremely critical to coordination with coalition forces and highlighted the need for both human and equipment interoperability in coalition operations. Both Army and Marine commanders have indicated the need for a standard, jump-capable communications package for liaison team support.

Organization and Management Issues

DISA is the single agency responsible for providing communications services to the National Command Authorities (the President and Secretary of Defense), to the DoD and to other authorized government agencies. The Defense Networks Systems Organization (DNSO) is the operational arm of DISA and is responsible for managing the world-wide Defense Communications System (now called the Defense Information System Network or DISN).

Within DNSO is the Contingency Support Branch with the task of engineering and implementing extensions of the DISN into crisis areas in support of deployed forces. DNSO also provides the Operations Center, which monitors and reports on the status of the DISN and directs restoral actions. These organizations, as well as other elements of DISA, including field offices in Europe and the Pacific and at CENTCOM and FORCECOM, supported CENTCOM J-6 during Desert Shield/Storm.

At the outset of the massive deployment for Desert Shield, a Crisis Action Team (CAT) was set up within the Contingency Branch of DNSO to act as a focal point for support to all participants. A contingent from this office, along with engineers from the Defense Communications Engineering Center, accompanied the CENTCOM J-6 to Saudi Arabia in early August 1990.

A systems engineering team was established in Washington during September 1990 to provide interface and integration engineering and to plan a regional communications architecture. A "Grey Beard" team was formed to monitor and document DISA support and prepare an after-action report.[9]

Throughout the conflict, the Defense Commercial Communications Office (DECCO), the Telecommunications Management and Service Organization

(TMSO), and the National Communications System provided assistance in establishing long-haul communications into the Gulf area. More than 600 telecommunications service requests were processed.

A number of unexpected problems were encountered as the operation unfolded. The size, operations tempo, and the complexity in terms of numbers of participants with varying interests, perspectives, and solutions were the first hurdles. Desert Shield/Storm was the first major operation to be conducted under the changes wrought by the Goldwater-Nichols Act, and this presented some fundamental coordination problems. The many communications support organizations were not accustomed to operating in a theater where the CINC and his J-6 were in firm and unquestioned control of all communications matters. However, the J-6 initially had neither the right numbers or skills on his staff to accomplish many of these new functions, and personnel were drawn from many sources to fill these voids. Many administrative procedures had to be altered or abolished and new ones improvised, on the spot. The point of emphasis is not the degree of management complexity or magnitude of problems encountered, but how quickly these issues were resolved in the field.

The role of DISA evolved in a much different way in this conflict than it did for its predecessor (DCA) during the Vietnam conflict. The difficulties of trying to integrate tactical and strategic communications were similar, but the solutions differed radically. In Vietnam, DCA was obliged (eventually directed by the JCS) to assume responsibility for theater switching and trunking systems. In the Persian Gulf, the J-6 gathered the necessary people and procedures to become an effective single manager. Key reasons for this success were the consistent use of this team and the establishment of proper support relationships with DISA—the only agency with the perspective, tools, and procedures to run a global telecommunications system.

DISA itself had to assimilate new skills to engineer and run an integrated network. The integration of strategic and tactical networks and heavy reliance on tactical systems to extend long-haul connectivity surfaced many shortfalls in knowledge about how tactical systems perform. DISA had few people with this background. Conversely, the tactical world had an incredibly simplistic view of how global systems—particularly space-based ones—were engineered and controlled. Furthermore, the control centers of the commercial carriers who became involved were suddenly immersed in a totally different and, to them, unstructured world. Everyone involved had a long climb up the learning curve. Fortunately, there was time to make this climb.

Every post-war analysis agrees that a mix of military and commercial networks is the only way to provide adequate communications support in the future. The task now is to institutionalize this newly captured management capability so that the learning curve need not be so steep the next time U.S. forces deploy into a communications wilderness.

Some Observations

The outcome of Desert Shield/Storm provides important guidelines for communications planning for military contingencies.

- The need for satellite connectivity is clearly demonstrated—no other broadband media can be moved into place so quickly.
- The total military SATCOM capability was exploited and was still grossly inadequate. The need for commercial SATCOM had been shown in Operation Just Cause and corroborated and emphasized in Desert Shield/Storm. The process for incorporating commercial capabilities into military operations must now be institutionalized.
- An integrated communications system successfully supported combat operations, but was barely able to keep up with the dynamics and high speed of maneuver, even in the most benign of environments. This will not be the blueprint for systems for the next war.
- Thousands of communicators around the world collaborated to improvise solutions to unforeseen problems. These skills can quickly evaporate in the drawdown in defense resources given its current emphasis on smart weapons and preserving force structure.
- We have seen a new form of warfare, and future communications systems should be assessed not only on what they can do but on how adaptable they are to being quickly reconfigured. This flexibility must be present not only in systems, but in the organizations that must plan, engineer and manage their use. Strong end-to-end performance won't just happen in an integrated system of such disparate parts.
- The DSCS was the principal multichannel transmission system for both intra- and inter-theater communications during early deployment. The DSCS entered and exited this operation on shaky legs and cannot be allowed to further deteriorate. Conversely, SATCOM remains uniquely vulnerable to a moderate investment in simple means for jamming, intercept, monitoring, and spoofing. A robust architecture must contain alternatives to such vulnerable repeaters, including guaranteed access to space.
- Data communications with global and near-instant connectivity will be the dominant demand on battlefield communications in the future.

There is room for both pride and modesty in what was accomplished in the Persian Gulf War. Potential adversaries of the United States will not be so foolish as to neglect glaring weaknesses in the systems that evolved over five months of improvisation and careful rehearsal. Active C[3] countermeasures against our systems are almost a foregone conclusion in future operations. Meanwhile, a large part of the military operations community is busy building doctrine and tactics based upon the assumed freedom to communicate.

"Just enough and just in time" may not be sufficient the next time.

Endnotes

[1] The JCSE is responsible to the Chairman, Joint Chiefs of Staff for providing tactical communications to Joint Task Force Headquarters and the Special Operations Command.

[2] Now called the Defense Information System Network (DISN).

[3] See the article *Silent Space Warriors* for details on these movements and reconfigurations.

[4] See the article *The First Space War* for details on SKYNET and other international

satellite systems.

⁵ See the articles *Information Systems and Air Warfare* and *Integrating Tactical and Strategic Switching Systems* for more details on degraded service in voice and message switching systems.

⁶ *Integrating Tactical and Strategic Switching Systems* contains further details.

⁷ Traffic saturation problems and their solutions are described in more detail in *Integrating Tatical and Strategic Switching Systems.*

⁸ Traffic loading on DDN is shown in Figure 3, *Integrating Tactical and Strategic Switching Systems.*

⁹ *DCA Grey Beards Lessons Learned: Desert Shield/Desert Storm*, August 1991, The MITRE Corporation.

References:

Brig. Gen. Dennis Beasley, USAF, and Major David Kovach, USAF, *Desert Storm: The Ultimate Jointness*, First Quarter 1991.

L. K. Wentz, *DCA Grey Beards Lessons Learned: Desert Shield/Storm*, MITRE MP-91W00024, August 1991.

Final Report to Congress, *Conduct of the Persian Gulf War*, April 1992.

USAISC Briefings, *USAISC Support to Desert Shield/Storm*, 1991.

Brig. Gen. Roscoe Cougill, USAF, *Desert Storm Communication*, AFCEA International Convention, 1991.

SIGNAL, Special Report: After the Storm, August 1991.

L. K. Wentz and Colonel Paul Patton, *Lessons Learned From the DCA Grey Beards Perspective*, MILCOM 91.

DCA Briefings, *Support to Desert Storm*, May 1991.

XVIII Airborne Corps briefing, *Operation Desert Storm*, May 1991.

VII Corps briefing, *Operation Desert Storm*, June 1991.

U.S. Army Training and Doctrine Command briefing, *Operation Desert Storm*, 1991.

C³I Experiences of U.S. Forces During Operation Desert Shield/Desert Storm. Briefing by MITRE Corporation for the Director, J-6, Joint Staff, October 1991.

Robert F. Weissert, *TCP/IP-The Hero of Operation Desert Storm Information Systems,* Connexions, Volume 6, No. 5, May 1992.

INFORMATION SYSTEMS AND AIR WARFARE

Alan D. Campen

To have command of the air means to be in a position to wield offensive power so great it defies human imagination.[1]

While air power alone did not win the war in the Persian Gulf, the relentless air strikes against command and communications left Iraq blind, befuddled, isolated and no match for the team of land, air, and sea forces that took but100 hours to envelop and disable what had been the world's fourth largest military force.

A combined air operation, unprecedented in military history, was orchestrated over the largest military tactical information network ever built: This network took a form radically different from that predicted by doctrine, and thus one not well provided for in pre-war planning or in the allocation of communications resources.

Over a period of five months information systems were constructed on the fly, by troops in the field, with few blueprints, with much desk-top engineering and employing many components never intended for the services they provided.

That these improvised networks worked at all—mind not that most worked well— is eloquent testimony to personnel readiness, responsive logistics, realistic training and the ingenuity and initiative of individuals who, as one U.S. airman put it, "drank a lot of tea" with their coalition partners and accomplished the seemingly impossible. They also rewrote the book on tactical air information systems.

Exercise in Reality

Most Americans—and probably Saddam Hussein as well—think the war began when Iraqi forces rolled over the border into Kuwait on August 2, 1990. They are wrong. There are those in the U.S. Ninth Air Force—the air component of U.S. Central Command— who will tell you that it began much earlier, when plans were developed by the U.S. Central Command at MacDill AFB, Florida, to deal with unexplainable and disturbing events in Iraq.

U.S. military intelligence could offer no rational explanation for the large military force being assembled by Iraq: one clearly beyond the needs for self-defense. A routine "Internal Look" readiness exercise in Florida in July 1990 utilized an exercise scenario built around an Iraqi invasion of Kuwait. This scenario was criticized as being unduly provocative by some in Washington who clung to the belief that diplomacy would lead Saddam Hussein to seek peaceful resolution of his differences with Kuwait and the United Arab Emirates.

However, criticism of that prescient scenario quickly faded when the intelligence events that had been scripted into the "exercise" began to overlap with real world events. What had begun as a military exercise rapidly turned into a rehearsal for a war that was now but a month away.

Resources Initially Overwhelmed

While Air Force communicators, computer and airspace management specialists were poised to support limited air operations in the Persian Gulf, they were nearly

---

SINGLE LARGEST COMMUNICATIONS MOBILIZATION IN HISTORY
- 12 Combat Communications Squadrons
- 2300+ USAF personnel
- Approximately 1500 short tons of equipment
- 7000+ radio frequencies

LARGEST DEFENSE COMMUNICATIONS SYSTEM (DCS) EXTENSION
- 26 SHF earth terminals
- 3 commercial T-1 satellite terminals
- 1050 USAF circuits
- 1000 miles of terrestrial systems
  — 29 tropo (AN/TRC-170) and microwave links
- 6 DCS entry points
- 19 automatic telephone switches (72 AUTOVON trunks)
- 17 manual switches
- 3 message switches
  — 132,012 messages transmitted
  — 1,293,775 messages received
- 59 communications centers
- 29,542,121 calls

AIR TRAFFIC
- 350,000 operations for Desert Shield
- 225,000 operations for Desert Storm
- Air Trasking Order often exceeded 950 pages

Table 1. Scope of USAF Activities

swamped by the scope and pace of escalation of Desert Shield and what eventually became the largest single communications mobilization in military history. (See Table 1.)

The quick reaction communications capabilities that routinely accompany deployment of air units (TSC-107 QRC package and TSC-94A ground mobile force satellite terminals) were no match for cascading requirements. Communications resources of the U.S. Tactical Air Command were soon exhausted. This explosive buildup of air power ultimately would consume nearly the entire storehouse of USAF tactical communications assets, along with some strategic communications resources as well. Well over 200 sorties of C-141s were needed to lift tactical communications equipment to the Gulf.

There were plans on the shelf for air operations in the Gulf region, but none matching the scale of the unfolding operation in Desert Shield, and there were no plans at all for data communications nets for the air units already surging into the Persian Gulf, laptops and PC's in hand.

The U.S. Central Command draft plan 1002-90 outlined the concept for early stages of a deployment as well as a guide for much larger basing options. But, that plan contained only "unstaffed" (read wish-list) communications requirements and, as yet, no Time Phased Force Deployment Data—the bible prescribing what units would be arriving, with what assets, where and when.

Tactical communications planners on the Air Staff in Washington thought they had sufficient resources to cover 13 airbases in the Area of Operations (AOR); the final count was 25. Compounding that serious shortfall was the fact that plans called for the Air National Guard to provide up to 30 percent of the tactical communications needs. The ANG would ultimately provide only two squadrons and just over 10 percent of the resources.

Although finely tuned and well rehearsed, USAFCENTAF Plan 1307 called only for the deployment of "show the flag" air forces to Riyadh. The Quick Reaction Package (QRP) of the 51st Combat Communications Squadron from Robins AFB, Georgia, was embarked within hours to set up the initial communications facility at that location. An advance management element departed from Ninth Air Force on August 8. It included a communications officer, frequency manager, technical controller, satellite control and combat airspace management team: A competent group, but one staffed only to direct and to operate, not to plan and engineer a theater-wide tactical network.

That rapid deployment was but hours old when Plan 1307 was overtaken by the sheer magnitude of air operations needed to defend against what was now feared to be an Iraqi invasion of Saudi Arabia.

The airborne warning and control aircraft (AWACS) would operate from Riyadh as planned, but the fighter aircraft—already enroute from Langley AFB in Virginia—were headed, instead, for Dhahran. The 52nd Combat Communications Squadron and its QRP package quickly were launched for that location, but had scarcely cleared home base when word came of fighter deployments to a third, airbase—this one in the United Arab Emirates—then a fourth, in Oman, and eventually, into an array of air bases deployed across nine countries and four continents. By January 1991, there would be 12 combat communications

SITE	FORCE ARRIVAL	COMMUNICATIONS INITIAL	SUSTAINING
Dhahran	9 August	12 August	21 August
Al Dhafra	10 August	23 August	1 September
Thumrait	10 August	22 August	23 August
Taif	17 August	28 September	28 September
K. Mushait	21 August	22 August	1 September
Doha	29 August	13 September	13 September
Tabuk	29 August	15 September	26 September
KKMC	14 December	11 December	17 December
Al Kharj	17 December	28 November	22 December

Table 2. Phasing of Deployments

organizations deployed across the Persian Gulf theater of operations—including the 1st Combat Communications Group (CCGp) from Europe and the 4th CCGp from the Pacific—and more than 2,300 people. (See Table 2.)

Improvising a Theater Network

Some fighter aircraft were in place and combat ready by the ninth of August, but these air units possessed very limited communications assets (see page 65, *SIGNAL*, August 1991) and could not connect into their controlling headquarters—the Tactical Air Control Center (TACC) in Riyadh. Further, it was not clear how the TACC could tie back into the United States; the nearest entry point into strategic communications and its world-wide connectivity.

A formidable task faced the communications planners at the USAF Tactical Air Command at Langley AFB, Virginia, and its Ninth Air Force at Shaw AFB, South Carolina. Their dilemma can be grasped by contrasting the assumptions in communications doctrine with "ground truth" rapidly unfolding in the Gulf:

• *A strategic communications gateway will exist in the AOR, providing the means to connect to the Defense Communications System and thence back to United States and Europe.* There was no such gateway in the Persian Gulf. Years of negotiations had failed to secure political agreement for installation of a strategic satellite earth station anywhere in the Gulf area. A transportable gateway communications package (called DCS-Central Area) existed, but it was in the hands of an Air National Guard unit that was never to be deployed. Thus, limited tactical Ground Mobile Force satellite equipment (AN/TSC-100A or AN/TSC-94A) had to be diverted to provide strategic gateways to the United States.

• *A terrestrial system made up of high capacity TRI-TAC switching and transmission equipment will interconnect the Joint Headquarters, its component air, land and sea commands and all locations in the Area of Operations.* Communications to construct the intra-theater network and to tie into the strategic gateways are supposed to be provided from digital tropospheric scatter radios (AN/TRC-170) and tactical microwave. However, 80 percent of Air Force tactical communications resources were in the hands of the Air National Guard units that had not been and, indeed, would not be called to active service. Further, even had these ANG units been activated, initial airlift was being allocated to support the buildup of combat forces and was not yet available to move bulky tactical switching and transmission systems.

What evolved then was a network of thin line tactical satellite systems that were stretched and stressed to provide the trunk-rich connectivity of a terrestrial, theater-wide communications system. It also was a network dependent upon satellites that were vulnerable to enemy exploitation, had Iraq (or anyone with a 22 meter dish and a 25 watt amplifier within the satellite footprint) chosen to do so.

Satellite Communications Network

Air Force communicators were hard pressed to provide an alternative means for adequate connectivity among the rapidly growing number of air bases and the TACC and to the nodes in the United States that provided those air units with logistics and intelligence. These connections had to be quickly made if air power could hope to blunt the expected Iraqi attacks into Saudi Arabia. High frequency radio was not the answer. Its capacity was far too limited and transmission reliability too low, especially in that part of the world and under bombardment from a sunspot cycle that peaked during Desert Storm.

The only solution to the intra-theater connectivity problem lay in use of Ground Mobile Force SHF tactical satellite communications. But this had to be done carefully and in ways that would not saturate the Defense Satellite Communications System (DSCS), thus denying capacity to the Army and Marine forces now beginning to arrive in large numbers in the theater.

A "hub and spoke" scheme was developed at a meeting of the USCENTAF and Central Command communications staffs. More subscribers would be added to the networks by reducing the voice channel data rates to 16 kbps from their normal rate of 32 kbps. Thumrait, Oman was selected for the initial hub location because it was believed to be outside the range of Scud or air attack. Soon the buildup of air power required a second hub at Riyadh AB, Saudi Arabia and then a third at Al Dhafra, UAE. This latter hub providing inter-theater trunking to Europe via a UK Skynet satellite and the Indian Ocean DSCS satellite. Figure 1 shows the network for the USCENTAF as it ultimately evolved. Commercial satellite communications eventually supplemented each of USCENTAF's satellite hubs, becoming the primary means of extending DSN, AUTODIN, weather and several other services from CONUS to the theater.

Airborne Communications

A key to success of this air operation—unprecedented in both scope and complexity—was the ability to plan, execute and monitor operations through tactical data links that enabled real time exchange of voice and radar displays. This network too had to be improvised. The challenge to USCENTAF communicators was to provide communications connectivity between the TACC in Riyadh and its eyes and ears now embarked on a growing family of aircraft, some of which were orbiting at greater distances from the Riyadh than could be reliably supported through conventional ground-air-ground communications nets.

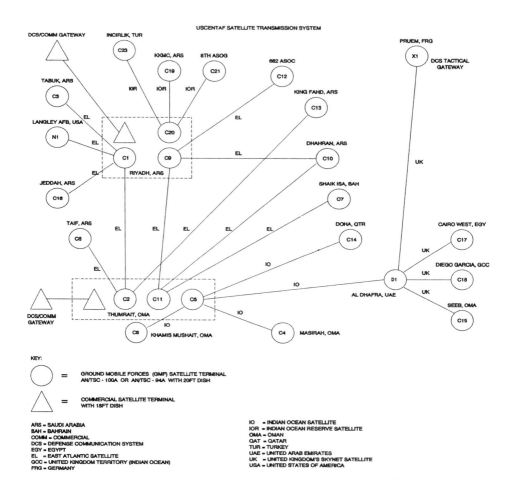

Figure 1. USCENTAF Satellite Transmission System

The airborne warning and control system (E3 AWACS), the airborne command and control center (ABCCC), the intelligence-gathering RC-135 Rivet Joint and eventually the airborne radar Joint Stars (JSTARS) aircraft, were often ranging or orbiting well beyond limits of UHF radio range from the TACC in Riyadh. To further complicate matters, the noise level in the UHF radio spectrum was higher than had been predicted, caused, in part by high local concentrations of emitters and the packing of networks onto the UHF satellites.

Air Force communicators solved the immediate range-noise ratio problem by installing ground-to-air radio repeater stations (one very near the Iraqi border) and through airborne relay aircraft—such as the EC-135L borrowed from the Strategic Air Command. The connectivity provided by this unique network of tactical data links connecting the TACC to its airborne elements is shown in Figure 2.

Nowhere within the USCENTAF staff was there an organization to oversee and manage the integration of ground and airborne command and control communications. The USCENTAF communications staff quickly formed a cadre from among communicators from the TACC and the Ninth Air Force communications and computer staff. This management element, known as the Airborne Communications Cell, has since been formally adopted as part of USCENTAF's wartime organizational structure.

Initially the GATRs—as these remote relays were to be called—could not extend secure voice from the TACC to its airborne elements. This was because the terrestrial links to the GATRs were using TRI-TAC equipment that was limited to a bandpass of 3 kHz, while ground to air systems were designed to pass either baseband voice at 12 kHz or diphase at 25 kHz. This configuration, in and of itself, would not permit operation of secure voice. This serious gap in operational capability was overcome initially when one of the GATR crews obtained a radio encryption device and connected it to one of the GATR van's backup radios. The crew then initiated a manual radio relay by receiving secure messages from the TACC over a digital secure phone and relaying this information over the now secured radio.

Eventually USCENTAF engineers and technicians developed an end-to-end secure capability which eliminated the need for message relay. This capability has been recommended for inclusion in future GATR system upgrades.

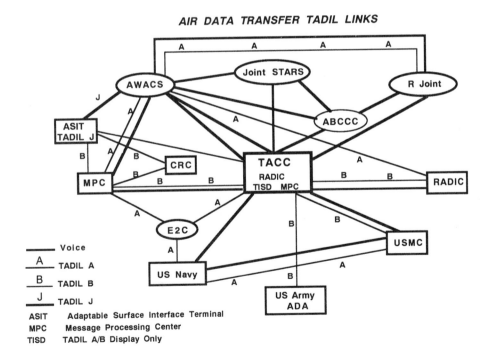

AIR DATA TRANSFER TADIL LINKS

Figure 2. Tactical Data Links

Terrestrial Communications

The interim theater network provided by Ground Mobile Force satellites provided an initial, if precarious capability. Communications were almost totally dependent upon the theater satellite hubs and would remain so until airlift could be obtained for the AN/TRC-170 tropospheric scatter and microwave terminals.

By mid-August, engineers from the 5th Combat Communications Group had completed initial studies and concluded that it was feasible to construct what would become the "longest tactical, digital, terrestrial transmission system ever assembled by the U.S. Air Force." Design parameters called for a transmission rate of 2,304 kbps with a link availability of .90 and a bit error rate of not more than 1×10^{-5}.

The initial increment of this tropo network would connect the communications hubs at Riyadh with Al Dhafra, through the tactical air bases on the eastern side of the Saudi Arabian peninsula. Later it would extend north through King Khalid Military City (KKMC) to Rahfa on the border with Iraq. This northward extension provided circuitry from the TACC in Riyadh to the radar control and reporting center at KKMC and to three air support operations centers co-located with the XVIIIth Airborne Corps, the VII Corps and other coalition ground forces. Figure 3 shows the final configuration of the air force terrestrial transmission system, consisting of 29 links of tropo and microwave, covering over 1,000 miles.

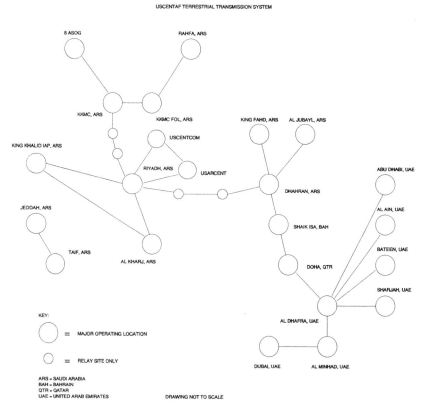

USCENTAF TERRESTRIAL TRANSMISSION SYSTEM

Figure 3. USCENTAF Terrestrial Transmission System

Voice Switched Network

Figure 4 shows the USCENTAF voice network that drew its trunking from the satellite and terrestrial systems already described. It contained 19 automatic and 17 manual switchboards and processed just under 30 million calls through 70 AUTOVON trunks. (By January 1991 there would be an additional 169 telephone switches brought into the theater by the other military services.)

Planning for telephone service in a theater of war is no easy task under the best of circumstances; there being no traffic models for any of the subscriber organizations. But, in addition, telephone service in the Persian Gulf was obliged to accommodate

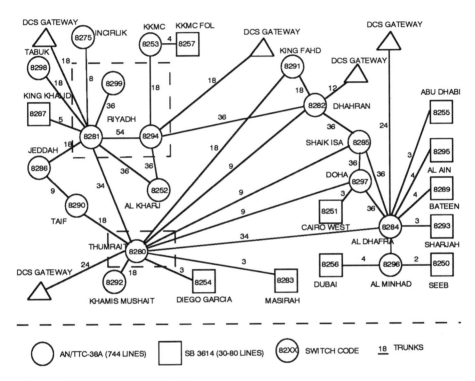

Figure 4. USCENTAF Voice Network

a new requirement in military operations: *morale telephone calls*. Morale calls during the Vietnam and the Korean conflicts had been limited to connections made through the Military Affiliate Radio System (MARS) to volunteer "ham" radio operators in the United States, or through bootlegged calls on the AUTOVON voice network.

The Ninth Air Force chief network systems engineer expressed the problem this way, "as you can imagine, boredom and loneliness coupled with free morale calls spelled disaster for call completion rates...by late September, we had a grid-locked, voice switched network."

The Air Force had set the following call completion objectives for cross border access into the strategic Defense Switched Network (DSN): Routine 80 percent,

Priority 90 percent and Immediate 96 percent. However, by late September, 1990, the switches were reporting worst case completion rates as low as 5 percent for Routine, 40 percent for Priority and 65 percent for Immediate. Administrative controls were immediately imposed, assigning each air base DSN and precedence allocations and also establishing "business" hours from 0900 in Germany until 1700 Pacific Standard Time, Monday through Friday. Morale calls were restricted to the remaining hours.

These administrative controls and some new routing and network balancing schemes brought call-completion rates near to the original objectives. However, as this engineer also stated, "we did not grasp the full impact of intermingled, unauthorized morale calls on the network until 17 January 1991, when morale calls ceased." He says that completion rates zoomed to 98 percent for Priority and 100 percent for Immediate.

Data Communications

Networks eventually evolved to satisfy customer needs for voice and message (AUTODIN) traffic, but little capability existed to handle large volumes of bit-oriented data traffic. Tactical communications planners had greatly underestimated the volume and the variety of data transmission that would be required by automated combat support systems.

Whereas previous experiences involved telephones and teletypes, the new battlefield environment included hundred, and later thousands, of personal computers. These computers were designed to be interconnected by local area networks (LANs), dial-up telephone circuits, leased data circuits, but those capabilities had not been adequately provided for in the development of tactical communications systems. As an Air Staff planner was to later say: "We had no plan for data communications."

Virtually every aspect of warfare is now automated, requiring the ability to transmit large quantities of data in many different forms. However, tactical communications networks could provide only dedicated, full-period circuits or message-switched (AUTODIN) service. They could by no means provide service comparable to the Defense Data Network found on home installations.

The Defense Information Systems Agency had fabricated a transportable version of a DDN MILNET packet switched node, but lack of a documented need held this switch out of the theater until January 1991.

That lack of in-theater data communications connectivity was a major headache for every organization above the level of a rifle platoon. Mission-critical deficiencies were satisfied only through extraordinary creativity by software and communications engineers both in-theater and in the United States—some of them reportedly working from home PCs and through the nights

Air Force organizations were hit particularly hard by the lack of data communications. Most base-level functions are automated on fixed Air Forces bases. Supply and maintenance functions are routinely conducted from computers on the flight line, which are, in turn, connected to centrally-located host computers. In the case of the Persian Gulf deployment, the flight line moved to a bare-base location in the desert, while the host base-level automation system remained in the United States. Because of limited initial communications, the automated umbilical cord could not be extended readily to deployed locations. The requirement to provide this support became a major focus of attention for Air Force communications and computer personnel.

In a matter of weeks, Air Force personnel had planned and procured a network of communications processors and multiplexers that eventually allowed a base-level computer at Langley Air Force Base (ordinarily designed to handle only local transactions) to serve as a central processing point for all Air Force supply transactions within Southwest Asia. This centralized computer at Langley AFB also provided an interface to the DDN to emulate maintenance, weather and other functions found at fixed Air Force bases. By war's end, there were over 3000 computers linked in one way or another to hosts in the U.S., in large part over full-period, leased commercial circuits.

However, this would not be the only form of data connectivity. The Secure Telephone Unit III (STU-III) came into its own in the Gulf War. While it provided readily accessible secure voice communications to war planners and operators, it was also used extensively to provide secure data communications. The STU-III allowed all echelons of command to transmit data, in a secure mode, to anyone worldwide who could be reached by telephone. In many cases, the STU-III provided secure data communications where no other means was available, short of a courier aircraft.

Airspace Management

Effective and efficient management of airspace was a key element in the spectacular air operations of Desert Shield and Desert Storm. It was effective because it kept the 900 or so aircraft in the air at any one time from running into each other and efficient because it did so without the wasteful block allocations of time and air volume that were seen in Vietnam.

The function of airspace management is not new—it has long been accomplished with wall charts and grease pencils—slowly, inefficiently and too often ineffectively. Computers made it possible to synchronize this planning process with the dynamics of modern air warfare during Desert Storm.

Airspace management is a critical concept of modern aerial warfare that is not well understood, even by some who fly in and through the protective envelope that it helps to create. Airspace management is a planning and deconfliction tool which is possible only if there is a single Airspace Control Authority: A controversial concept long advocated by the Air Force but never before employed on such a large scale. By way of contrast, there were at least four air authorities in the Vietnam war, with virtually no means for coordination and with deconfliction achieved only through wasteful reservations of time and airspace. It was never efficient and all too often not effective.

Airspace management in the Ninth Air Force is a function, heavily supported by automation, that permits airspace managers to visualize how the airspace from the ground to about 100,000 feet is being used by missions planners and others and to deconflict airspace by time, location or altitude.

In certain respects, airspace management is not much different from the air traffic control corridors and procedures around any large municipal airport. In point of fact, military airspace management during Desert Shield/Storm was conducted by Air Force Senior NCO's and officers. But there the similarity ends. Unlike civil airways, tactical airspace is not *controlled* : Its use is *coordinated*. The final responsibility remains with the pilot to "see and to avoid."

Airspace managers are one of the instruments through which the single Airspace Control Authority deconflicts multiple demands for use of the airspace and thus achieves an integrated operation. Airspace managers must understand not only airspace but also the technical demands (speed, altitude, etc.) that will be made upon that air volume by the planners for manned and unmanned aircraft, artillery and tank shells and tactical missiles. They must compile and display this knowledge in such a way that all mission planners can quickly visualize potential conflicts that would otherwise occur.

Precise instructions are issued to mission planners in the Air Control Order (ACO) portion of the single daily Air Tasking Order (ATO). The ACO often exceeded 100 pages in length during Desert Storm. There were as many as 980 daily sorties to be deconflicted during Desert Shield and over 2,800 sorties during the 100 hours of Desert Storm. These sorties involved 122 different air refueling tracks, 660 restricted operating zones, 312 missile engagement zones, 78 strike corridors, 92 combat air patrol points and 36 training areas alone, spread over 93,600 square miles.

All of this had to be superimposed upon and thoroughly coordinated with the continually shifting civil airways of six independent nations. This civil coordination step involved placing 357 USAF controllers, 55 of which were liaison personnel at the air traffic control and ground control intercept facilities of the host nations in the Gulf region.

However, dynamics in the air war and frequent changes in the fire support coordination line during Desert Storm did not permit all potential conflicts to be foreseen and contained in the daily ATO. As many as 100 daily changes were passed by message directly to mission planners. In some instances it was necessary to pass advisories through AWACS or the ABCCC's directly to missions already in progress, Airspace management in the Ninth Air Force was accomplished through its Combat Airspace Deconfliction System (CADS); using commercial hardware and unique software written and maintained by the 1912th Computer Systems Group. CADS depicts, analyzes and deconflicts airspace by time, by location and by altitude. Then CADS automatically compiles the Airspace Control Order and inserts it into the Computer Assisted Force Management System (CAFMS) where it becomes one element of the daily ATO.

CADS uses enhanced graphics and a data base that contains maps of the entire world. The airspace needs of each weapon systems are manually entered into CADS, enabling the airspace manager to instantly see airspace use over the combat area, by time, and in three dimensions. The system will also detect conflicts so airspace managers can propose safe alternative areas. CADS minimizes the risks of fratricide by deconflicting airspace before the aircraft leave the ground.

Summary

While obviously delighted over the decisive application of airpower in the Persian

Gulf, the Air Force is concerned over the delays and difficulties encountered in building the supporting information structure that underwrote that victory.

A potentially disruptive disconnect in Air Force planning allowed combat forces to arrive in the Persian Gulf without the communications equipment needed to plan, launch and control air operations. And when the resources did arrive, they provided only marginal support for critical data communications—the service needed most in modern air warfare. The ingenuity of highly trained and motivated people, along with extraordinary cross-service cooperation, allowed all of these problems to be solved.

The outcome might have been otherwise but for a benign electromagnetic environment and an opponent who could not or did not choose to disrupt vulnerable satellite communications.

The Air Force Chief of Staff asked his deputy for computers and communications, LTGen. Robert Ludwig, to begin "with a clean slate" and to map out changes required to provide more adequate information service support to future air operations. These are some of the actions under study:

• Repackaging equipment so that it is light enough to accompany tactical air units.

• Examining the allocation of resources between active force and national guard combat communications units.

• Reorganizing active force combat communications to put critical skills within deploying tactical air units.

• Providing tactical units with earth terminals that can access commercial satellites and establishing procedures so this can be done routinely and quickly.

• Building a tactical data communications network capable of handling secondary imagery dissemination and connecting data terminals to their CONUS-based hosts.

• Rethinking the point of interface between strategic and tactical communications and how it should be managed.

• Providing the TACC with a more comprehensive communications planning, control and operating capability.

• Examining ways to reduce vulnerability of tactical communications.

• Providing for greater use of contractor personnel for operations and maintenance of strategic systems; freeing personnel for tactical systems.

• Finding ways to more fully exploit bandwidth in present communications systems: that is, integrating voice, data and imagery transmission; use of demand assigned (DAMA) access, pre-processing and data compression to reduce volume of traffic introduced in networks; elimination of redundant traffic, etc.

Endnote

[1] Giulio Douhet, *The Command of the Air.*

CAFMS GOES TO WAR

John Paul Hyde, Johann W. Pfeiffer and Toby C. Logan

"The mechanism used to provide daily tasking to all the bases and units supporting the theater air campaign is the Air Tasking Order, or ATO. The ATO gives detailed instructions to each unit, answering the questions of who does what, where and when. The ATO contains an enormous amount of information. Targets, TOTs [time on target], ordnance loads and fuzing are all specified. Identification routes and procedures, IFF squawks and radio frequencies are directed. Air refueling times, altitudes and contact points are established. There may be a long section of "SPINS," or special instructions. Rules of Engagement are often stated or amplified in some way.
Naturally, the ATO must be received by the tasked units in time for it to be read and understood—no small task for a document of its length and complexity—and in time for the unit to generate and load aircraft, select a mission commander and aircrews, do flight planning and target study, coordinate with other units, etc. As a rough guide, we would like to transmit the ATO at least 12 hours before the start of the execution day."[1]

For the Desert Shield/Desert Storm air campaign, USAF Lt. Gen. Charles A. Horner, Commander, USCENTAF and 9AF Tactical Air Command, was designated as single Joint Forces Air Component Commander, with authority for all ashore air tasking and responsibility for using a single ATO.[2] Horner turned to CAFMS, the transportable Computer-Assisted Force Management System developed by TAC to help generate that ATO.

How CAFMS Works

CAFMS, born in 1979, was the first successful step toward transforming the labor-intensive manual operations of a Tactical Air Control Center (TACC) to a modern, computer-based system.[3] [Following the 1992 Air Force reorganizations, the TACC will become the Modular Air Operations Center (MOAC).] According to TAC Pamphlet 55-43: [4]

> "The Computer-Assisted Force Management System (CAFMS) provides an automated assist to the planning and mission-monitoring functions of the Tactical Air Control Center (TACC). It expedites information exchange between the TACC and lower echelon Tactical Air Control System (TACS) elements, such as the Wing Operations Center (WOC), Air Support Operations Center (ASOC), and Control and Reporting Center (CRC), as well as between sections within the TACC. CAFMS fulfills the functions of Air Tasking Order (ATO) preparation, mission monitoring, immediate tasking, and end-of-day reporting. Collocated with the TACC, the CAFMS is mobile and housed in an S-280 shelter.
>
> CAFMS is capable of handling up to 26 ATOs, 10,000 missions each, 20 local terminals, and 11 remote terminals. It is capable of disseminating ATOs to remotes or through organic communications. It allows units to maintain the status of aircraft, aircrews, base weather, and ammunition. It provides combat operations with mission monitoring, immediate tasking, and immediate update of daily mission end-of-day recaps."

CAFMS *assists* in performing functions in Combat Plans and Combat Operations, but doesn't do them by itself. The ATO, for example, is the product of a process that begins with the commander's guidance on how next he wants to engage the enemy and a master attack plan that lays out where air forces should be going, what they should be attacking, and when, in a logical format.

For Desert Storm, planners conceptualized five airpower objectives and twelve target classes to meet them. The daily tasking process began at 0700 with updated objectives from the commander, which planners worked with new intelligence information, bomb-damage assessments, weather forecasts, and other considerations into a revised master attack plan—complete with target names and priorities—by 2000 hours that evening.

Next, intelligence experts specified aimpoints for each target to be struck, while planners from all airpower components met to assemble force packages—groups of attacking and supporting aircraft—to exploit coalition force strengths and enemy weaknesses.

By 0430 the next morning, planners could begin using CAFMS: to record individual tasking assignments, based on resident force status data; to build and organize the ATO, assignment by assignment; and to blend in still more factors, such as tanker tracks, the Airspace Control Order, and other SPINS. The completed ATO was ready for transmission by 1700-1900 that evening for execution for the next day beginning at 0500.[5]

CAFMS Goes To The Gulf

In August 1990, the USAF had three CAFMS in vans: 9th and 12th Air Forces were authorized one van each (containing primary and backup processors), assigned to the 507th and 602nd TACC Squadrons respectively; and the Blue Flag organization was authorized a van (with a single processor), assigned to the 727 Tactical Control Squadron—Test. The 1912 Computer Systems Group had a fourth set of CAFMS equipments, installed in racks without a shelter.

What USCENTAF took to the Gulf in August 1990 was one van, from the 507th TACCS, connectivity and terminals for 11 remote sites (WOCs, units of the TACS, or headquarters elements), 20 local workstations, and one 600 line-per-minute printer. The goal was to establish command and control for the USCENTAF TACC, to produce, distribute, and track a theater ATO, and for everything that flew to be in it.

Members of the USCENTAF advance party, who had arrived several days earlier, were using PCs and the program FRAGWORKS, designed by the Air Force Data Systems Design Center, to create a daily ATO, which was sent to the initial wing/squadron operating locations over Saudi high-speed secure facsimile and AUTODIN.

The first CAFMS processor came on line at 2300 hours on August 17, followed by the first remote—in the WOC at Dhahran—the following day. WOCs were brought into the system by "road teams" comprised of a system operator/trainer and a maintainer, both from the 507th. These teams packed the equipment, delivered it to the assigned location, installed and tested the equipment and trained local personnel in its operation. Terminals in Europe and Turkey were installed by teams from the 1912th CSGP.

Despite on-site training, some users were uncomfortable with CAFMS and were reluctant to use it, except for receiving the ATO. This obliged Combat Operations to telephone some units for information they should have been receiving over CAFMS.

The ATO was produced and distributed by CAFMS for the first time on 20 August: 200 computer-screen pages, 14 AUTODIN sections. By August 25th the number of deployed units exceeded CAFMS' capacity of 11 remotes. Headquarters TAC tasked 12th AF to deploy its van so that up to 11 more remote sites could receive and track the ATO.

The TACC was now forced to produce, distribute, and track a single theater ATO from two identical, but completely separate systems. The problem was minor to units in the field, but within the TACC planners, controllers, and duty officers had to check both systems to determine alert postures, aircraft availabilities and facility status or to ensure the accuracy of data.

A database management cell was established to re-key updates from one system into the other. A print routine inserted into selected applications programs copied changes to the management cell where an operator entered them into the other system. But even small, 2-3% error rates produced significant differences in reporting parameters such as sorties "scheduled/flown." So, manual transfer was abandoned in favor of collecting data from both systems and consolidating them on PCs for reporting.

By late November, the third CAFMS, from the 727th TCS-T was shipped to the Gulf. In December, TAC scooped up the CAFMS equipment at the 1912th CSGP and the equipment for another system (without shelters), enough to serve a total of

	CAFMS 1
Dhahran	726TCS (CRC)
Al Dhafra	363TFW, 306SW,1705ARS, IAF
Al Minhad	388TFW
Dhahran	1TFW, RAF (F-3)
Shaik Isa	35TFW, 52TFW, 152 TRG
Taif	48TFW, 366 TFW, 1704SRS
Incirlik	USAFE Command Post
Al Kharj	4TFW, 36TFW
KKMC	728TCS
Khamis Mushat	37TFW
Tabuk	33TFW
	CAFMS 2
Rafha	682ASOCS
Shaik Isa	3D MAW, MAG-11
King Fahd	354TFW, 193SOG, 23TFW
KKMC	712ASOCS
Doha	401TFW
Ras Mishab	MTAOC
Al Kharj	169TFG, 1670TASP
Jubial	MTACC
KKMC	A-10 FOL
Muharraq	RAF, 3D MAW
VII Corps ASOC	8ASOG
	CAFMS 3
King Fahd	AFSOC
KKI	FAF
Al Ahsa	FAF
Bateen	41ECS, 1620TAW
Sharjah	1650TAW
Al Ain	1630TAW
Masirah	1640TAW, 1707ARS
King Fahd	1682ALCSP
Al Qaysumah	2nd MI BN
Thumrait	1660TAS
	CAFMS 4
Doha	CAF
Riyadh	Joint STARS
Riyadh	552AWACS, 1612MAS
Riyadh	MODA
Riyadh	Logistics Readiness Center
	CAFMS 5
Cairo West	1706ARS
Diego Garcia	4300ARS, 4300BWP
Abu Dhabi	1712ARW
Dubai	1713ARW
Moron AB	801AREFWP
RAF Fairford	806BWP
Jeddah New	1701ARW
KKI	1703ARW
Seeb	1702ARW
Riyadh	7ACCS, 1700SRS

Table 1.

55 remote locations. Three programmers deployed earlier from the 1912th to the Gulf for software maintenance and were tasked to make the interface and software changes necessary for all five systems to share a common database. Local technicians assembled the pieces and, by February 7, 1991, all five systems were operational and interconnected, serving 60-65 local workstations and 47 remotes. Table 1 shows the distribution of the remotes.

Communications Connectivity

Communications for CAFMS was high on the priority list. The goal was to get a voice circuit to each new site, followed immediately by a link for CAFMS. The most successful medium was SHF satellite, which functioned well, even on circuits which had to pass through as many as five ground stations. Connectivity via TRI-TAC TRC-170 [tropospheric scatter] radios was also successful in most cases. For connectivity to the French air forces at Al Ahsa, the circuit traversed a combination of U.S. and French military circuits. Saudi telephone lines were less effective; 13 were leased, but only 4 successfully passed traffic

Making The System Work

CAFMS deployed with known software deficiencies. These were soon highlighted and had to be fixed. The most serious problem prevented remote terminals from storing the ATO on disk or getting a printout in any reasonable time. It forced remote users to print the ATO one screen at a time—a lengthy task. Consequently, most WOCs preferred to get the ATO hardcopy via AUTODIN. This was the first problem worked, and the fix was completed by November 11, 1990.

In all, 81 major software changes were made—fixing problems that had been brought to the field, some that only appeared during Desert Shield, and some that grew from the growing scale of the operation. For example:

• The entire database was reworked for more flexibility to support the many changes the environment forced on the system.

• Five hundred pages of special instructions were added.

• Capacity was increased to handle four times the number of units.

• Maximum allowable length of the ATO was increased from 999 to 9999 pages.

• The "impossible network" was built, allowing all five systems to link to a common database.

The only hardware change was the installation of higher capacity disk drives one week before the ground war began, increasing storage capacity from 256 megabytes to more than 2 gigabytes and decreasing response time accordingly.

The Mini-ATO Distribution System (MADS)[6]

When the first CAFMS van reached its limit on remotes, an alternative was urgently needed to distribute the ATO. The STU-III secure telephone provided that alternative. Several PC-based systems in the theater were already using the STU-III's data port to transfer files, securely, over the voice switched networks. A quick test showed this to be a viable way to send the ATO. It was suitable for sites as a commercial backup to the tactical communications network.

The ATO in the CAFMS processor was converted to an ASCII file, compressed onto a floppy disk, and transmitted, using Pro-Comm [commercial protocol], PC-to-PC, secured by STU-IIIs. Since most WOCs already had STU-IIIs and PCs, they needed only interface cables, software, and training—all of which were furnished by late October.

As Desert Shield progressed, many WOCs had trouble downloading the ATO from CAFMS and asked that it be sent via the STU-III system. While CAFMS connectivity was still needed to report force-status, the STU-III backup became a preferred means of getting the ATO because it could be printed faster. [Editor's note: this had an adverse impact on grade-of-service in the telephone systems noted in the essay on Air Force communications.]

Much earlier, the 5th Combat Communications Group had designed a KY-68-to-computer interface cable, but few had been produced. More were delivered in late November to those sites without STU-IIIs, thereby completing the MADS. Designed as a commercial backup, MADS became a critical supplement to CAFMS and AUTODIN for distributing the ATO. The MADS kit, composed of an IBM-compatible laptop, a STU-III, cables (for both the STU-III and KY-68), and software made an indispensable asset to WOC deployments.

Army Connectivity

Although the Air Support Operations Centers (ASOCs) had CAFMS terminals, the Army aviation units subject to tasking and airspace coordination—forward-deployed fixed-wing and helicopter units and echelon above corps forces operating from fixed bases—did not. Vital mission data—times on target and station times, special EW mission tracks, and transit route approvals—had to be obtained through secondary sources, and were reportedly sometimes too late for mission windows. Even in the ASOCs themselves, the CAFMS database couldn't be downloaded and manipulated. In the end, ASOCs such as the 682nd attached to the XVIII Corps got the ATO over MADS, converted the message file to a database file with a computer program written locally, and then massaged it to extract relevant information. Army aviation units got the ATO over AUTODIN or by collocating with or commuting daily to Air Force units with CAFMS connections.[7]

Navy Connectivity[8]

As widely reported in the media, CAFMS was not interoperable with Navy units afloat. Early on, Navy liaison officers in the TACC learned how to pass the ATO to the Command Ship USS *Blue Ridge*, PC-to-PC, secured by STU-IIIs. Transmission took 2 to 3 hours, but this worked only when the *Blue Ridge* was in port and had access to landlines. For broader distribution to ships afloat, CAFMS operators cut two teletype tapes:

• An abbreviated version of the ATO including only naval aviation and tanker tasking, and SPINs. Sent over the FLEETFLASHNET at 75 baud, it reached recipients by 0200 local (8-9 hours in transit).

• The entire ATO. Sent over the Computer Processing and Routing System (COMPARS) with a manual relay and format conversion from AUTODIN in Guam, it reached addressees by 1000 local (16-17 hours in transit), 5-6 hours into the day of execution. Eventually CAFMS was reprogrammed to produce the COMPARS-compatible format (JANAP 126) directly, shortening the overall transmission time by 6 hours.

Over time, Navy and Air Force personnel explored many alternatives:

• Putting CAFMS terminals aboard ship. This didn't work because the ships had no SHF satellite communications.

• Connecting CAFMS terminals aboard ships via UHF satellites. There were no CAFMS-to-remote handshake protocols for half-duplex UHF SATCOM, and no spare UHF frequencies.

• Using dual UHF SATCOM channels to simplify the handshaking. This would require designing a new handshake anyway. In any regard, there were still no UHF SATCOM channels available.

• PC-to-PC connectivity over MARSAT [commercial maritime satellite] telephone. The circuit quality was not adequate to sustain synchronization, and the cost was high ($10/minute).

• Streamlining the FLEETFLASHNET abbreviated ATO even further, cutting out the non-Navy-supporting tanker tracks and SPINs. This didn't shorten the overall delivery time, but it did reduce transmission time on the net itself.

In the end, shuttling the ATO in hardcopy and floppy-disk forms each night from the TACC to command carriers in the Red Sea and Persian Gulf, and from there by helicopters to other carriers and ships afloat, was the fastest (arriving by 0100 local) and most reliable, and became the primary distribution means for Desert Storm.

How Well Did CAFMS Work

How does one measure the performance of a C^4 system? Technicians can take pride in a system that was up and working 98% of the time, but availability is but one criterion. For CAFMS, time of ATO delivery is another critical measure. Delivery times to Naval units have already been discussed. In mid-November it was taking (on average) 2.5 hours for Air Force tactical telecommunications centers to get the ATO; 3.5 hours for fixed telecommunications centers outside of the theater; and approximately 7 hours to other Service telecommunications centers.

At a CAFMS remote terminal, a typical unit could extract and print out its portion of the ATO and SPINs in 40 minutes to 2 hours. But, downloading the entire ATO could tie up the terminal for 4-6 hours more, and printing it, page by page, could take another 8-14 hours. So those units wanting the entire order either got it via MADS or waited for the AUTODIN message version.

Another measure is expandability: the ability to cope with overloading. Sorties surged from 980 per day in Desert Shield to over 3000 per day during the ground campaign, and the ATO grew in size accordingly.

CAFMS' first ATO, published August 20, 1990, was 200 computer-screen pages and 14 AUTODIN sections long. By November a typical Desert Shield ATO was 300 pages, or 40 sections long. During the air campaign (January 1991), the length had increased to nearly 900 pages (actually 874, just before the fix was made increasing the maximum length above 999). Peak length during the ground war (February 23-27) was 982 pages (over 100 sections).

So too did the number of ATO addressees grow. The number of direct addressees with CAFMS remote terminals rose from 11 in August 1990 to 54 (of 55 possible) by the time of the ground offensive. Total ATO addressees numbered around 150 in November and exceeded 175 at war's end.

Looking at it operationally, over 120,000 sorties were flown in Desert Shield, over 110,000 in Desert Storm, and "an airplane didn't fly unless it was in the Air Tasking Order."[9] And later it was the Air Force Chief of Staff's view that "no commander was ever stopped from doing anything he needed to do because of lack of communications."[10]

Conclusions

CAFMS went to the Persian Gulf war an 11-year old, sent to do an adult's job. It was too small, too slow, and capable of too few planning functions. Not all of the tactical commands in the U.S. Air Force were standardized on it, and the Army, the Navy, the Marine Corps, and our coalition allies used yet other systems, albeit no better.[11]

It was not designed to handle the number of air bases or the size of the ATO required in Desert Storm. It worked because people made it work, and had the luxury of five months time to enhance it with additional processors and storage devices, some of them newly acquired, and linked together with software changes engineered on the spot, in the desert.[12]

Gaining air superiority early in Desert Storm gave coalition forces a relatively static enemy, hunkered down and awaiting our moves; a permissive battlefield allowing us to prosecute the campaign with a 72-hour planning-execution cycle and ATOs scripted by CAFMS. "A more aggressive and determined enemy might have done much better by exploiting the inherent lags."[13]

A new, modular Contingency Tactical-Air-Control Automated Planning System (CTAPS) is being fielded now by the Air Force to succeed CAFMS, to interoperate jointly, and to automate more planning functions in order to help reduce the planning cycle.[14] And joint USAF/Navy tests of the CAFMS segment, from TACCs shore to carriers at sea worldwide, have been remarkably successful.[15]

But, that's all in the future. For Desert Shield and Desert Storm, CAFMS was there—just enough and just in time.

Endnotes

[1] General Merrill A. McPeak, USAF: "For the Composite Wing," *AIRPOWER JOURNAL*, Fall 1990.

[2] James P. Coyne: *Airpower In The Gulf*, Air Force Association, Arlington, Virginia, June 1992.

[3] General Robert D. Russ, USAF: "The Eighty Percent Solution," *AIR FORCE MAGAZINE*, January 1991.

[4] TAC Pamphlet (TACP) 55-43: "Operations: Tactical Air Control System," Headquarters, Tactical Air Command, September 18, 1987.

[5] Coyne, ibid.

[6] Edited from an article of the same name by 2nd Lt Michael Pervere, USAF, published in *Air Force Tactical Communications in War: The Desert Shield/Desert Storm Comms Story*, Headquarters USCENTAF, March 1991.

[7] *CALL Newsletter 92-1*: "Joint Tactical Communications," U.S. Army Combined Arms Command, Center for Army Lessons Learned, January 1992.

[8] Captain Lee Patton, USAF: "Getting the Air Tasking Order (ATO) to the Navy," *Air Force Tactical Communications in War: The Desert Shield/Desert Storm Comms Story*, Headquarters USCENTAF, March 1991.

[9] Major General John A. Corder, USAF, CENTAF Director of Operations, quoted in Coyne, ibid. See also "Single Air Tasking Order in Desert Storm Puts USAF in Driver's Seat for Air Plans," *Inside the Air Force*, February 22, 1991.

[10] General Merrill A. McPeak, USAF, quoted in Policy Letter from the Office of the Secretary of the Air Force, May 1991.

[11] Coyne, ibid.

[12] Major Richard M. Jensen, USAF, Headquarters USAF/SCMCT in a talking paper prepared for General Merrill A. McPeak, USAF, April 4, 1991.

[13] Norman Friedman: *Desert Victory: The War For Kuwait*, Naval Institute Press, 1991.

[14] Russ, ibid.

[15] Interview with Lt. Col. Michael Whitehurst, USAF, Headquarters TAC/DOYY, June 26, 1992.

Appendix

CAFMS Hardware

The CAFMS host computer is a 32-bit mini-computer with access to 10 megabytes of RAM, four removable disk drives (two with 67-megabyte capacity each; two with one gigabyte each), and a high-density one-gigabyte tape drive. Each shelter contains two computers, the second for backup. When necessary, a single operator can bring CAFMS back on-line in about 5 minutes.

The primary input/output terminal, local or remote, is a PC workstation with 12 inch display. Paired to each terminal is a dot matrix printer. Line printers capable of 600 132-character lines per minute are used in Combat Plans and Combat Operations.

Local terminals and printers connect to the host computer through RS-232 fiber optic links, supported by six 8-port fiber optic multiplexers. Remote terminals are connected to CAFMS through tactical communications links (satellite or microwave) or wire lines using KG-84As for data encryption and Model C-86A Communications Controllers for error checking and flow regulation. Although they do many of the same functions, the local and remote terminals actually operate in fundamentally different ways, use different protocols, and can't be substituted for one another.

The primary communications connectivity to subscribers without CAFMS terminals is through AUTODIN, reached by direct digital interface between the CAFMS host computer and TRI-TAC TYC-39 Message Switch. The host can also output standard teletype tape.

CAFMS Software

Applications programs are written in COBOL; system-level programs are written in Fortran and Assembler. The operating system is a C3 Systems' OS/32 for scientific applications. All programs are modular and relatively easy to modify when necessary.

The database structure is hierarchical, designed for speed of access. Over the past eight years, nearly 1.5 million lines of application-program code have been developed. The complete CAFMS application occupies 60 megabytes of disk. Once configured, the database occupies 400 megabytes spread over two disks.

Local terminals use a terminal emulator in C language especially developed to emulate the Perkin-Elmer Model 1251 terminal. The emulator was converted to Pascal during Desert Shield to support 386 and 486 PCs. Remote terminals use an off-the-shelf IBM bisync emulator well suited for cryptographic synchronous communications. Both emulators support downloading CAFMS information to printers, floppies, and removable hard disks. Local terminals support uploading mission data from floppies and hard disks created off-line.

CAFMS Control and Operation

The entire system is controlled by the Computer Operator's Station located in the shelter. It allows accesses and grants permissions to selected local and remote terminals; delegates read/write authority to appropriate workstations; operates KG-84 encryption devices and modems supporting communications interfaces; and monitors overall system performance.

CAFMS is a template-driven system. Users are given display skeletons on their screens, allowing them to input or modify data only in certain unprotected areas. There are four basic types of displays:

• Selection Criteria display, when a command is entered and the computer needs more information.

• Blank Template contains empty data fields, is normally used to create a new record and cannot be used to purge an existing record.

• Information display contains data from a single record (e.g., a single mission) and normally is used to update or purge an existing record.

• List display contains data from two or more records (e.g., all CAS missions), and database cannot be updated from this display.

Within CAFMS, up to 26 separate ATOs can be constructed and maintained simultaneously. The designated terminal operator assigns an alphabetic identifier and specific time period to each ATO. Time periods for individual ATOs are completely flexible; they may overlap or even coincide. The database can handle up to 9,000 missions at one time. Individual parts of an ATO may be constructed in any order, using blank templates or by modifying an existing ATO. ATOs can be reviewed before dissemination. Once notified, units with remote terminals can access the ATO directly from the database. ATOs outgoing via AUTODIN or paper tape are formatted according to USMTF rules.

Combat Operations monitors missions using mission schedules. Once generated, they can be updated from local or remote terminals. A wide range of selection criteria is available for calling up and displaying missions. Except for individual mission displays, all schedule displays are updated automatically as new information is received.

THE ELECTRONIC SANCTUARY

James M. Burin

Electronic warfare (EW) is one of the most significant but least understood success stories from Desert Storm. The conflict in the Persian Gulf offered our first glimpse of the profound impact of a new warfare area formed by the Chief of Naval Operations in 1989. Called Space and Electronic Warfare (SEW), it was to play a major role in the overwhelming victory in both air and ground operations by allied forces.

SEW is the combination of space, electronic warfare, and C⁴I. And much more! SEW is a textbook example of synergism at work. When these elements are combined and today's technology added, the result is *information warfare* in its purest form. It has put a powerful and dynamic tactical tool in the hands of the operational commander.

As with any warfare area, SEW has a specific target set—this one composed of the enemy decision makers, who might be as diverse as radar operators in vans, signalmen at communications sites, commanders in command posts or political leaders in underground bunkers.

The object of SEW is the same for all targets: to reduce or eliminate their effectiveness by interrupting, modifying or blocking the information flowing to, from and among these nodes. This may be achieved through *hard kill* (bombs or anti-radiation missiles) or *soft kill* (jamming, deception, computer intrusion, intimidation, etc.), depending upon the mission objective.

SEW in Desert Storm was proof of a theory—ironically one originally called Radio-Electronic Combat and proposed by the Soviet military over two decades ago. Information to and from Iraqi decision makers was modified or eliminated, and they became largely ineffective. Electronic warfare played a major role in this attack on information and in the overall success of the war.

While electronic warfare is not new—it has been standing on the sidelines for a long time, its status not unlike that of an offensive lineman in football—it is always there, very powerful, absolutely necessary, but rarely acknowledged or appreciated.

As a result of this faulty perception of its potential, EW has been exposed to a pattern of peacetime reductions and continuous demands to justify EW equipment, which is always difficult because EW does not go supersonic, does not look great in glossy photos and does not have measures of effectiveness that are easy to calculate or to prove.

Nevertheless, there are constant demands in wartime for more and better EW. [Editor's note: the U.S. Air Force has reconsidered its pre-Desert Storm decision to phase out its Wild Weasel squadrons. It now plans to retain at least one squadron in the force structure.]

Concurrent SEAD

During Desert Storm we saw a new dimension of electronic warfare. Historically, EW has been defensive, planned and waged at unit level, and usually passive in nature. However, the current SEW trend—as evidenced by Desert Storm—is to make electronic warfare more offensive, planned and executed at force level and preemptive in nature.

We had just a glimpse of this new look during the attacks on Libya in 1986. In that incident a relatively modern air defense network was deftly countered by EW, enabling Navy and Air Force strike aircraft to conduct their attacks with only one combat loss.

This new offensive approach to EW was dominant throughout Desert Storm, but particularly during the first few strikes. In a classic approach, suppression of enemy air defense (SEAD) consists of a sequential type roll-back campaign, where the defenses are systematically rendered ineffective before attacks are made against tactical and strategic targets. However, in *concurrent SEAD*—as seen in the initial strikes of Desert Storm—the strike and the SEAD effort are carried out simultaneously in an integrated plan.

Concurrent SEAD is not possible without a strong and effective EW effort—as exemplified by allied air forces that rendered impotent the vaunted Iraqi defense system.

Offensive electronic warfare was a major part of this effort. Yes, the allied aircraft still had EW sensors and defensive electronic protection devices. However, for the first time, we also had offensive electronic warfare tactical actions; that is, coordinated preemptive jamming, air launched decoys, and anti-radiation missiles. The combination of these offensive hard-kill and soft-kill systems was very effective. In just a few days, Iraqi electronic emissions needed for a reasonable air defense posture were reduced from an impressive pre-war level to virtually nothing. The reasons are many: a sound strike plan that targeted critical nodes; good weapons and superb execution by aircrews; and, a not-to-be-neglected psychological risk factor that reduced the desire of Iraqi operators to use their equipment and invite near-certain targeting by anti-radiation missiles. This risk factor was high for Iraqi decision makers—and particularly for those in and around radar sites!

We do not know and probably will never know the full story of why electronic warfare was so successful. Was it because of jamming of signals, or destruction of transmitters and communications or intimidation of operators? The answers to those questions may be of marginal use and possibly irrelevant. The bottom line is that this unprecedented execution of electronic warfare shut down one of the most sophisticated air defense networks in the world. That led, in consequence, to a spectacularly successful air operation and the quick and low-loss ground campaign.

EW At War

It is particularly important to note that this EW effort was truly a joint operation, with EA-6Bs of the Navy and Marines and the EF-111s of the Air Force providing jamming support and the Navy's A-7, EA-6B, A-6, and F/A-18 Harm-shooters working hand in hand with the Air Force's F-4G Wild Weasels providing anti-radiation missile support.

Let me give you a typical mission sequence for a Persian Gulf carrier air wing strike. It is early in the war and the air wing is assigned to hit an Iraqi airfield. The strike is a daytime strike and is made up of 8 strike aircraft, 4 HARM aircraft, and 2 EA-6B Prowlers.

The planning involves a high altitude ingress, with the Prowlers in separate standoff jamming orbits just on the edge of the threat envelopes to cover the two major strike groups' attack axes. An additional aircraft is carrying four air launched radar decoys (TALD) to try to stimulate the electronic environment for the HARM shooters. A fighter sweep is planned prior to the strike (later in the war, because of the reduced air-to-air threat, these aircraft would double as HARM shooters). Since it is early in the war, several preemptive HARM shots are planned.

After the strike leader briefs all the participants in the strike, 18 aircraft total, including tankers and the E-2, launch and proceed up the Gulf. Tanking is accomplished and check-in with the E-2 completed. The strikers are carrying four 1,000-pound bombs each, the SEAD aircraft 2 HARM each, and the Prowlers have the appropriate pod mix for the threat and one HARM each for "pop-up" emitters.

As the strike group approached the coast, the aircraft carrying the decoys accelerates ahead to ensure the radar decoys are in the heart of the threat envelope when the fighter sweep first penetrates the envelope.

As the EA-6Bs approach the coast, there is minimal electronic activity, even though it is only a few days into the war. The TALD are released, and as they enter the heart of the threat envelope, the preemptive HARM are launched against critical surface-to-air radars. The fighter sweep passes through the target area, finds nothing, and heads outbound. As the strike group approaches the coast, the Prowlers start jamming, first against early warning, then fire control radars. They set up their orbits and continue jamming as the strike group enters the threat envelopes and proceeds to the target. The electronic activity, minimal on ingress to the coast, now goes to virtually zero after the jamming comes on and several preemptive HARM are fired.

As the strikers hit their target with stunning accuracy and start to egress, one point defense missile radar comes on. The Prowler waits to ensure it is not just a transient emission, and when it stays up they target the HARM against it. The last strike aircraft is egressing the target area, and the threat radar still remains active. The HARM is away! The actual results of the HARM shot are not conclusively known, but at the calculated impact time the target radar abruptly stops emitting. The Prowlers continue to jam and cover the strikers' egress until all have checked safely back in with the E-2. At that time jammers come off, and the EA-6Bs proceed back to the ship, another successful mission completed.

Due to their superb capability and the relatively low number of jamming-capable aircraft available in theater, at times the Prowlers would do double duty by tanking after a strike and proceeding to a designated orbit point to provide support for another strike group—one that could have aircraft from the Air Force, Marines, or the allies.

This scenario, and many very similar, went on day and night from all the Navy carriers as the highly trained flight crews planned and executed strike after strike. The tactics and EW support combined to produce impressive results during the 43 days, with only two aircraft from the 4 carriers in the Persian Gulf lost to enemy fire. One of these had no EW support since it was on a surface reconnaissance mission.

The aircrews never got comfortable or complacent, and rightfully so, but they did have supreme confidence in their aircraft and in the EW sanctuary that was created for them.

In assessing the quality of the EW effort, the loss rates speak for themselves. Until just near the end of the war, jamming support from EA-6B or EF-111 aircraft was normally a "go/no go" criteria for a strike. In addition, aircraft like the EP-3, RC-135, and EC-130 provided invaluable support to all strike activities across the entire Desert Storm theater of operations.

This intensive EW effort created an electronic sanctuary in which the allied aircraft operated during the air and ground operations. This sanctuary enabled strike aircraft to proceed to and from their targets and to fully exploit their modern technology weapons in relative safety.

The results of this impressive, astute and aggressive employment of electronic warfare should speak for themselves. The vast majority of the Iraqi surface-to-air missiles and anti-aircraft artillery were fired in a ballistic mode with no electronic guidance at all, thereby greatly reducing their effectiveness and at the same time, significantly enhancing the survivability of the strike aircraft.

With an obvious insight to the future, Admiral Gorshkov, former Admiral of the Soviet Fleet, stated: "The next war will be won by the side which best exploits the electromagnetic spectrum."

In that regard, Desert Storm was the "next" war and, as the pivotal role of SEW becomes better known, there can be little doubt but that it will play a role of increasing importance in information warfare and in future conflicts.

COMMUNICATIONS SUPPORT TO INTELLIGENCE

Alan D. Campen

When signalman Captain Alexander wigwagged a warning to Colonel "Shanks" Evans on Sunday, July 26,1861, his message spoiled General McDowell's scheme to encircle the Confederate army, dashing hopes that Bull Run would be the first and only major conflict in a civil war. The warning that Union infantry and artillery "could turn his flank" was succinct, precise, and, above all else, timely. Battlefield geometry at Manassas helped: The sensor, the sensed, and the command and control node were all within eyesight of one another. General Beauregard immediately shifted his forces, changing the outcome of this battle and the course of the Civil War.

Saddam Hussein received no warning that his right flank was about to be turned by Coalition forces storming across the desert to spring the trap on the Republican Guards. He did not yet own space-based sensors that could see the largest mechanized army in history sweeping into Iraq at speeds up to 40 kilometers per hour[1]. Deception, false radio signals and strict operational security by Coalition forces had tricked Iraqi leaders into believing that the U.S. XVIIIth and VIIth Corps were still poised at the berms and barriers along the Saudi border with Kuwait and that amphibious forces would soon swarm over the beaches.

Even if the Coalition strategy had been detected, the relentless aerial bombardment had flattened Iraq's electrical and telephone system and left intact little other communications through which a regrouping of forces might have been managed. Ignorance, misjudgment and high technology had left Iraqi forces pinned under the sand and in the path of an oncoming juggernaut.

In stark contrast to Iraq's information wasteland, commanders of Coalition forces were receiving a level of intelligence support far greater than furnished military commanders in any previous conflict.

But however good that intelligence support may have been—and much was excellent—some commanders still complained that the information (imagery in particular) lacked the precision and timeliness to support the maneuvers being executed.

Secondary dissemination of imagery was a major problem and most of the blame for that can be laid upon tactical communications systems that lacked proper connectivity, interoperability and capacity to cope with a downward deluge of bit-oriented data traffic.

Even when operating under the benign, almost peacetime conditions—the most serious interruptions to communications were self-inflicted—and although functioning at design speed, the tactical information systems installed in the Persian Gulf still could not satisfy the expectations of users below the corps level.

The expanding scope and pace of modern warfare has fractured the always tenuous link connecting the commander with his scouts. Signal flags that once readily conveyed timely warnings have given way to electrical communication media that can be exploited by an enemy willing to make an investment in technology; and, that cannot carry the ever increasing volumes of data spewing forth from all-seeing sensors. These are not trivial problems, and the search for solutions will take more than frantic scrambling for new technology or engaging in peevish turf battles over ownership of communications networks.

Senior defense officials say the blame must be shared for this serious shortcoming in tactical communications. They stress the need for much closer cooperation and coordination between the intelligence and communications communities as designs are laid down for new systems to collect, process and disseminate intelligence.

This search might begin by reexamining some basic notions about how intelligence actually flows on today's battlefield.

Bottom Up or Top Down

Military maxim holds that the best intelligence comes from soldiers in contact and that reports from these engagements flow up the chain of command, being filtered and consolidated at each echelon along the way. One can almost conjure a picture of an anxious and distraught President Lincoln perched in the telegraph office in Washington, D.C., awaiting news from his latest choice as Commander of the Army of the Potomac.

It is precisely this perspective of data flow that drove a *bottoms-up* approach to the design of the communications systems to collect and disseminate intelligence. Doctrine held that systems should be tailored to the specific needs of the tactical commander and placed under his direct control, but that paradigm is no longer useful. It does not match how intelligence information flows to, from and around the area of operations.

Weapons and tactics have expanded the battlefield well beyond the range of human eyes, ears and of the electronic sensors owned by battalions, brigades and regiments. Maneuver warfare absolutely depends on accurate and timely intelligence about entities and events that are no longer easily nor quickly sensed from the front lines: events at the full depth of the theater of operations and often beyond the reach of sensors under the direct control of combat commanders.

Infantry no longer trudges a dozen miles a day. They ride swiftly into battle at speeds up to 40 miles per hour, at night and in poor weather, when optical sensors are blind. Further, well-disciplined forces may ride silently into new formations, limiting the usefulness of sensors sweeping the spectrum for signs of activity.

These new, deep threats can be detected only by air- and space-borne systems. These are controlled at theater or even national levels, serve multiple users and other purposes and their use must be prioritized. Spy satellites are a good example of sensors that have other, often competing, tasks to perform.

Tactical communications networks designed to pass an upward flow of voice and message SITREPS (*situation reports*) cannot handle the downward flow of data-intensive photographs and charts; kilobit circuits are no match for megabit images.

Further, the most skillful of analysts and photo interpreters now sit hundreds or even thousands of miles from the scene of battle. A discrete event on the battlefield may convey entirely different meanings to evaluators who sit at tactical, theater and strategic levels. The rancorous arguments between Washington and Riyadh over the percentage of tank kills during the air phase of Desert Storm is one illustration of differing perceptions from intelligence reports.

Satellite-based and airborne sensors sweep volumes of data from across enormous arcs of the Earth's surface. Impressive progress has been made in converting that raw data into useful information, but these improvements go for naught when the knowledge they impart cannot be delivered to those most in need, when they need it, in a format they can readily use.

"Precision weapons need precision intelligence," said a high ranking military intelligence official, who admitted that much remains to be done before intelligence collection and dissemination systems are brought to the level of performance demanded by modern AirLand battle doctrine and by *one-shot, one-kill* weapons.

Knowing the Extended Battlefield

There was a good match among technology, procedures and some customer demands for intelligence during Desert Shield. While it took a bit of a scramble to assemble Iraqi order of battle, the U. S. Central Command credited OOB as timely and accurate. Sensor technology—satellite and aerial photography, supplemented by signals and communications intelligence—pinpointed major maneuver units of the enemy force.[2] This task was simplified when Iraqi forces dug into the sand, seldom moved during the prolonged buildup of forces, remained in view of overhead systems and thus bided well within intelligence cycle times.

But, order of battle is only the first step in a continuing intelligence cycle that is expected to help the operational commander answer four questions: what may happen; what is happening; what does it mean, and what should I do about it?

Battlelines are constantly changing in high mobility warfare. During one intense period in the 100-hour Desert Storm ground campaign, the Fire Support Coordination Line—that is the boundary for free fire—shifted three times in less than 24 hours. This disrupted deconfliction procedures that had been designed and rehearsed to prevent Blue on Blue engagements and undoubtedly contributed to friendly fire casualties.

Portraying Sense of Battle

Sensor technologies excel at collecting and disgorging raw data and richly deserve plaudits for intensive development in satellite photography and signals exploitation in the past two decades. Nevertheless, while intelligence support may begin with data collection, it does not end until these data are transformed into militarily useful *information* and delivered to key command and control and fire support nodes in time to be used to direct maneuver forces or execute strikes.

Intelligence support to operational commanders was uneven. Some complained that the intelligence delivered during Desert Storm was not timely, nor accurate, nor did it cover the battlefield in sufficient depth to support the military operations being executed.[3] Others lauded the "battlefield templates" as portraying exactly which forces and weapons were encountered when they breached the berms.[4]

The *sense* of an extended and expanded battle can be accurately garnered best by fusing of the data from sensors on the battlefield with that from sensors and analysis centers thousands of miles distant. While the military effectiveness of Patriot intercepts of Iraqi Scuds has been criticized, those intercepts stand as striking examples of what is technically possible through coupling the output of strategic and tactical sensors into a real-time information network.[5] While the notion of coupling the output of the strategic Defense Support Program (DSP) sensors to Patriot was not new, the technical interface was improvised in an extraordinarily short time and during the heat of battle.

Communicating With Movers

Mobility on the battlefield presents another challenge for communications systems that must couple commanders to intelligence flowing down from above. Combat units moved so often and so quickly during Desert Storm that they broke the umbilical connecting them to their intelligence nodes. This was true even where intelligence terminals had been installed in vans that were to accompany combat forces into battle. These large vehicles could not keep up with commanders. FM voice was the best that most commanders could count on when on the move.

The problem was further compounded by the extreme mobility of some enemy forces. Some weapons moved so often and quickly they almost never remained inside the engagement window of the countering weapons. For example, many Scud missile launchers did not remain in position long enough to be fixed and engaged. Further, they moved at night or under the screen of weather or smoke from oil fires that blinded most sensors. The search for Scuds—conducted in the unforgiving spotlight of global television—was a singularly frustrating challenge for national technical means. Government sources later admitted that the most useful information about Scud launchers came not from electronic sensors, but from human intelligence (HUMINT)[6] and from analysis of launcher capabilities that reduced the search area to manageable dimensions.

As one senior intelligence official described it, high technology sensors provide, "a view of the battlefield as if seen through a straw." He concluded that "synoptic sensing" of the battlefield was the only answer for combat commanders who ask what lies over the next hill and who expect the answer to come in something other than days-old photographs. However, passing 600 frames of high-resolution imagery each day to a corps on the move, or 50 frames to a division, is beyond the capacity of most communications systems now in the field and some still on the drawing board.

Capacity and Vulnerability

Those who engineer communications systems are being asked not only to increase the capacity of communications systems, but to reduce vulnerabilities to enemy exploitation as well. That involves techniques that are often mutually exclusive. Accordingly, communications engineers are urging the intelligence community to pay more attention to *pre-processing* of data at the sensor and upon data *compression* techniques to reduce the total number of bits to be transmitted.

In combination, preprocessing and compression could reduce throughput demands by a factor of 100 (some say 1000) or more. Experts point, for example, to commercially available fractal-based compression, which claims a 75 to 1 compression ratio. This permits large images to be packed into small data files and leads to techniques that will allow full-motion video to run on a personal computer.

Connectivity and Capacity

Communications experts use the terms *connectivity* and *capacity* to explain the anguish suffered by military intelligence in the Persian Gulf. Connectivity is not a new term in the lexicon of communications. However, it is a condition that is far more difficult to assure in the digital age than it was in the era of analog telephony and the telegraph, when physical continuity in a circuit was usually sufficient. A host of technical and procedural interface criteria must now first be satisfied if user terminals are to exchange information over an otherwise contiguous path.

Communications engineers are quick to point out that most of these inhibitors to connectivity are not inherent in the transmission segment. They are imposed by the user terminal or its protocol-dependent application program and are beyond the control of the transmission or even the network systems engineer.

Emphasis on terminals and on user foremats and protocols is not to imply that *capacity* in transmission systems was not a problem in the Gulf. Fortunately, most of the satellite telecommunications resources of the Free World were marshalled to satisfy data-intensive demands for imagery down to the level of the theater commander and the component commands (ARCENT, AFCENT and MARCENT).

It is the tactical networks that were usually unable to adequately support the insatiable demands for high quality imagery to combat echelons below the level of the tactical air force and the army corps. Many units were served only by hard copy photos couriered by helicopter or truck. This clearly did not meet the high and probably unrealistic expectations of their customers.

Data communications with the naval units afloat was a potentially serious problem that was bridged initially by courier service and later with satellite and computer terminals borrowed from the Air Force. The Navy had already commenced a crash program to equip all of its carriers with SHF satellite terminals, but none of those ships had been deployed to the Gulf.[7]

Another point of concern is that consumer complaints abound despite the fact that all communications systems were performing at near design speeds and in a benign electromagnetic environment. A senior Navy official noted[8] that interference with one UHF satellite would have seriously interrupted the flow of intelligence and altered the outcome of the war.

Data Transmission

The personal computer has become the instrument of choice, not only for command and control, but in performing the most mundane logistic, financial and personnel support functions. The Defense Data Network (DDN)—a packet switching system—is the cardinal means by which thousands of computers are normally connected in peacetime to their hosts and to each other. This is accomplished through one of several hundred packet switch nodes (PSNs) in the DDN, consisting of the MilNet (unclassified) and the DISNET (actually several distinct classified networks).

Unfortunately, this migration away from the telephone and traditional message traffic had not been adequately accommodated for in the planning for tactical transmission and switching systems. Contingency plans did not reflect this need and PC users searched in vain for a DDN node in the Persian Gulf. Improvisation abounded.

The Army constructed a MILNET-like capability and reached back to a CONUS connection to DDN through dedicated channels. The Air Force reprogrammed several nodes at CONUS airbases to extend packet-switch capability to tactical units.

The DISA had fabricated a PSN that was capable of supporting SECRET traffic, but it was late in January 1991 before that node was finally ordered into the theater.

Some fortunate users had also shipped their STU-III and DSVT (KY-68) secure telephone instruments and were able to make secure file transfers through the data port of those instruments. But this alternative was slow, wasteful of precious bandwidth and it often disrupted the network for voice users.

Data Links

Communications difficulties were not limited to satellites or to terrestrial trunking or switching systems. A senior official in the defense department believes that a principal weakness in battlefield communications lies with the "data links" which, in terms of intelligence support, are those communications paths that connect the sensor to the analyst and, often, the analyst to the customer.

Data links have been aptly called the "step-child" of sensor programs. This is because the focus of research and development has been on detection and discrimination, not on how the sensor product would be delivered into the hands of operational users, in a man-readable format and in time to be of operational use.

Data links seem often to have been an afterthought in the development chain, perhaps because they involved technologies unfamiliar to the program staff. As a consequence, the data links that accompany most sensor systems into the field bear some common burdens:

• Data links were unique and incompatible with those of other sensor systems. Data elements, message formats, protocols, etc. were usually specific to the host system. In fact, many are not so much data links as they are character-oriented bit streams, often in machine readable-only format. In that form they are often worthless to an operational commander and his staff. The data must be manually extracted, interpreted and converted before it can be correlated with that from other sensors and then fused into a useful display for the commander. These manual processes imposed time delays that may be acceptable for strategic intelligence, but are unrealistic in a tactical scenario where target dwell times are measured in minutes[9].

• Most sensor platforms are not equipped to perform on-board processing of the data they collect. Accordingly, their communications down-links must transport huge volumes of raw data to earth-bound analysis centers[10]. Communications systems must operate in the line-of-sight radio frequency range (UHF, SHF and EHF) if they are to handle such volumes of data[11].

• Data links from sensors have traditionally beamed down to fixed or semi-mobile nodes, usually far removed from the battlefield. Those that were down-linked directly into the combat zone were installed in vehicles that could not keep pace with the fast-moving mobile command centers they were to support. The AirLand doctrine delegates initiative to divisions, armored cavalry regiments and maneuver brigades, resulting in many independent combat actions on a non-linear battlefront. Intelligence officials have concluded that data links that provide targeting support to such units must be installed either in the command vehicle or in ones that can keep pace[12].

• Communications links do not now have the capacity to pass large numbers (in the hundreds each day) of high resolution images among intelligence nodes, in or out of theater or with customers below the theater level in the Army. This limitation was partially overcome in Desert Storm through the liberal use of dedicated military and commercial satellite-based channels (such as the Army Trojan system). This expedient worked in the Persian Gulf but over paths and modes that could easily be exploited or interrupted by an enemy (or any third-party) equipped and inclined to do so.

• The immense size of the AOR in the Persian Gulf war far exceeded anything envisioned in planning for control of tactical air warfare. Aircraft employed by AWACS (air warning and control), JSTARS (radar surveillance of moving ground targets), Rivet Joint (signals intercept) and ABCCC (control of close air support) aircraft, that were absolutely dependent on data and voice links to the Tactical Air Control Center in Riyadh, were orbiting well beyond line-of-sight ranges of the normal complement of air-ground-air radio links. The Air Force was obliged to insert communications relay aircraft into the network—including EC-135L aircraft borrowed from the strategic missile program—and to install remote radio ground stations in the forward combat zones, to maintain connectivity between the TACC and the orbiting fleet.[13]

Demand vs Capacity

Demand for communications seems always to exceed capacity and engineers who have labored to increase throughput are now looking elsewhere for relief. Ruthless enforcement of administrative controls—as was successfully done with the AUTOVON voice network—is one constraint on input. The Navy practice of purging outdated traffic in store-and-forward networks is another. But, these measures are band-aids at best.

Digital transmission techniques permit more efficient utilization of communications bandwidth than does analog, but these improvements in capacity continue to lag the traffic demands brought on by advances in sensor technology. Further, the U. S. Navy, among others, intends to acquire communications techniques that are much less vulnerable to enemy exploitation than those widely employed by all services in the Persian Gulf. However, barring some fundamental breakthrough in physics, the techniques to achieve low probability of intercept (LPI), exploitation (LPE), and detection (LPD) in communications must invariably come at the expense of capacity. This is why senior defense officials cite the need for complementary actions by both the communications and the intelligence communities: The one to reduce vulnerability while improving throughput; the other to acquire pre-processing and compression algorithms that will compress data by a factor of hundreds.

Summary

Information technology unveiled in the Persian Gulf war gave combat forces a tantalizing glimpse of what commanders have hungered for since the dawn of human conflict: A "God's Eye" view of the battlefield, providing the same comprehensive and real-time perspective of battle given to those generals who once commanded from horseback and hill top.

Technology has filled the skies and heavens with sensors. Data from those sensors was fused and disseminated by electrical means down to the theater, using the abundant bandwidths available from civil and military SHF satellites. But the electrical flow halted at the level of the theater army and tactical air force. Trucks and helicopters took over at that point to get the templates and photos to the troops about to go into combat.

That this plethora of sensors does not now provide more useful decision-making support to tactical commanders is due, in no small measure, to faulty employment of technology. The intelligence community did not pay adequate heed to admonishments that their "wish lists" exceeded capacity of communications systems by orders of magnitude. While the intelligence community employed only 3% of the earth terminals in the Gulf War, they consumed over 17% of satellite capacity.

Experts in both communities agree that these are some of the changes that must be made:

• *Curbing appetites.* Commercial satellites offer the only near-term potential for substantial increases in capacity and military units will be furnished the necessary terminals. Milstar is the only new survivable, military long distance communications capability on the horizon. Milstar is a system that began life as a rugged, low data-rate means for connectivity in a high stress environment. It is now being redesigned to make it more useful in conventional environments, but the changes will only modestly increase capacity—perhaps to T-1—(the useful bandwidth remains classified). No one is suggesting that Milstar will carry the volume of image traffic passed by the Defense Satellite Communications System and allied and commercial carriers during Desert Storm. Combat commanders should be weaned from over dependence upon imagery that might not be deliverable in future contingencies.

• *Tailoring products for "on-demand" delivery to users.* Users complained that not only was much of the intelligence received of little use, but that they received the same information over and over. One study estimated that 80% of intelligence traffic was redundant. Argument is growing for an end to "provider-push" concepts for dissemination of intelligence in favor of "user-pull" that will allow the customers to extract what they need from the intelligence data base.

• *Exploiting available bandwidth.* Peering apprehensively into a resource-limited future, communicators see no option but to wring every bit of capacity from present systems by exploiting integrated, common-user, packetized networks and *on-demand* systems: that is, systems that automatically reconfigure to meet demand. The days of the dedicated, full-period circuit are fast disappearing. The Navy Copernicus[14] approach may be the harbinger for future defense communications.

• *Standards for data links and user terminals.* There were 17 different digital data entry devices employed in the many fire support planning and control systems and none were compatible. Standard data links must be deployed so that the input from many sensor systems can be integrated into a single user terminal.

• *Pre-processing and data compression to reduce demands for throughput.* Technology now in the commercial marketplace easily provies 75 to 1 reduction factors. Reduction factors of 100 to 1000 are claimed. Reductions of this magnitude may be needed if images must be delivered over the tactical communications now in the field.

• *Acquisition and management of commercial systems.* Military services plan to equip combat forces with transportable or mobile terminals that can directly access commercial satellites. Desert Shield/Storm provided compelling evidence of the need for centralized defense-wide management over the acquisition and allocation of these resources.

• *Theater-wide packet switching and transmission system.* It took months to improvise the packet-switching networks needed to disseminate data in the theater. A solution to this problem—Integrated Tactical Strategic Data Networking—evolved within the intelligence community, has reportedly been blessed by the Joint Staff and may finally be on the front burner with the implementing agency, DISA.[15]

Endnotes

[1] Prior to the Gulf War, Iraq agreed to buy from Brazil a reconnaissance satellite being developed in China. Had the satellite been available in time, it could have revealed the allied flanking maneuver that won the ground war. *SIGNAL*, April 1992, p. 11.

[2] Not all OOB was lauded. One commander was sharply critical of intelligence, in general, and order of battle in particular. "... we were tracking the Iraqi 80th Tank Brigade for months...because of the T-72 tanks, it was a major threat...but it turned out that this unit wasn't in our sector after all. It had left Kuwait months before and we didn't know it. The intelligence was not accurate." Major General J. I. Hopkins, USMC, commander 7th Marine Expeditionary Brigade, U. S. Naval Institute *Proceedings*, November 1991, p. 58.

[3] Said one commander, "One of the failures of the whole damn war was intelligence...absolutely terrible...when battalion commanders and regimental commanders...crossed the line of departure, they didn't know what was in front of them..." *Proceedings*, November 1991, p. 58.

[4] "We were able to get imagery about 14 hours before we hit the Tawakalna (Division) showing exactly where and how they were set up...We knew what they were going to do before the avrage Iraqi soldier did,"...Desert Storm After Action Review. "A Swift Kick," by Steve Vogel, *Army Times*, August 5, 1991. Other favorable reports about battlefield intelligence will be found in "The Dreadnoughts' Rip the Saddam Line," Lt. Col. Gregory Fontenot, January 1992 issue of Army, p. 31.

[5] In one extraordinary incident, foreign missile experts in Huntsville, Alabama were sending on-line queries about the technical characteristics of specific Iraqi Scuds to their counterparts in Saudi Arabia, while those missiles were still in flight.

[6] "Among the most potent threats to GLCM [ground launched cruise missile] was a combination of *Spetsnaz* (Special Forces) reconnoitering an area on foot and calling in air strikes on units they located. This was also an effective tactic in Desert Storm." Lt. Col. Michael E. Rogers, USAF (Ret.), Letter to Editor, *Air Force* Magazine, June 1992.

[7] This was not the first instance where "blue water Navy" communications were inadequate for joint operations. Navy had declined an Army proposal for a system of semaphores prior to the Civil War, claiming that its system of flag hoists was adequate. Consequently, it was normal practice for Army signalmen to be put aboard ships where "ship-shore coordination was required." C. Kenneth Allard, *Command, Control and the Common Defense.* Yale University Press, 1990, p. 61

[8] *SIGNAL*, August 1991, p. 69.

[9] In fairness, until recently there has been no directive from the defense department that even encouraged compatibility of these data links. Defense guidance has now been issued that mandates compatible data links and the Defense Information Systems Agency has been tasked to assure development of and enforce use of standards to that end.

[10] As a point of reference, environmental sensors associated with the Mission to Planet Earth Program will send *terabytes* of data earthward.

[11] UHF is extremely vulnerable to jamming. Commercial SHF systems—widely used for the most vital military functions during the war—are also vulnerable to interference. The military SHF system (DSCS III) has means to mitigate interference, but most of those satellites have yet to be launched and future improvements in the SHF range are uncertain. Only EHF affords much protection from enemy detection and exploitation and it will be late in the 1990s before the MILSTAR system is deployed in useful numbers.

[12] One benefit from the drastic downsizing of the US Army is the availability of excess Bradley Fighting vehicles, some of which may be converted into *electronic fighting vehicles.*

[13] Some of the limitation on line-of-sight and high frequency radio range can be explained by abnormal propagation conditions in the Gulf region and on an unusually high peak in sunspot activity. Also, the background noise threshhold was raised for some users by the intense concentrations of UHF radio activity.

[14] The Copernicus Architecture, Michael S. Loescher, Chapter II, *Naval Command and Control: Policy, Programs, People and Issues*, 1991, AFCEA International Press.

[15] The intelligence community has complained for years over the lack of means for rapid data transfer (bit-oriented message traffic) in the tactical arena and with the aid of the Congress, obtained a mandate to the DoD to take corrective action. The Integrated Tactical-Strategic Data Network (IDTN) is an initiative of the INCA project office and is currently under development for implementation by the Defense Information Systems Agency (DISA).

An excellent summary on military intelligence can be found in a report by Maj. General John F. Stewart, Jr., entitled "Desert Storm, The Military Intelligence Story: A View from the G-2, 3d U.S. Army."

EXTENDING REAL-TIME INTELLIGENCE TO THEATER LEVEL

Harry E. Soyster

During the months of Desert Shield, communicators and intelligence specialists collaborated to deploy an intelligence system capable of providing a real-time product to the theater commander. This system, an extension of the Department of Defense intelligence information system, or DODIIS, was only grinding along in the research and development phase when Iraqi forces stormed across the border into Kuwait on August 2, 1990.

While the quickly deployed system was rudimentary, its use during the war provided some national-level, theater-level and tactical intelligence assets.

Motivating Factors

Intelligence planners recognized years ago that future battlefield commanders would rely more and more on national-level intelligence as a basis for their decision making. Operation Just Cause in Panama during December 1989 and January 1990 reaffirmed this notion, but operations Desert Shield and Desert Storm drove the point home.

Faced with the prospect of an extremely fluid battlefield ranging over thousands of square miles of desert, U.S. and allied commanders quickly recognized how seeing deep would enhance their ability to fight deep. The list of intelligence lessons learned from Desert Storm already is replete with the cries of commanders for additional battlefield imagery that can be distributed in a timely manner. Moreover, deployed forces expressed a need for sufficiently redundant and interoperable communications systems to ensure intelligence data did not become lost in the system, thereby rendering it dated and useless.

Gen. H. Norman Schwarzkopf, USA, commander of the U.S. Central Command, recommended in testimony before the Senate and House Armed Services

Committees in mid-June 1991 that the intelligence community immediately begin developing systems "capable of delivering a real-time product to [the] theater commander when he requests that."

Support Teams

During operation Just Cause and in other crises, the Defense Intelligence Agency has tried to satisfy similar needs expressed by other operational commanders primarily by deploying national military intelligence support teams, or NMIST. These specially trained and equipped three-person groups facilitate the transmission and receipt of intelligence-related information between national-level and theater-level assets. In many instances, the national military intelligence support team provides the only secure-voice capability in a region, along with the capability of rapidly exchanging intelligence-related text, imagery, data and facsimile materials.

A national military intelligence support team arrived in the Persian Gulf on August 8, 1990, with the first contingent of U.S. forces and established the first secure-voice links to the area. By war's end, the extra teams that the Defense Intelligence Agency rapidly configured, trained and deployed had processed more than half of all the requests for intelligence information sent to the national Iraqi regional intelligence task force, which was established in the Pentagon shortly after the invasion of Kuwait. That amounted to more than 2,700 separate requests, compared to the 166 information requests the national military intelligence support team processed during operation Just Cause.

Interoperability

While the various individual systems worked well independently, the direct handoff of data between the teams and other systems was not always possible. National military intelligence support teams also suffered from data receipt and transmission rates that were too low to accommodate the volume of imagery products that analysts and technicians were trying to pass.

To overcome these factors and to distribute national-level intelligence products effectively further down the tactical chain, the Defense Intelligence Agency extended DODIIS, which previously supported the timely and comprehensive presentation of intelligence and intelligence-related information to military commanders and national-level decision makers at 52 sites worldwide.

Through the years, the Department of Defense intelligence information system has proved itself a valuable composite of telecommunications, automated data processing equipment and personnel. It uses a packet switching network with worldwide connections to establish virtually instantaneous links between national intelligence systems and commands in the field, over which most data currently available can be passed to supported force commanders.

Although these connections join unified and specified commands worldwide, they have been limited to strategic-level commanders and generally do not reach tactical echelons at corps level and below. With the advent of newer, more lightweight technologies, however, the Department of Defense intelligence information system extension was developed to provide similar secure intelligence connections to tactical commanders.

The long challenge, encountered once again during the Gulf buildup and war, was one of finding an efficient way of sending a significant volume of timely, national-level intelligence to tactical decision makers. By the end of the war, the expanded use of the Department of Defense intelligence information system extension was meeting this challenge.

Gulf Deployed System

The prototype system fielded during Desert Storm was a transportable and quickly relocatable connection to the existing worldwide defense data network backbone. The system was built using a 2.4-meter Ku-band communications satellite dish integrated by California Microwave of Annapolis Junction, Maryland; a packet switching node and gateway loaned to the project's overall integration contractor, J. G. Van Dyke and Associates of Bethesda, Maryland, by Bolt, Beranek and Newman (BBN) Communications of Cambridge, Massachusetts; and personal computer systems provided by the military.

The equipment was configured in an Army S-250 shelter with the satellite dish mounted on a trailer. Through the use of two existing 64 kilobit per second satellite communications channels, connections quickly were established with the defense data network backbone, allowing access in the area of operations to continental United States-based intelligence systems. An early prototype system was nearly identical, except that the satellite dish was not trailer-mounted, but it was transportable.

Once deployed, the intelligence information system extension was installed at the Army Central Command headquarters, where it provided connections with both Army intelligence and national-level agencies and systems within the continental United States. The system extension used during the conflict gave intelligence officers in the field quick and reliable access to the best, most up-to-date data. Much of this data, which previously would have been available only by courier, was being passed directly to those who needed it in a matter of minutes.

Personal computer-based local area networks using off-the-shelf, network operating systems and electronic mail software were connected to the intelligence information system extension links. With the addition of plotters and printers, this configuration provided the means to pass text, images, map overlays and virtually any other type of intelligence data expeditiously to the Army Central Command headquarters. From there, tactical communications methods quickly moved the data to the corps, divisions and armored cavalry regiments. Using these same connections, national-level agencies quickly could respond to requests for data from the field. The Department of Defense intelligence information system extension equipment, operated by no more than 3 to 4 people, effectively linked the Army Central Command headquarters with the entire Department of Defense intelligence information system network and created the means to move intelligence data around the globe within minutes.

For the first time, deployed commanders and intelligence officers had the same access to data previously available only in fixed facilities. They gained access without the huge logistical overhead required to deploy, operate and maintain large main frame-based intelligence data systems. Connections quickly were established, easily maintained and continuously operated on their behalf.

The system performed admirably during the war, and now that the equipment and its operators have returned to the United States, the Defense Intelligence Agency is examining ways of integrating key lessons learned into its planning for future intelligence communications architecture.

The Defense Department intelligence information system extension experiment demonstrated that the best performance came from equipment that allowed for quick deployments and easy replacements. Several systems never made it to center stage during the war because they were too large. Portability now has emerged as a requirement for any future system the agency intends to deploy.

Management Program

The Defense Intelligence Agency is considering establishing an executive agent to blend the intelligence communications support programs that succeeded during the Gulf War into a coordinated, viable program.

This executive agent would ensure configuration management, standardization, interoperability and technology sharing and could manage the program's funding while also providing program direction. Operations people as well as communications experts from both the military and commercial sectors who can provide insight into the specific communications requirements for tactical intelligence will be integral to this program.

The intelligence community must plan smartly for the integration of a properly configured system linking tactical commanders with national-level intelligence assets. The United States and its allies were fortunate to have a considerable amount of preparation time before they launched the ground war. The next crisis might not afford defense intelligence a similar luxury.

This article originally appeared in the September 1991 issue of *SIGNAL.*

EARS OF THE STORM

Robert S. Hopkins III

As the big RC-135 jet moved from its parking place, Capt. David Lawlor saw the crew chief standing at attention, rendering a solemn salute. Captain Lawlor returned the salute; the crew chief gave a thumbs-up and hurried to his remaining duties. "It was then that it struck me we were really going to war," said Captain Lawlor, an RC-135 Rivet Joint commander with the 38th Strategic Reconnaissance Squadron (SRS).

The men and women who flew and maintained the highly classified RC-135 Rivet Joint (RJ) reconnaissance platform in the Persian Gulf War understand that the story of their contributions might never fully be told. Nonetheless, the RC-135 mission was central to the prosecution of coalition combat operations. Whereas the much-publicized E-3 AWACS was popularly considered the "Eyes of the Storm," the shadowy Rivet Joint aircraft might best be called the "Ears of the Storm."

Rivet Joint was a crucial part of the coalition's intelligence collection capability. It provided real-time intelligence data to theater and tactical commanders, in coordination with such assets as AWACS, E-8 Joint Stars aircraft, the EF-111A, and the Navy's EA-6B Prowler.

Even in peacetime, the mission of the RC-135 is shrouded in secrecy. Assigned to Strategic Air Command's 55th Strategic Reconnaissance Wing (SRW) at Offutt AFB, Neb., RC-135s have routinely flown worldwide peacetime strategic aerial reconnaissance missions directed by the Joint Chiefs of Staff on behalf of national intelligence organizations as part of the Burning Wind program. Pilots and navigators on board the "Wind" were part of the 38th SRS. Electronic warfare officers, known as "ravens," were assigned to the 343d SRS, and in-flight maintenance technicians came from the 55th SRW. Mission personnel were selected from Electronic Security Command units worldwide.

The RC-135 is a specially configured variant of the Boeing KC-135 Stratotanker. There are currently five different variants of the RC-135 in use, two of which—the RC-135V and the RC-135W—are in the Rivet Joint configuration and participate in the Burning Wind program. The other three support special technical reconnaissance programs.

Hog Nose and Cheeks
Rivet Joint RC-135s are capable of air refueling, enabling them to remain aloft for extended missions over intercontinental distances. They have four TF33 turbofan engines and are covered with a variety of fairings and antennas. The most obvious external characteristics are the airplane's elongated nose (called a "hog nose" by RJ crew members) and its "cheeks," large aerodynamic fairings along each side of the forward fuselage.

Wind crews often see adversaries "up close and personal." Not all these confrontations have ended peacefully. In July 1960, for example, a 55th SRW RB-47H, a predecessor of the RC-135, was shot down by a Soviet MiG over the Barents Sea. The two surviving crewmen were captured and eventually repatriated. In April 1965, a pair of North Korean MiG-17s attacked and badly damaged another SRW RB-47H, but it managed to escape with no casualties and landed safely in Japan.

RC-135s participated in Operation Urgent Fury in Grenada in 1983, Operation Eldorado Canyon against Libya in 1986, and Operation Just Cause in Panama in 1989-90, all significant combat operations. According to one raven with over a hundred peacetime RC-135 missions, these encounters definitely improved the RC-135 crews' operational discipline. The chance to display this discipline in the Gulf War came early in August 1990.

The first Rivet Joint aircraft came to Riyadh Military AB, Saudi Arabia, on August 11, 1990. En route to Saudi Arabia, the airplane conducted an operational reconnaissance mission, establishing the uninterrupted intelligence link that the RJs would provide to theater commanders through the end of the war and long after. Additional RC-135s and crews flew nonstop from Offutt to Riyadh. These RC-135s were part of the 1700 Strategic Reconnaissance Squadron. Mission support personnel came from RC-135 detachments at Kadena AB, Japan; Eielson AFB, Alaska; and RAF Mildenhall, England.

Crews initially stayed in Riyadh hotels but soon moved to a large compound thirty minutes from the air base. Accommodations were Spartan. Given the crews' twenty-hour duty periods on alternating days, there was little time to do anything other than eat and sleep between fifteen-hour missions.

Aloft Twenty Hours
During Desert Shield, RJs flew continuous, twenty-four-hour coverage in a single orbit along the Saudi-Iraqi border. An airplane and crew were on station for twelve hours (or until relieved), with an additional three hours total transit time to reach and return from the orbit area. Any malfunction of a replacement jet meant that the on-duty place would have to fly an extended orbit, as Maj. Jerry Orcutt's crew discovered one night in January 1991, when it set an unofficial Desert Storm RC-135 record by staying airborne for more than twenty hours.

Crews flew fifteen-hour missions every other day. Staff personnel filled gaps in manning that occasionally arose, particularly due to illness. The most common ailment among the RJ flyers was an insidious sinus infection caused by extremely low humidity, high dust content, and time spent breathing recycled air while flying. Flight surgeons were able to treat all but the most serious illnesses without grounding the flyers.

This demanding pace was not entirely new to the 55th SRW's maintenance personnel. In addition to RC-135s, the wing operated SAC's EC-135C Looking Glass airborne command post, which until July 1990 had an airplane continuously airborne. Applying lessons learned from the Looking Glass operation significantly reduced major maintenance problems.

Foremost among these problems was the effect of windblown sand on the airplanes. Sand and grit permeated any opening or panel not tightly sealed. Despite the strict use of engine intake and exhaust covers, engine compressors and fan blades were gouged and scarred from the sand and debris ingested during engine start and takeoff or landing and taxi back. Even at high altitude, the planes encountered so much dust that paint on wing leading edges was stripped off in a single flight.

The incessant flying schedule was generally beneficial to airplane maintenance. Crew chiefs are quick to say that a jet that flies a lot breaks very little, while a plane that sits a lot breaks a lot. Nonetheless, there were recurring maintenance requirements such as phase inspections after, say, 250 flying hours. Approximately every three weeks, an RJ reached this limit of safe flying without a major inspection and overhaul and was rotated back to the US.

The long Rivet Joint missions in the Gulf were a mix of boring flying and moments of confusion, excitement, and concern. For pilots, the only break from the tedium generally came during the two air refuelings necessary to stay on station for twelve hours. At the outset of Desert Shield, these refuelings were major events. Problems with new autopilot software in the KC-135 precluded autopilot-on refueling, and tanker crews lacked experience in long autopilot-off contacts with fuel offloads in excess of 100,000 pounds. The fatigue felt by most RJ pilots made these refuelings even more challenging. By the beginning of the war, however, experience levels had improved dramatically and air refueling had become routine.

The navigators on board the RJs worked continuously to maintain precise positioning throughout the mission. Using systems as advanced as stellar-inertial and global positioning systems (GPS) satellites and as basic as dead reckoning, the two RJ navigators kept the airplane in the optimum orbit for data collection and coordinated with the mission crew members for special orbit requirements.

The Work of the "Backenders"

The Rivet Joint reconnaissance mission was conducted by the ravens and other US personnel. Using the RC-135's sophisticated and powerful sensors, these "backenders" located, identified, and cataloged electronic threats that could have affected the coalition's combat forces. At first the Iraqis were relatively careless with their electronic emitters, but eventually they "ran silent," turning them on only for brief periods in the early morning and late evening.

"The Iraqis were good," said one RJ mission specialist, "but they weren't good enough." By that he meant that the RJ already had picked up the most vital data.

In the Iran-Iraq War, Iranian F-14 Tomcats with their powerful radars were used like miniature AWACS planes, reporting Iraqi fighter operations to Iranian air defense commanders. To counter this capability, Iraqi Mirage F1-EQ fighters flew high-speed, low-altitude missions well beneath the Tomcat's radar limits. Based on timing, the Mirage F1-EQ would pop up directly beneath the Tomcat's orbit, briefly illuminate the F-14 with its radar, and fire one or two air-to-air missiles at it. Iran lost several Tomcats this way—a fact not lost on RJ crew members.

During the months of Desert Shield, Iraqi fighters flew teardrop shaped tracks that worked well with this tactic. When the planes were launched from forward Iraqi bases, these fighter tracks ended directly beneath Rivet Joint and AWACS orbits. There was little doubt in the mind of RJ crew members that the Iraqis planned to try to destroy these important aerial assets, so Desert Shield flights were as tense as those during Desert Storm.

On one occasion, just before the start of the war, an RJ reported unidentified radar contacts during the rendezvous with a tanker. The local AWACS was unaware of any coalition aircraft in the vicinity, although some high-speed, high-altitude Iraqi planes (probably MiG-25 "Foxbats") had been reported minutes earlier. US F-15s were quick to scour the area with their powerful radar but found nothing. The Foxbats had disappeared. The radar returns persisted.

At the same time, a US ground unit near the Iraqi border reported it was being surrounded by unidentified ground forces and requested immediate assistance. With tanker in tow, the RJ headed for the beleaguered ground unit. The mysterious radar blips also accelerated and began a course that would intersect that of the Rivet Joint plane.

To everyone's relief, it turned out that the ground unit had mistakenly identified a returning patrol as hostile troops. The mysterious radar returns turned out to be rare, spurious radar returns of the RC-135 and its tanker. As the RJ accelerated to rush to the aid of the ground unit, so too did its enigmatic pursuers. Only the discipline brought about by training and operations under pressure prevented shooting at ghosts.

The War Begins

On the eve of the war, the replacement RJ under the command of Capt. Paul Hutchinson taxied out and launched amid the usual radio chatter and air traffic control calls. If the Iraqis were monitoring the radio traffic, they would hear nothing unusual about that night's launch.

Shortly thereafter, in absolute radio silence, a second RJ, commanded by Major Orcutt, launched and hurriedly established itself in a new, second orbit. Iraqi radar remained silent and thus ignorant of this second, ominous development. Until the war's end, there would be two RJs airborne at all times, taxing the system and its crews to their limits.

To alleviate this strain, additional crews and every available RJ in SAC were relocated to the Middle East for Desert Storm or for missions along the Turkish-Iraqi border in Operation Proven Force. In Saudi Arabia, primary crews moved from the compound into field conditions at Riyadh AB, sleeping in tents. On the first night of the war, air raid sirens awoke crew members trying to sleep prior to their next-day combat sortie. There were worries that Iraqi Su-24 "Fencers" carrying chemical weapons might hit Saudi air bases. The attacks never came.

Crews often wore flak vests during takeoff and landing to ward off possible small-arms fire. To reduce the vulnerability of the RC-135, the 55th SRW Combat Tactics Division developed unique takeoff and approach procedures. Combined with the extremely bad weather, these radical tactics were very unsettling compared to traditional peacetime departure and recovery profiles, but they seemed effective.

Iraq's Scud missile proved to be a major annoyance. "I don't know how many times the airfield at Riyadh came under Scud attack," said Captain Lawlor, "but it seemed as if it was always when my crew and I were out trying to launch."

Capt. Mike Canna, an RJ intelligence officer, was nearly hit by Scud debris. "It happened so quickly," he said. "I saw the Patriot launch, dove for cover, and seconds later a big chunk of Scud missile landed right where I had been standing."

The US Patriot intercepted one Scud missile directly in the flight path of a landing RC-135, which narrowly avoided debris and down wash.

The RC-135 is not well suited for direct combat operations. It has no defensive armament and must rely on its "eyes" and "ears" for protection. During operations in the Gulf, however, the RJs were never alone. F-15s routinely orbited nearby and were quick to react to potential threats. Prior to the war, Iraqi fighters would often fly right up to the border. The RJ would withdraw to a safe distance while the Eagles clustered along the border waiting for a chance to shoot, a chance that never came. Other fighter coverage came from Navy F-14s, British Tornado F. Mk. 3s, French Mirage 2000s, and Saudi F-15s and Tornado ADVs.

The Iraqi Fighter Threat

On the first night of the war, an AWACS plane detected a fast mover—probably a MiG-23 "Flogger"—heading south across the Saudi-Iraqi border directly toward an orbiting RJ. As the RC-135 began evasive action, F-15s from the 33d Tactical Fighter Wing, Eglin AFB, Fla., responded to the RJ's calls for assistance. The MiG-23, its radar warning gear no doubt illuminated like a Christmas tree and alerted to the F-15s, fled back across the border. A similar event took place on the same night in the other RJ orbit. This time, however, the F-15s shot down the threatening Iraqi Mirage F1-EQ.

On the night of January 23, an RC-135 was shot at by an unidentified type of surface-to-air missile. "I was standing behind the pilot and looking out the window when I saw the launch," recalled Capt. Tim Spaeth, an RC-135 instructor navigator. "As the missile guided closer, the pilot prepared to take evasive action. Suddenly, just a few thousand feet below us, the SAM detonated prematurely."

Among the RJ's least-known accomplishments is its role in search-and-rescue (SAR) operations. The airplane's sophisticated sensor suite allows it to pinpoint a downed aviator's emergency rescue beacon. Under hostile conditions, the flyer might transmit on his beacon only for extremely brief periods, and local terrain can dramatically reduce the beacon's range. The RJ's sensors can find the beacon, track its azimuth over time, and thus give an accurate position of the flyer.

Working with SAR forces, the RJ can direct rescue helicopters to the flyer's position with less wasted time and effort and help the SAR forces avoid enemy troop positions or antiaircraft threats. RJ crews participated in several such rescues during Desert Storm. On one occasion, the RJ required air refueling during a critical phase of an SAR mission. The available KC-10 tanker flew right up to the border, joined up with the RJ, offloaded its fuel, and allowed the SAR operation to go on uninterrupted.

Eyewitnesses to War

Rivet Joint orbits often placed an RJ and its crew in unique positions to witness the campaign firsthand. On the first night of the war, a huge package of five KC-135s refueling twenty F-15Es en route to targets in Iraq flew through the RJ orbit. Later, RC-135 crew members would count the number of southbound contrails passing over the Saudi-Iraq border. Even numbers usually meant that all of the strike package was returning; odd numbers often meant that a jet had been downed in Kuwait or Iraq and that the hunt was on to rescue the mission aviator. Each night the B-52s struck targets in Kuwait and Iraq, RJ crews saw the small flashes of antiaircraft artillery at low altitude followed by the exploding bombs dropped from the B-52s and, on occasion, the secondary explosions that followed.

On one night, as an RJ banked in its orbit, the aircraft commander witnessed the launch of four Scud missiles. As he turned toward Kuwait, he saw four parallel streaks of fire rising from northwest Kuwait. At first he thought they were SAMs launched at the RJ, but they continued upward out of sight. "I then realized they were Scuds," said the commander, "and I looked at our navigation systems to determine a bearing from us to their launch site and quickly worked up an approximate launch position with the nav. We then called AWACS with the data." Soon coalition "ScudBusters" were dropping iron on the transporter-erector-launchers.

The hunt for Scud missiles almost brought in another of SAC's RC-135s. Assigned to the 6th SRW at Eielson Air Force Base, Alaska, the RC-135S Cobra Ball was configured to gather data on ballistic missiles. US planners briefly considered using the Cobra Ball's sensors to help locate the Scud launch sites, and 6th SRW crews were briefed, equipped, and made ready to deploy to Riyadh. Coalition forces, however, had by this time eliminated most of the safe havens from which the Iraqis launched Scuds (and Scud attacks had decreased to almost nil), so the Cobra Ball was not needed.

Throughout the buildup for the war, the days of combat, and the aftermath, Rivet Joint RC-135s flew missions vital to the development and execution of the coalition's combat operations. The RJs flew over hostile territory and came under fire from ground and aerial threats. Still, not one RC-135 was lost, and there were no combat casualties among its crews, maintenance, or support personnel.

The success of the RC-135 in Desert Storm has caused the Air Force to plan to convert additional airplanes into RC-135s, and theater commanders are now committed to making the Rivet Joint RC-135 an integral part of their arsenals. The RC-135's peacetime mission, however, remains the same.

RESPONSIVE COMMUNICATIONS KEY TO ARMY INTELLIGENCE

Paul E. Menoher, Jr.

Military intelligence is planning to field several collection and processing systems over the next few years that offer enhanced visibility of the battlefield with targeting accuracies to the depth of the battlefield. Desert Storm provided a glimpse of this future intelligence and targeting capability when the United States deployed three such systems: the ground station module, which is an interim configuration, as well as the joint surveillance target attack radar system and unattended aerial vehicles, which are prototypes.

The new systems will incorporate the timeliness and accuracy parameters necessary to back commanders and their fire support elements. Where possible, the designs will link the collection platform directly to key command and control and fire support nodes.

Meeting the Mission

Responsive communications are critical to intelligence's fundamental mission of supporting commanders. Regardless of the amount of data collected, the targets identified or the accuracies achieved, information has no value unless the commanders and appropriate fire support elements receive it in time to react, either through fire, maneuver or both. The joint surveillance target attack radar system with its ground station module and the Guardrail common sensor with its commander's tactical terminal are examples of the types of systems to meet these needs.

The ground station module will be deployed to each corps in sufficient numbers to provide key command and control and fire support nodes down to division, armored cavalry regiment and even maneuver brigade. The module is designed to downlink raw radar data from the joint surveillance target attack radar system aircraft and tailor the data to the echelon and function of the node it is supporting.

Army intelligence intends to build into the ground station module the ability to downlink live video (television or forward looking radar) from its family of unattended aerial vehicles. The module also will allow users to view the unattended aerial vehicle video through windows on the same screen depicting the joint surveillance target attack radar system moving target indicator and/or synthetic aperture radar data. Over time, Army intelligence will downlink additional sensors to the ground station module, as it evolves the station to the common ground station.

The commander's tactical terminal brings in signals intelligence reporting from the Guardrail common sensor and the U.S. Air Force's TR-1 aircraft collection platform in near real time and will provide data to multiple users in each corps.

Despite efforts to provide communications downlinks to key users from as many collection systems as possible, the capability is not always appropriate because of the type of data collected or the inherent accuracies in some systems. In other cases, Army intelligence has been able to provide direct downlinks or near real time reporting links, but the expense of building the system has limited the service's ability to proliferate the downlink below the corps or, in some cases, division level. Tactical exploitation of national capabilities systems is an example of these situations.

Army intelligence has established the corps as its national interface and, in some cases, has extended that to divisions with systems such as the tactical high mobility terminal. Army intelligence also intends to do the same with the future common ground station.

To handle situations when data from collectors cannot be provided directly to command and control and fire support nodes or must be analyzed and correlated with other data, Army intelligence is developing processors and fusion systems, such as the all-source analysis system, which have organic communications processors. Some of these link directly with collection systems through dedicated communications net radio protocols. In other cases, the processors obtain the data through the area communication systems. Dissemination of these data to key users, as well as much of the communications necessary to steer or manage organic collection assets and to request support from higher, lower and adjacent collection agencies, must be passed by the area communication system.

No single echelon has all the assets it needs to satisfy the intelligence requirements of that echelon. To compensate, the Army doctrinally has created an intelligence system of systems in which echelons mutually support each other, primarily on the basis of the higher echelon supporting the lower. To make this system of systems work requires robust, flexible communications capable of skip echelon connectivity. This communication system will allow national, departmental and theater capabilities to be leveraged in support of the tactical warfighter. Lower echelon to higher headquarter reporting and requests for support also can be orchestrated effectively over the same communications means.

In the past, Army intelligence tended to state its communication requirements for corps and below units on a selected system-by-system basis. The intelligence organization is now at a point in its architecture development and understanding of technological advancements where it must broaden its communication requirements in support of this complete top-to-bottom national-to-maneuver brigade architecture.

While many of these ideas and requirements were born out of work in defining how military intelligence would support the AirLand operations concept, they apply equally as well to any operation involving power projection from the continental United States base and where warfighting is highly mobile and fluid. The majority of these ideas and requirements were validated in Desert Storm.

Cooperative Efforts

The Army Intelligence Center, Fort Huachuca, Arizona, works with the Signal Center at Fort Gordon, Georgia, to articulate its communications by data rate, volume, classification and virtually all other measurable parameters for each system ranging from the all-source analysis system to front-end collectors. Operations Desert Shield and Desert Storm have indicated that a set of new requirements must be considered if Army intelligence is to support adequately the emerging AirLand operations concept and future operations in accordance with its doctrinal tenets.

Intelligence assets, in general, were not the first to arrive in Saudi Arabia to support Desert Shield. Once deployed, most corps and division intelligence assets, less deep-looking aerial collection platforms, were kept away from the Iraqi border as was the bulk of the combat force. As a consequence, intelligence and even targets were being pushed into theater from national and departmental intelligence agencies in the continental United States. Requirements from both Desert Shield and Desert Storm and AirLand operations doctrine make the need to support deploying forces from the continental United States a test of intelligence capabilities and communications connectivity. This split base requirement demands that the entire intelligence structure of the United States, from national to tactical levels, provides tailored support to deploying forces. Frequently, this support will have to be provided in a skip echelon mode to ensure timeliness and guaranteed receipt by those most affected by the intelligence provided.

Imagery Requirement Grows

Within the context of the split base intelligence operations that supported the Gulf War, the most pressing cases for enhanced communications support were for dissemination of both hard and soft copy imagery to enable commanders to see their areas of operations/responsibility; signals, imagery and human intelligence data base transfer necessary to support collection operations against threats in the area of operations; and communications to synchronize collection and processing priorities throughout the national, Defense Department and Army intelligence communities.

The greatest stress intelligence put on the communications system was created by the almost universal demand by commanders for imagery. As an order of magnitude, each corps requested about 600 frames of imagery per day, and each division needed an additional 30 to 50 frames. This volume collectively was significant in terms of communications. Signals intelligence data bases of several megabits of data also had to be transmitted between national and tactical users.

It became apparent early in the deployment that, because of the vast areas over which communications had to be provided and the relative lack of communications that could be provided by the host country, the area communications systems would be severely challenged to support all of the intelligence requirements. Consequently,

Army intelligence began to develop alternative solutions to provide direct real-time connectivity between key intelligence nodes in theater and in the continental United States.

Solutions were coordinated with appropriate communications authorities. First, working with the Army space program office and major commands, the Army began to redistribute tactical exploitation of national capabilities assets that were capable of receiving national, departmental and theater imagery and signal intelligence products over satellite broadcasts to units in theater. Then Department of Defense intelligence information system connectivity was made between Army Central-G2 and Defense Intelligence Agency/Army Intelligence Agency for direct access to data bases and dissemination of tailored intelligence products. Next, the Army provided Forces Command goldwing high-frequency radios to help mobile forces keep connectivity with senior headquarters that were providing them intelligence support. Finally, Army intelligence provided special purpose integrated remote intelligence terminals, part of the Trojan program, which uses satellite technology to import foreign languages through front-end systems, for language training. This provides high capacity on-line voice, data and facsimile connectivity between deployed units and the intelligence activities in the continental United States.

This system was capable of handling bulk data transfers and secondary imagery dissemination, and it provided point-to-point, broadcast and conference connectivity. The Trojan special purpose integrated remote intelligence terminals system also was capable of flexible baud rates up to 32 kilobits per second and was secure at an appropriate level to handle all operational and tactical intelligence requirements. In one case, it passed joint surveillance target attack radar system video from one ground receive site to another that did not have radio line of sight to the aircraft. In another case, it passed bulk data back to the continental United States that required expeditious processing of data for support to operational commanders. In another example, software updates were sent from the Intelligence Center at Fort Huachuca via the system to all holders in theater of an artificial intelligence processor called Hawkeye.

Changing Structures

As U.S. forces become based increasingly in the continental United States, intelligence from national, departmental and theater assets will have to carry the burden while tactical forces deploy to the theater of operations. On arrival in a theater, intelligence assets must be synchronized within a system of systems architecture to support the full range of intelligence requirements.

The Army is in the process of assessing all of its intelligence structure and requirements. The Signal Center is working with the Intelligence Center throughout this process to ensure the two groups corporately develop the best and most affordable solutions for the Army. Jointly, the centers will develop an architecture that enables commanders at all echelons to see the battlefield so they can focus and leverage their combat power to fight smart and win.

This article originally appeared in the October 1991 issue of *SIGNAL.*

ELECTRONIC TEMPLATES

Alan D. Campen

The computer-driven network that fed all-source intelligence to U.S. troops about to plunge across the Saudi Arabian border on February 24, 1991, did not even exist on that day, barely six months earlier, when Iraq invaded Kuwait. Like so many other computer networks that came on-line during the five-month build-up in Saudi Arabia, this one also sprang from the fertile minds of innovators.

Army officials and their support contractors had gathered at Fort McPherson, Georgia, in August 1990 for an "in-process" review of a program for an architecture to upgrade internal intelligence automation for the Army Intelligence Agency (AIA). Their meeting came to an abrupt halt when a call to war sent participants scrambling to support the Army forces already mobilizing for what would be the largest military operation since World War II.

What began as a peacetime network to interconnect Army intelligence activities in the United States ended up as the primary means by which, among other invaluable products, the much-lauded *battlefield templates* were delivered to troops about to breach the berms and barriers along the Saudi Arabian border.

The computer and communications networks that would eventually connect analysts across the world into one "virtual environment" were improvised in less than six months by a group of innovators who discovered how to bend the rules, end-run the bureaucracy and exploit off-the-shelf hardware and software to get the job done, promptly.

AIANET epitomizes the Yankee ingenuity that lies behind the success of information systems support to Desert Shield and Desert Storm.

The AIANET

AIA is the U.S. Army's departmental intelligence producer. In August 1990, it consisted of the Armed Forces Medical Intelligence Center at Aberdeen, Maryland, the Foreign Science and Technology Center in Charlottesville, Virginia, the Intelligence and Threat Analysis Center (ITAC) in Washington, D.C., and the Missile and Space Intelligence Center in Huntsville, Alabama.

AIA began a program in 1989 to upgrade its internal intelligence automation capabilities and to improve support to consumers. The program was called AIANET, and it would tie the four intelligence production facilities together with a high-speed T1 communications net, so that all analysts could share all-source data on a virtual network. War in the Persian Gulf changed all that.

Demands for up-to-date intelligence on the situation in Kuwait and Iraq were rapidly getting out of hand as planners and operational units in and enroute to Saudi Arabia deluged AIA with requests for information. Some of the data were available, more were quickly being collected, but that data and the experts to interpret them were at widely dispersed and poorly connected locations, turning correlation and dissemination into a major headache.

AIA's ITAC had become the focus for analysis and production of intelligence on ground activities in Kuwait and Iraq. That center, at the Washington Navy Yard, had been augmented by specialists from other AIA centers in scientific, technical and medical intelligence. And it was soon producing daily summaries of military activity, estimates of Iraqi strength and capabilities, and updates of Iraqi troop dispositions.

Current maps of the Kuwaiti Theater Operations were grossly inadequate, and a first priority was to improve upon these maps with what are called products for Intelligence Preparation of the Battlefield (IPB).

Cross Town Communications

The concept of a CONUS-only net was quickly expanded to include the Army Operations Center and Army Deputy Chief of Intelligence (both in the Pentagon) and the G2 (intelligence) of Army Forces Central Command in Riyadh, Saudi Arabia.

The first task was to establish an electronic link between the ITAC and the Pentagon and to install workstations, printers, communications bridges and cryptographic equipment throughout the Washington area that would provide specialists in the Army and Joint Intelligence centers with on-line access to the AIA data base and its applications programs.

ITAC became the focal point for what soon became known as AIANET Extended. Using on-site government and contractor personnel in Charlottesville and Huntsville, an AIANET task force used commercial software to set up an automated mail system over the defense data networks' DSNET3 (for classified traffic). That solved the CONUS problem. Getting to Saudi Arabia presented a challenge.

Communicating With Riyadh

Now that the Potomac River had been successfully bridged with electronics, the task force faced a far more difficult challenge: finding communications channels to extend AIANET into Saudi Arabia and then outward to corps and divisions. Enter TROJAN SPIRIT (Figure 1).

TROJAN SPIRIT consisted of commercial communications satellite terminals that had been installed on military vehicles to support training exercises. Now these were used to extend AIANET, through MacDill Air Force Base in Florida, to Riyadh and the advanced echelon headquarters of the Central Command, Army Forces Central Command and to the newly formed Joint Imagery Production Center (JIPC).

DESERT STORM
TROJAN SPIRIT SYSTEM

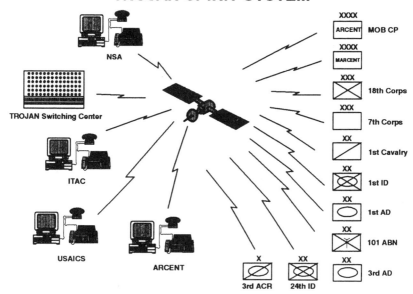

Figure 1. TROJAN SPIRIT in Desert Storm

This connectivity allowed rapid transmission of current intelligence reports, data, graphics products and the forwarding of electronic mail messages. However, it was basically a one-way system that did not allow users in Riyadh to interact with data through the network. Also, limitations in tactical communications networks would not allow the network to be reliably extended down to the critical users at the headquarters of the corps and divisions. Delivery of products below theater level—an area roughly the size of the Eastern United States—was by foot, truck and helicopter.

An AIANET team visited ARCENT (Forward) in Riyadh in December 1990 and decided to build a local area network from readily available hardware and software. A contractor team operating out of Tinton Falls, New Jersey, rounded up government owned modems and cryptographic devices and designed, developed and tested interfaces to the various communications links. Engineering advice for these efforts was being passed back from Riyadh by electronic mail. After a successful test of the network between New Jersey and Washington, and a shake-down of the LAN at the Washington facility, the new ARCENT LAN and a duplicate set for the Joint Imagery Production Center (JIPC) was moved to Dover Air Force Base, Delaware, and airlifted to Saudi Arabia in early January 1991.

A team of military and contractor personnel accompanied the shipment and installed, tested and monitored operation of this system through the remaining days of the war.

Meanwhile the Defense Intelligence Agency had been brought into the AIANET and, through that agency, another satellite path to Riyadh had become available.

Timely Templating

From the outset of Desert Shield, ITAC had been using satellite photos to produce overlays of Iraqi troop dispositions and barrier construction in Kuwait. In many cases these overlays revealed Iraqi positions down to the level of individual fighting positions. Hundreds of copies of paper or acetate templates were produced manually in Washington, on individual sheets, at a 1:50,000 scale. From there they went by Defense Courier Agency pallet to Saudi Arabia for further manual distribution to Army, Air Force, Marine Corps and allied units.

The ITAC templates soon became "best sellers," representing the most accurate ground force intelligence available on Iraqi forces in Kuwait and southern Iraq. The accuracy was applauded, but the timeliness criticized. Production, reproduction and dissemination took from 12 to 14 days.

Within 90 days another contractor effort produced a system that allowed ITAC analysts, seated at graphics terminals, to interactively enter or update intelligence about Iraqi dispositions and facilities, generate the map symbology needed to depict the facilities and fortifications, and add comments and marginalia for the templates.

Once quality control was performed, templates were electronically transmitted over the AIANET to ARCENT. Here hard copies were made for further distribution to planners, targeteers, and operational units within the theater. Eventually, graphics

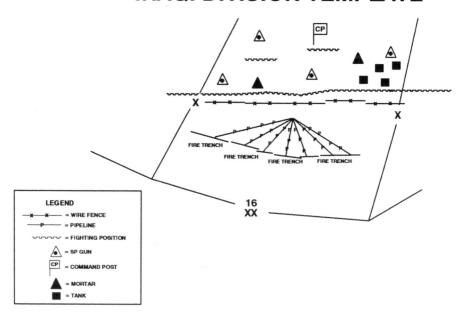

IRAQI DIVISION TEMPLATE

Figure 2. Iraqi Template

plotters were airlifted to ARCENT so that tactical intelligence collected within the theater could quickly be added to the templates. They were bought and enroute within 3 days.

By the time the Desert Storm air campaign began, automated templates were being received in theater in as little as 13 hours after the raw information had been received at ITAC.

Back to Normal

The key to AIANET (Extended) was use or adaptation of existing hardware and software. All of the components, from personal computers and software through communications devices and cryptographic equipment, were off-the-shelf, non-developmental items already in the inventory when Desert Shield began. Existing contract vehicles were used creatively and flexibly, and strict accountability was maintained over inventories of equipment, software, and supplies.

Contractor personnel from Booz-Allen & Hamilton, Intergraph and Van Dyke provided yeoman service, acting as systems designers, installers, shipment escorts, on-site technicians and trouble shooters.

What began as a peacetime system had quickly evolved into a near-real-time system for direct support to combat planning and operations. The proof of value of AIANET comes from these user comments:

• "(Template) products so good...so fast...we killed them at maximum range."

• "We always knew where the enemy was."

• "The reason we destroyed the 48th Guards...with minimum casualties...[was] the templates."

An after-action report on this highly successful enterprise ends with this footnote: "We may not have 6 months to fix the system the next time we commit U.S. forces."

DESERT WAR: CRUCIBLE FOR INTELLIGENCE SYSTEMS

James R. Clapper Jr.

Desert Storm not only proved to be a dramatically decisive military operation, but it also served as a crucible for systems that collect, analyze, fuse and disseminate intelligence. The successes and pitfalls of the war in Southwest Asia will shape the way the U.S. Air Force does business for years to come.

Successful Air Force operations depend on the knowledge of enemy force capabilities, dispositions, intentions and operations as well as the battlefield environment. This requirement is the basis of the primary Air Force intelligence mission, which will provide information and intelligence on foreign military and military related capabilities, intentions and operations. The mission also will support commanders and staff, those responsible for developing and implementing national security policy and structuring and employing military forces.

The methods and capabilities for providing intelligence to users significantly have improved during the last 20 years, and senior Air Force officials believe this trend will continue.

Stovepipe Systems

In the past, intelligence organizations have been characterized by a proliferation of stovepipe collection, processing and analysis organizations. Stovepipe is a term given to vertical organizations that collect, process, analyze and disseminate one category of intelligence without integrating other types of intelligence into the final product.

Another characteristic of the past has been the proliferation of command-unique intelligence organizations and systems. For example, a variety of secondary imagery systems are scattered throughout theater commands that are not interoperable. As a result, the intelligence community has difficulty providing an integrated all-source product tailored to users' needs.

Another limitation to timely dissemination of intelligence is the lack of robust communication networks to a wide range of consumers from the national to the tactical level. The Air Force's ability to provide intelligence support to the operators has, for the most part, been a manual process. For years, wing and squadron intelligence organizations have been plotting order of battle updates on maps with grease pencils.

When operations Desert Shield and Desert Storm began, many intelligence systems, in various states of development, were thrust onto center stage. Air Force intelligence personnel at Central Command Air Force (CENTAF) in Saudi Arabia were forced to bring together a number of different systems into an architecture that would provide the operators with a timely, fused product. In order to do this, a variety of collection assets were employed from the national to the theater level. Once the information was collected, some of it was processed and analyzed at intelligence centers in the United States, and some of it was done in-theater at the joint intelligence center and component command intelligence organizations.

Intelligence Systems

Two developmental unit-level systems called upon to do this force-level job were Constant Source and Sentinel Byte (SIGNAL, September 1990, page 46). Constant Source provided near real-time multisource signals intelligence, while Sentinel Byte provided a reference source for air and missile orders of battle. Together, they supplied tactical air situation updates. Customers included Air Force, Marine and Navy flying units, as well as special operations units and Army Patriot missile batteries.

The dissemination of intelligence information was accomplished primarily in two ways. One method was via an in-theater backbone tri-service tactical communications (TRI-TAC) network, using the secure telephone unit (STU)-III and the KY-68 for encryption. This was how the Sentinel Byte at force-level passed order of battle data to the Sentinel Bytes at unit-level.

The second method was by broadcasting intelligence updates to wings and squadrons directly from the collector or its associated ground processing facility. Constant Source and tactical information broadcast service were two systems used to receive these broadcasts.

At the unit level, the Air Force used Sentinel Byte to receive the order of battle data base from its force level counterpart, to pull together other pieces of the intelligence picture and to provide the mission planners with both a graphic depiction of the threat and the data necessary to support automated mission planning. Operators used the tactical digital facsimile to send and receive imagery—originating stateside and in-theater—for pre-mission planning and post-mission analysis.

Overall, the Air Force was able to provide timely, quality intelligence support to the flying units prosecuting the war. As with all functional areas, however, a number of lessons learned exist that will color the way the Air Force intelligence does business in the future. The Air Force did not have a well-integrated architecture for intelligence operations throughout its Desert Storm units. Some of these intelligence units used one kind of hardware to process and disseminate intelligence, while others used something different.

Some units were familiar with using computer-based data, while others still primarily used hard copy reports. It is no surprise, then, that many of the units had trouble coordinating and passing data efficiently. An overall concept of operations and associated systems architecture will help ensure a common baseline of intelligence systems that meet the interoperability, timeliness and information requirements of combat operations.

One area where the Air Force suffered from an overabundance of different systems was imagery dissemination. More than a dozen secondary imagery systems supported headquarters U.S. Central Command and its components during the conflict. Very few of these were compatible because they were not equipped with the national imagery transmission format or common communications protocols. The resulting hodgepodge of systems injected time delays into distribution of time-critical imagery and imagery derived intelligence. Air Force intelligence needs to ensure standardization of secondary imagery transmission systems not only for the Air Force but also for all services.

Tactical Reconnaissance

Tactical reconnaissance demonstrated it had an important role to play in the combat planning cycle. The tempo of future operations is expected to dictate more timely receipt of tactical reconnaissance data. Film processing techniques used by the RF-4C cannot meet this need, so the follow-on tactical reconnaissance system is being developed to take advantage of today's technology.

Another lesson learned is that the CENTAF intelligence staff had difficulty sending and receiving intelligence data essential to development of the air situation assessment and targets. This was primarily because of the limited enemy situation correlation element, a system designed to receive and fuse large amounts of raw data into a coherent picture of the battlefield. This and other experiences demonstrated that the air component intelligence staff must have direct access to secure intratheater data communications capable of supporting simultaneous transmission of order of battle, threat and target data from the component command's intelligence nodes to all units.

At the unit level, dial-up, point-to-point communications equipment was not totally satisfactory for the job because of time delays in moving information. Twice daily during the war, intelligence personnel electronically transmitted data files sequentially to each of the 30-plus units in-theater. This process, which took four hours under ideal conditions, must be improved for future operations. Communications will continue to be a priority for Air Force intelligence.

When Air Force intelligence was assessing the capabilities of enemy units during hostilities, the reports tended to reflect the amount of equipment destroyed without assessing the impact on enemy combat effectiveness. A commander is vitally interested in the current combat effectiveness of the enemy force, which is more than a simple count of equipment damaged or destroyed. This process will be improved by ensuring development of standardized methodologies and automation tools that assess battle damage against desired objectives of the commander. This shortcoming is not new and becomes apparent after every major conflict. It is an area that is not amenable to peacetime training.

Pushing And Pulling

During Desert Storm the flow of intelligence largely followed the traditional "push" system. This means tactical flying units primarily received intelligence data when the air component headquarters pushed information downstream that it believed the units needed. Air Force intelligence now is in the process of changing this system. This is not only because of the experiences of Desert Storm but also because of the changing threat, budgetary constraints and advances in communications and information systems technology. There also is an increasing appetite for greater amounts of detailed intelligence—smart weapons and in-flight cockpit updates.

Air Force intelligence is creating a "pull" system for the flow of future Air Force theater intelligence to supplement the "push" system. The dissemination of collected, processed and analyzed data will be more widespread and timely. More onboard collector processing and broadcast systems will send the data out to consumers in near real time from both collector and all-source organizations.

When data needs to be analyzed, Air Force intelligence will use all-source intelligence organizations composed of experienced analytical and targeting personnel who are connected directly to units being supported. They will use standard automated systems that are integrated with command and control as well as mission planning and rehearsal systems. Intelligence personnel then will have the capability to access theater and/or national imagery and textual data from a variety of intelligence centers.

Deployable Assets

Deployable communications and automated data processing systems also will be key elements for force-level intelligence organizations. This robust capability will permit Air Force intelligence to execute operations anywhere in the world. The objective is for intelligence to be a key part of an integrated command and control system, supported by communications and focused on the effective and efficient application of air power.

One of the programs that will help Air Force intelligence achieve this objective is the tactical Air Force linked operations/intelligence centers Europe capability, or TAFLC. Despite the connotation of having the word "Europe" in the title, this program includes Pacific Air Forces operating locations as well as those responsible for operating in and around the European theater. TAFLC is based on the tactical forces' need to exploit time-sensitive, high-volume, multisensor information rapidly. As collection means and communications improve, the ability to process the raw data manually is falling behind the requirement for an effective operational response.

While the commander never will operate on a basis of absolute certainty, more timely analyzed data will reduce the uncertainty to more tolerable levels. The objective of the TAFLC program is to field a baseline capability to provide intelligence and operations personnel with the precise location of an opposing force structure and graphic display of the ground situation through correlation and aggregation of all-source intelligence.

Common View

Additionally, the program will be interoperable with the Army's all-source analysis system, thus supporting Air Force intelligence's goal of providing systems that give a common view of the battlefield. TAFLC also will supply users with a common capability consistent with Air Force plans for upgrades in the intelligence data handling system (IDHS).

The data handling system is composed of processing systems used to analyze, process and disseminate vast amounts of intelligence coming into national, theater, component and unit organizations. At the national level, the system processes data used to perform strategic warning, develop the single integrated operational plan and construct data bases used by the Defense Intelligence Agency. At the theater or component level, the system provides intelligence used for indications and warning, situation and threat assessments, target development and weapons selection as well as reprogramming of electronic warfare assets. At the unit level, this system provides targeting information, threat alerts and current air defense situations. It will continue to evolve because of advances in technology and increasing demands for more effective information processing.

Air Force intelligence will head into the future with five concepts. Customers will have "one button to press" to get the information they need. All-source intelligence organizations will provide tailored organic support to the force level and below. Intelligence units will have a demand or "pull" system that will filter data. Air Force intelligence will operate standard and deployable systems. Finally, Air Force intelligence will be able to deliver near real-time intelligence to mission planners as well as directly into the cockpit.

These strategies mean that Air Force intelligence must be flexible and have the capability to provide more timely and effective support to the operators as they organize and plan to execute the Air Force's concept of "global reach, global power."

Air Force intelligence must support a commander responsible for planning and execution, a commander who may be working with mission orders that assign objectives to a unit rather than to specific targets and one whose assets will be highly trained and rapidly deployable. As a result, Air Force planners believe that intelligence and operations will work together to meet the requirements of a new national military strategy by improving rapid force projection.

This article originally appeared in the September 1991 issue of *SIGNAL.*

INFORMATION, TRUTH AND WAR

Alan D. Campen

The military used half as much communications satellite bandwidth in prosecuting the Persian Gulf war as the press did in reporting it.

The first skirmishes that U.S. military forces fought in the Persian Gulf War were not with Iraq but with their own press corps. The battle cry of some journalists—they came to number nearly 1,400 by the start of the ground war—was one that has attended most wars: "Truth, the first casualty of war!"

Still smarting from criticism over its ham-handed treatment of the media during in the Grenada operation and negotiating with a skeptical Kingdom of Saudi Arabia over admission of *any* reporters, the Department of Defense had invoked a controversial "press pool" concept.

Fully engaged in bitter argument over that issue, both the government and the media apparently failed to foresee the implications of direct, real-time reporting by journalists over commercial communications satellites. Technology and suitcase-sized earth terminals had added a new and unexpected dimension to information warfare and exposed a void in military security policy.

Modern communications technology thrust television reporters into a role they might not have sought: One which has some of them on the defensive and seeking both moral support for their actions as well as ethical guidance.

Arthur Lubow, writing in *The New Republic* says: "In modern war, reporters must be permitted at the front, and they must submit to sensible censorship. Mutual mistrust is part of the shared heritage of soldiers and journalists in time of war. So is mutual accommodation." Satellite technology makes moot the issue of censorship.

Television reporters have become a critical instrument in a totally new kind of warfare. Satellite technology that allows commentators to report instantly on military action can transform reporters from dispassionate observers to unwitting, even unwilling, but nonetheless direct participants. As the coverage of Patriot intercepts of Scud missiles over Israel so graphically showed, technology endows these journalists with the awesome ability to shape events even as they report upon them.

This was the first war to be televised live. It will not be the last. Satellite technology allows reporters to free themselves from military controls in filing stories and images, should they choose to do so. And looming on the near horizon are civilian space imaging capabilities that will give journalists—and "talking heads" anywhere in the world—the opportunity to literally peer over the shoulders of the combatants.[1]

AFCEA's *SIGNAL* Magazine reported in its April 1992 issue that "[W]ithin a few years, it will be possible to build or buy a small reconnaissance satellite total system with a 2.5 meter resolution for about $60 million. This resolution makes it possible to pick out individual vehicles on Earth. When combined with infrared, the resolution can detect camouflage and provide targeting information."

Those whose business is oversight and reporting on U.S. military affairs must now give serious consideration as to how they will handle these extraordinary capabilities and attendant responsibilities—perhaps even choosing sides. [2]

Real Time Attack Assessment

On the evening of January 20, 1991, television audiences around the world—including those in U.S. military command posts in Riyadh—witnessed a unique if giddy form of instantaneous attack assessment. From rooftop reporters and goading anchors half a world away, the airwaves were filled with rumor and speculation, badgered from harassed military officials by armchair strategists and gushed to the world without forethought. Some wrap this behavior in the First Amendment and chant that "the public needs to know." Perhaps it does, but in real time?

There has always been tension between those who would cloak military operations and those who would roam unfettered in the footsteps of Pyle and Maulden to discover and report "truth."

Our Civil War was contested almost as fiercely in the press as it was in the field. Journalists accompanied the troops of both North and South on even the most trivial expeditions and used military telegraph lines to file their stories. However much military commanders may have been aggravated by this intimate and often critical press coverage, the reports almost certainly lagged events by days or weeks. Stories from a critical press probably influenced national policies, but the dispatches themselves could have had no impact on the conduct of any given battle; nor could they have put the lives of soldiers at risk.

Television removes the cushion of time. Instant reporting by satellite can insinuate viewers directly into the planning and decision cycle of military commanders, on both sides.

Responsible Reporting

History shows that the sword and the pen need not inevitably parry in anger and mistrust. Unable to secure a military billet with the 4th Hussars, a young Winston Churchill joined the Malakand Field Force as a correspondent for *The Daily*

Telegraph, recording—under the byline "young officer"— "the facts as they occurred, and the impressions as they arose, without attempting to make a case against any person or any policy."[3]

Churchill's dispatches were informed and informative; timely, perceptive, accurate and, often brutally critical. He was not dismayed to discover that military tactics sometimes failed; nor astonished at human frailty; nor shocked that innocents suffer in war. He wrote honestly of the chaos of night operations; of gallant officers who lost their heads; of regiments becoming instantly terrified and useless; of brutality and bravery. He told of the moments of "wild enthusiasm, savage anger and dismay."

"Slender wires and long-drawn cables carried the vibrations to the far-off countries of the West," but his candid commentaries could have no direct impact on current military operations. That day would not dawn for another 90 years.

Information and War

Armies that seek victory by fighting smarter—and this is now the foundation of U.S. military doctrine—will quickly falter and die if the flow of battle information is interrupted or distorted. Always a factor in separating winners from losers, combat information now rivals weapons as the commodity most vital to success in war. Modern "smart" weapons are useless until instructed over information systems.

Command and control is a phrase newly come to the public lexicon. Information is the essence of command and control. Accurate, precise and timely information lies at the heart of military endeavor on the battlefield. "What is happening; what does it mean; and what must I do about it." Each commander struggles to answer those questions, even as he actively seeks through countermeasures to deny that advantage to his opponent. The winner is the side that first comes to *know* the battlefield and is able to cloud or confuse the vision of the opponent.

Commercial television is an important tool in informing as well as in deceiving. Unfortunately, the technology is non-partisan: Global television feeds friend and foe equally.[4]

Fraud and the Press

Thomas Hobbes spoke to the issue of truth in war when he wrote "Force, and fraud, are in war the two cardinal virtues." Disinformation is the military euphemism for Hobbes' fraud. The press—whether naive, unwitting, or reluctant—has, at least since the Civil War, played an adjunct role in the sowing of disinformation. "To confuse his enemies, Johnston had first to mislead his friends...," writes Shelby Foote[5] about the successful efforts of a Confederate general to hide weaknesses of his Kentucky army. This he did by planting false reports on his strength and campaign strategies with the Southern press, knowing they would be parroted in the North—as, indeed, they were.

Paul Fussell has brought the question of truth into contemporary context in his introduction to *Modern War*[6]: "From the days of the Trojan horse, war has necessitated ruses, espionage, deceptions, misrepresentations, and other elements of fiction, and a modern war can be distinguished from others by the extent, depth, sophistication, and technological expertise of these operations."

Key to the spectacular end-run around and behind the Republican Guards was the false belief by Iraqi leaders that the main threat was from a direct frontal assault and amphibious landings into Kuwait. The press played a useful role in that deception.

Called by whatever name, deception remains a necessary virtue in war, and while methods have changed, the principles have not; nor has the role of the press in both informing and misinforming.

The Right and Need to Know

Objections to the short leash that the military has placed on the media rest on two arguments: One, firmly on the rock of the First Amendment and the other on the quicksand of assertions about the rights and needs of the public to know. The *right* to know and the *need* to know are quite different. Polls about military censorship, taken by the *Washington Post* shortly after the Gulf War, suggest that the public understands the difference.

The public has both the right and need to know about those affairs of government which the citizens of a republic can hope to influence.[7] The First Amendment protects the right of the press to inform the public in such matters. Vietnam is held to be a notable example of the role of a free press in changing faulty national policy. *But, while the public can put an intimate knowledge of a current military operation to no useful purpose, an opponent can, and will.*

Risks to military operations from instant reporting are not contrived. Communications satellite technology has eliminated a principal means by which the military was able to monitor and control the flow of news from the battlefield.[8] Civilian space-based reconnaissance systems will soon give the media unencumbered access to the battlefield. Any controls over what journalists report from future war zones must be self-imposed.[9]

Truth need not be a casualty in a system based on self-discipline. A free, informed and responsible press can tell the whole story and do so without endangering current military operations. Journalists have had the wisdom and maturity to do so in the past: Reporters with the empathy of Churchill, the wit of Maulden, and the eloquence of Ernie Pyle, who knew not to ask "silly questions...in the presence of the dead."[10]

Endnotes

[1] "Any country that desires to have a space-based reconnaissance program can acquire one over the next decade." Rear Admiral Thomas Brooks, Director of Naval Intelligence, as reported in *Technology Review*, April 1992. The same article also reports the admiral as stating that the following countries can attain space reconnaissance capabilities (some with 1 meter resolution) by the end of the decade: Canada, Germany, Israel, Italy, Pakistan, South Africa, South Korea, Spain and Taiwan. In addition to the United States, the following countries now have imaging satellites: Commonwealth of Independent States (USSR), France, Japan, China and India. *Aviation Week & Space Technology* reported in its May 18, 1992, issue that a major news organization had expressed interest to the U.S. Commerce Department in orbiting its own remote-sensing satellite.

[2] "As for censorship as opposed to criticism of cable news coverage 'helping the enemy', no amount of control in the Pentagon, in Riyadh, or Dhahran would have prevented international television crews from working in Baghdad, Cairo, or Amman. If there had been

censorship in the United States, it would not have applied to India, Turkey, Israel, Western Europe, or the Soviet Union. Television works past censorship. Television news is with us, and the genie cannot be put back in the bottle." John R. Whiting, War-Live!, *Proceedings*, August 1991.

[3] *The Story of the Malakand Field Force*, Winston Churchill, pub. W.W. Norton, New York. 1990.

[4] "This was, after all, an enemy that had virtually as much access to American news reporting as our people had here at home...for the sake of the operation and the lives of those American, British, and French troops, we absolutely could not have let the enemy learn that [refers to flanking movement of XVIII Corps]. "The Press and the Persian Gulf War," Pete Williams, Assistant Secretary of Defense for Public Affairs, U.S. Army War College Quarterly *Parameters*, autumn 1991.

[5] *The Civil War*. Shelby Foote, p. 130. Vintage Books

[6] *The Norton Book of Modern War*, ed. Paul Fussell, pub. W.W. Norton & Co. 1991.

[7] "Had there been Cable Network News coverage of the Battle of the Somme in World War I with tens of thousands of lives being lost each day, it is inconceivable that the battle would have been allowed to continue." Admiral Sir Julian Oswald, First Sea Lord, in a speech to the AFCEA conference in San Diego, California, on January 6, 1992.

[8] The Department of Defense says that of 1351 print pool reports filed during the war, only five were forwarded to Washington for review, and all but one was quickly cleared.

[9] Career Journalist Richard Halloran is not sanguine about self-reform. Writing in the spring 1991 issue of the Army War College Quarterly, *Parameters,* he says that military officers "should accept the press as it is, whether that seems fair or not." He goes on to cite Elie Abel, Television correspondent and later dean of Columbia's Graduate School of Journalism who once wrote this about the press: "Its instinctive rejection of self-improvement schemes as far back as the Hutchins Commission in 1947 leaves little room for hope of wholesale reform."

[10] The Death of Captain Waskow. *The Retired Officer Magazine*, February 1991.

On April 17, 1992, the Associated Press (AP) reported that a media group, formed to negotiate new rules of engagement between the press and the military, had reached agreement on nine of ten principles for press coverage of war. The military agreed to curb the use of pooled coverage and to prohibit escort officers from interfering in reporting. The two sides did not agree on the military's right to review and censor articles and pictures. The AP story does not discuss the impact of direct reporting by satellite.

Readers who desire more information on press coverage of the Persian Gulf War are referred to nine articles on this subject in the August 1991 issue of *Proceedings*, U.S. Naval Institute.

COMMUNICATING ON THE MOVE

Wayne M. White

["In the order of march the telegraph detachments and their heavily laden wagons often found themselves relegated to the rear of the columns..."[1]]

The success of the 141st Signal Battalion system was the result of quickly adapting to a new operational environment and changing its way of doing business to meet the commanders' needs.

The overwhelming success of Operation Desert Storm was also a success for theater-wide command and control systems, which gave commanders a decisive edge in the coalition forces' victory.

For many Signal units, the desert campaign was business as usual—fighting the way they had trained. But for others, specifically divisional Signal battalions equipped with multichannel communications, or PCM, the Gulf War created a new array of operational demands forcing some to change their ways of doing business.

The 141st Signal Battalion faced such a challenge supporting the 1st Armored Division during Operation Desert Storm. Old Ironsides' offensive, with its speed and intensity, made doctrinal PCM communications almost obsolete. Attempting to install and operate multichannel systems for subscribers while trying to keep pace with a charging armada across miles of sandy wasteland appeared to be a losing battle.

In response to the division's communications needs, the battalion threw away the book on conventional Signal doctrine. It developed a multichannel network completely different from its wartime Signal mission that provided commanders a vital command and control asset throughout the operation.

Until its deployment to Southwest Asia, the 141st Signal Battalion supported the 1st Armored Division's European wartime mission. The battalion had been

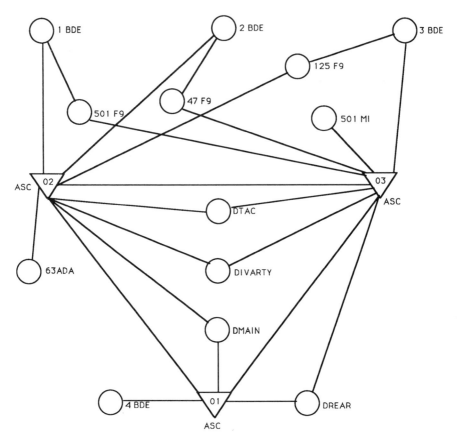

Normal system. 6 to 10 hours to engineer and install.

Figure 1. Normal System

organized similarly to other heavy division Signal battalions with its three line companies assigned specific missions. Company A, Command Operations, serviced the division command posts: Main, Rear and Tac. The forward operations company, B Company, linked the maneuver brigades, division artillery and separate battalions into the network. The division Area Signal Centers (ASC) provided by the three large platoons of Company C, were the backbone of the 1AD Signal architecture providing the common user links to all command posts. The ASCs also provided, at times, a corps gateway for the divisional system. Because of its size and the area coverage required to support the division, six to ten hours were normal for engineering and installing the entire system under the best conditions (Figure 1).

The 141st continued its traditional support of the 1AD during the division's five-week desert train-up in Tactical Assembly Area (TAA) Thompson, east of King Khalid Military City, Saudi Arabia. That was until the battalion received the division's plan to support the corps' armored offensive. The battalion realized then a new approach to its Signal support was needed.

The VII Corps plan to attack into the flank of the elite Iraqi Republican Guards was considered, by many, very ambitious. At the forefront of the attack, the 1AD would race 144 km in 18 hours to its initial attack position (Python) where the division would link-up with adjacent corps units for the operation's main effort.

The division's plan would require an extensive command and control endeavor that was beyond the normal operational capabilities of the 141st multichannel systems. However, the commanding general mandated that he have PCM telephone service with his commanders whenever possible during the operation. Besides the redundancy in communications, the CG required the multichannel systems in order to reduce the use of FM combat net radio for signal and operational security purposes, as well as to allow communications for future planning without interfering with current operations on the division FM radio nets.

Because of the speed and scope of the plan and the CG's intent, the battalion knew there was no way to maneuver ASCs to keep systems on the air as the division advanced. Any attempt to do so would have left the battalion in the dust of the division's charge right from the time most units would cross the line of departure.

The Simple Solution

In the final analysis of the division's order, the battalion's solution was simple—reduce the size and the service of the multichannel system and make it a sole user system dedicated to commanders's needs. The resulting strategy was a linear multichannel network linking brigade command posts directly to the Division TAC CP (DTAC) with point to point and long local access telephone service. Although the initial installation would only provide a few selected sole-user circuits, the system would be flexible enough to expand it for common users as time permitted.

The battalion plan centered on the division DTAC. From this forward command post, the Assistant Division Commander, Maneuver, ADC (M), would control the division wedge, the maneuver formation used to conduct its attack. Maneuver brigades were positioned to the front and flanks of the wedge with divisional CPs, force artillery, and mobile CSS units situated inside the formation for security. Because of the compact size of the wedge (20 km wide by 50 km deep), and with the DTAC centrally located with force artillery tucked in behind the 1st Brigade (division's advance guard), direct multichannel links could easily be made to the maneuver units and the division's main CP from the Signal platoon that normally supports this command post (Figure 2).

The DTAC Signal platoon became the hub for the battalion's new system. Multichannel shots from each brigade would be terminated at the DTAC CP on TA-312s inside the command tracks, M-577. These telephones would provide point to point sole user circuits for the ADC (M) to each brigade commander. In addition, a long local access circuit from the DTAC switchboard (SB-3614A) would be provided to each brigade system for redundancy in service. Another multichannel link from the DTAC to the DMAIN would provide additional point to point and long local circuits linking the G3 staff sections that operate the two divisional CPs.

The nonstandard multichannel system was designed for flexibility and allowed for expansion as determined by the operation's METT-T. Once divisional and subordinate command posts were set following a halt in the division's advance, a

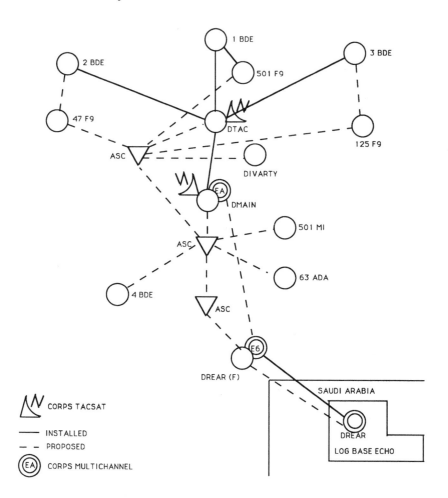

Figure 2. The Solution

common user system would be built using the battalion's area Signal centers to provide connectivity to other regular subscribers.

After installing the priority systems to the brigades, the forward ASC, 02, would link other units in its vicinity into the system. Additionally, ASC 01 would tie-in other units to the system as needed and establish a backbone link with ASC 02. ASC 03 was held in reserve and would provide on-call service to units as necessary to include lateral shots and terminating corps systems.

The division wedge formation would also facilitate the combat PCM plan minimizing the area coverage required of the battalion's system. With the A and B Companies' platoons advancing as part of the subscribers' movement orders and the three ASCs convoying with the divisional CPs, PCM links could be easily installed when required. From these positions, FM radio contact was easily maintained, and all battalion elements could be tracked during the advance.

As part of the plan, the S3 officer would maintain control from the battalion during the attack. The S3 section, through the systems control element (SYSCON), trailing the DTAC along with ASC 02, would track the units's move and manage the engineering and installation of the systems. Platoon leaders would have assigned frequency pairs for each system. Upon closing on a CP location, platoon leaders would report their subscriber's location by FM radio to the SYSCON, where the S3 staff would determine the azimuth for each shot. This information would be provided to the DTAC platoon leader who would coordinate the installation of each system and provide systems status to SYSCON once the shots were on the air and the circuits were logged-in.

Under the plan, the DTAC Signal platoon actually became a mini-area Signal center, and equipment adjustments had to be made within the battalion for the platoon to support the plan. By MTOE, the platoon was only authorized two AN/TRC-145 multichannel vans and no switchboard vans. Therefore, two AN/TRC-145s from the B and C Companies along with a switchboard (AN/TTC-41) from B Company were added to the platoon. Besides terminating the additional systems, the extra equipment would provide backup equipment if needed.

Because installation time would be critical to the success of any Signal support, the DTAC platoon modified the AN/GRC-103 radio antenna kit for quick erection. When the battalion swapped its fleet of CUCV, M1028s for HWMMV shelter carriers, M1037, the antenna launchers were welded to the bumper of the vehicles. The operator only had to install the fly swatter antenna and the coaxial cable to put the system on the air and could easily raise and lower the antenna as needed. With the antenna rigged this way, the DTAC platoon was usually installing systems within 10 minutes after the CP was established.

As part of the system's future expansion, it was critical that the plan include additional communications links for intelligence and logistics that were so vital to the operation's success.

Intelligence reports would be provided to the G2 at the DMAIN via a corps TACSAT link provided by Company A, 34th Signal, 93d Signal Brigade. That information would be provided to the DTAC through the division system. As the battalion expanded the division system, all corps links would become direct dial access.

The battalion's system also had to provide a tie-in to the division's logistics rear at Log Base Echo in Saudi Arabia. A division PCM system serving as a tail to the Corps UHF system at the log base was installed giving division subscribers common-user access to the division and corps systems. This also enabled division logisticians to talk directly to the forward element of the division Rear CP. However, this would only be possible during the attack if the battalion's system had time to mature. For redundancy, the division would rely on the Corps TACSAT link that would be provided to the division during the attack.

Final Rehearsal

A final rehearsal for the division's movement to contact came as Old Ironsides moved from the TAA to its forward assembly area (FAA) Garcia, 20 km south of the Iraqi/Saudi border, ten days before the start of the ground campaign. The 165 km maneuver abrest of the 3d Armored Division would replicate the corps' planned move into Iraq.

As the division began closing at FAA Garcia, the combat PCM system was installed between the DTAC and the brigade CPs within two hours. It was not known how long the wait would be before the ground war began. The PCM system was, therefore, expanded exercising the rest of the battalion's plan for combat. In the next 24 hours, all MSC and separate battalions had telephone service as all switchboards were added to the network as the remainder of the division closed in the FAA. The system was also successful tying-in the corps system providing the division direct dial access throughout the corps network.

Two days before the start of the ground war, a battalion after action review on the move to Garcia was conducted with company commanders, platoon leaders, and sergeants. The battalion combat PCM plan was also briefed as part of the division operations order. Platoon leaders were given frequency pairs, a system installation priority listing, and system contingencies if fighting prevented the division from positioning itself as planned and command posts were out of multichannel planning range.

Corps intelligence summaries up to this time indicated resistance was very light in the division's initial zone of attack. Division planners noted that the corps estimate was very optimistic and determined that the division might be given the go-ahead to attack early.

G Day (24 Feb 1991):

From the very first hours of the allied ground offensive, it was apparent that the operation had launched at lightning speed and would continue this pace throughout its duration. With the 1AD crossing the line of departure (the Iraqi/Saudi border) 18 hours ahead of schedule, there was considerable doubt whether multichannel communications would ever play a part in this operation. It was almost a foregone conclusion that, during this attack, when push came to shove, communications would simply be push-to-talk, FM combat net radio.

Few enemy forces were encountered by the 1AD the first day as division units drove 30 km into Iraq. The corps halted the attack that evening to maneuver the 2d ACR east of the 1AD, which gave the 141st the opportunity to employ its combat PCM system.

Within two hours following the refueling and repositioning of division units, multichannel links were installed between the DTAC and 1st and 3d Brigades. These systems were first priority as the two brigades were synchronizing their scheme for the planned penetration into the lead battalions of the Iraqi 26th Infantry Division the next day. Units within the division wedge were still moving, and with the attack scheduled for first light there was no time to expand the system.

G+1 (25 Feb 91)

The division's torrid pace continued with the attack commencing at 0630 (VII Corps LD time), with fierce fighting throughout the day. As darkness closed on a long day of combat, the commanding general decided to conduct a deliberate attack early the next morning, as heavy rain threatened all vehicle trafficability and made preplanned U.S. Air Force close air support (CAS) impossible.

In the midst of choking dust, smoke, and periodic downpours, the battalion again was successful providing communications for the division on the move. The barebone PCM system was installed to all three brigades and DMAIN from the DTAC as the division halted its advance. Planning was critical as the division coordinated the next day's attack against an Iraqi Corps log base at Al Busayyah (defended by an infantry battalion and a commando battalion in heavily fortified positions), with follow-on attacks into the Republican Guards Tawakalna and Adnan (Mechanized Infantry) and Medina (Armored) Divisions.

G+2 (26 Feb 91)

At first light, the division destroyed elements of the Iraqi 26th Infantry Division and an elite commando battalion, as it captured the Iraqi VII Corps logistics base at Al Busayyah by noon. As the division now maneuvered east against the first two Republican Guards divisions, the DTAC ordered a pause in the attack to reorganize, conduct hasty refueling operations, and push division reconnaissance elements deep.

In a driving sandstorm, the DTAC platoon again installed PCM systems to the 1st and 3d brigades as their forces consolidated for their attack into elite RGFC enemy forces later that day. Within ten minutes of positioning their vehicles within the perimeter of the DTAC, the platoon had telephones installed in the command post. However, within an hour DTAC and the forward elements of the Signal battalion were again on the move as the VII Corps commander ordered a resumption of the corps offensive east against the RGFC.

G+3 (27 Feb 91)

The ensuing pursuit of the Iraqi Republican Guards carried into the early morning of the battle's fourth day. The pace of the attack was now taking its toll, and throughout the 27th, the division faced critical fuel shortages due to extended CSS lines of communications and the rapid operational pace.

As the attack was again halted at 2100 hours, the Signal battalion went to work, and telephone service from the DMAIN to the DTAC and brigade command posts was installed in less than two hours.

Division planners were alerted that a cease-fire was imminent the next day. The CG's intent was to continue to attack early the next morning, with an intense artillery barrage and Apache Brigade (two battalions) deep strike preceding the ground maneuver attack.

G+4 (28 Feb.)

The artillery prep began at 0530 and continued for 45 minutes before the division began its final assault on the retreating Republican Guards. When the cease-fire was called at 0800, two brigades of the Median Armored Division and remnants of 17 other Iraqi divisions fleeing to the north were destroyed.

Because of Old Ironsides' furious, swift-paced offensive, the 141st was able to provide the division with only limited multichannel communications during the operation. Under the demanding combat conditions and the harsh desert environment, the battalion's combat PCM network was installed during the division's four operational halts in its attack. The system never matured beyond the limited point to point and sole user circuits connecting the brigade CPs to the DTAC and the DMAIN. The ASCs and other battalion support slices were only able to tie into the system once the cease-fire was declared.

Nonetheless, the battalion's tactical telephone system provided maneuver commanders an effective means to coordinate firepower and logistics support while on the move.

Commanders were quick to point out during after action reviews that the limited direct line access system was an extremely valuable C^2 asset and significantly contributed as a combat multiplier to their units' successful destruction of enemy forces.

The success of the 141st Signal Battalion system was the result of quickly adapting to a new operational environment and changing its way of doing business to meet the commanders' needs.

By modifying conventional Signal support doctrine, the battalion played a major role in Old Ironsides' victory by simply applying the bottom line to all communications doctrine: "whatever works."

And work it did.

This article originally appeared in the Summer 1991 issue of *Army Communicator.*

Endnote

[1] "Uber die Ta"tigkeit der Feldtelegraphen in den jüngsten Kriegen" 1880.

C² IN A HEAVY BRIGADE

Randolph W. House and Gregory L. Johnson

The 2d Brigade, 1st Cavalry Division deployed to Saudi Arabia on Operation Desert Shield and closed on its tactical assembly area in early October, 1990. Tough, realistic training to maintain our combat readiness was the goal. The brigade developed contingency plans from which full-up orders processes, terrain walks and table briefs, a command post exercise (CPX) and a command field exercise (CFX) were conducted. The brigade CFX provided a means to practice command and control in a *wedge* formation moving quickly over great distances.

As a combined arms maneuver battalion brigade, 2d Brigade is permanently task organized with one balanced task force (two tank companies and two mechanized infantry companies) and two tank-heavy task forces (three tank companies and one mechanized infantry company). The brigade's main command post (CP) and tactical command posts (TACs) are outfitted with the Standard Integrated Command Post System (SICPS), Single-Channel Ground and Airborne Radio System (SINCGARS), maneuver control system (MCS) and mobile subscriber equipment (MSE).

In this CFX, the brigade battle task force (TF) was required to quickly travel across rugged desert terrain with no road network. A distance exceeding the widest boundaries at the National Training Center was covered by a full brigade formation in one morning. Under these conditions, systems were stressed and lessons learned in a way not previously experienced.

Our present doctrine and force structure was developed primarily for a European scenario. Changes in basic doctrine and force structure will undoubtedly occur as a result of Desert Shield and Desert Storm experiences, but the brigade had to make some adjustments in the desert as it prepared for Desert Storm. This article will describe how the brigade developed the concept and trained for employment in a brigade wedge formation for movement to contact in the expanse of desert terrain.

Our present doctrine allows for flexibility in tactics, techniques and procedures. Full advantage of this flexibility had to be utilized to meet the challenges presented by the vast stretches of desert terrain. For the movement to contact CFX, the brigade battle TF task organized as outlined in Figure 1.

```
┌─────────────────────────────────────────────────────────────────────┐
│                          BRIGADE CONTROL                              │
│ Improved Tow Vehicle Company from the Balanced TF                     │
│      Ground Surveillance Radar Platoon                                │
│      Combat Observation Lasing Team  from Headquarters, Headquarters Battery Direct Support Field │
│      Artillery Battalion                                              │
│ FA Battalion (155mm SP) (DS)                                          │
│      Avenger Platoon from HHB, Air Defense Artillery Battalion        │
│ ADA Battery                                                           │
│      2 Stinger Teams                                                  │
│      2 Foward Area Alerting Radars                                    │
│ Engineer Company                                                      │
│ Chemical Reconnaissance Platoon (Decontamination)                     │
│ Military Police Platoon (DS)                                          │
│      Two MSE Signal Sections, (Small Extension Node) (DS)             │
│ Forward Support Batalion (DS)                                         │
│      2 Stinger Teams                                                  │
│                                                                       │
│                     BALANCED TASK FORCE (TF) (-)                      │
│ 2 Tank Companies                                                      │
│ 2 Mechanized Infantry Companies                                       │
│      Vulcan Platoon (+)                                               │
│      4 Stinger teams                                                  │
│      Chemical Reconnaissance Section (FOX)                            │
│                                                                       │
│                        TANK—HEAVY TF                                  │
│ 3 Tank Companies                                                      │
│ 1 Mechanized Infantry Company                                         │
│      Vulcan Platoon (+)                                               │
│      3 Stinger Teams                                                  │
│                        TANK—HEAVY TF                                  │
│      Vulcan Platoon (+)                                               │
│      4 Stinger Teams                                                  │
│               Other Participants in Brigade CFX                       │
│ Attack Helicopter Battalion to support Joint Air Attack Team (JAAT)   │
│ Electronic Warfare Liaison Officer (EW LNO) and communications jammers│
└─────────────────────────────────────────────────────────────────────┘
```

Figure 1. CFX Organization

One of the main training objectives of the CFX was to test the concept of the brigade wedge. The wedge consists of three maneuver battalion TFs, one artillery battalion, an engineer company and an air defense artillery battery. Brigade planners had templated this wedge formation down to company and battery level and found it to be 9 kilometers wide by 7 kilometers deep (discounting the three TF scout platoons, which move 4 to 7 kilometers forward). We tested this wedge formation during the CFX by taking Global Positioning System (GPS) readings during the battle and later plotting them on a 1:50,000 map and comparing it to our "doctrinal" template.

We determined that the wedge is an excellent means of maintaining control at all levels while maneuvering a brigade battle TF over long distances in desert terrain. It allows the commander to keep the force postured for rapid application of combat power at the critical point on the battlefield. The brigade zone was 17 kilometers wide on the CFX and was divided into three equal battalion TF zones. The brigade wedge is only 9 kilometers wide with all elements keying on the lead TF: Maneuver units found they did not need wider TF boundaries for the scouts.

This formation was found to be excellent for a force-oriented objective. The brigade commander can order the lead TF to alter its direction according to the situation, and the rest of the brigade battle TF can easily follow its lead without detailed explanation. It also provides the brigade commander with the option of executing a small number of brigade "plays." The flank TFs can quickly and easily swing left or right, or come to the support of the lead TF.

The brigade commander can mass his forces at the critical point and time with a minimum of confusion. The formation also provides a flexible, on-order company-size brigade reserve from either the left or right wing TF.

Even though the M1/M2/M3 (Abrams main battle tank and Bradley infantry and scout fighting vehicles) fleet can move across the rugged desert floor at high rates of speed, the brigade could only move at a sustained speed of 15 kilometers per hour. Command post tracked vehicles (M577s) proved to be the weak link. The brigade's other tracked vehicles (M113 armored personnel carriers, M901 improved TOW vehicles, M109 155mm self-propelled howitzers, field artillery ammunition support vehicles, fire support team vehicles, combat engineer vehicles and armored vehicle launched bridges) were all able to move faster than 15 kph and did not hamper momentum. At faster sustained speed, both the battalion TF and brigade formations became more difficult to control and critical M577 vehicles began to fall behind.

The brigade wedge facilitates maximum command and control from brigade to platoon level. TF commanders had developed three or four TF-level "plays" that

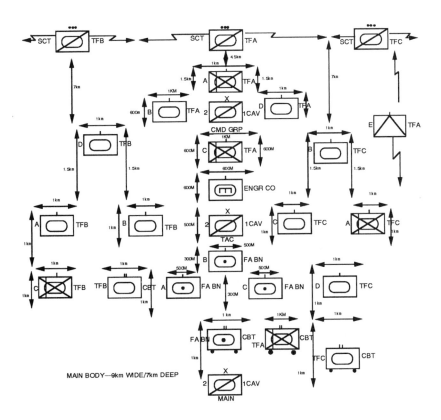

Figure 2. 2d Brigade Wedge

were practiced in the weeks prior to the CFX. When executed from the brigade wedge formation, these maneuver plays were relatively easy to control. Spatial relationships between elements of the entire brigade battle TF are easily understood all the way down to individual track commanders. Reaction time is decreased and battle drill or execution of TF plays is facilitated at all levels.

The brigade commander's workable options are increased significantly, without his having to worry about whether the artillery can support a flank swing maneuver, or that the trail TF is too far to the rear to get into the battle. Time and distance factors are known at all levels and each and all elements can keep up.

Using the antitank company (improved TOW vehicle-equipped) as a brigade flank screen worked well. On order, they moved immediately to the flank and entered the brigade command net. They were to sustain the screen with the brigade wedge traveling at 15 kilometers per hour. The brigade commander was able to relay instructions through the flank TF to maintain communications with the screen force when they were in communications dead space.

The brigade wedge facilitates good communications within the formation. SINCGARS radios on single channel have been especially reliable. Battalion TF commanders were extremely responsive and never lost communications with the brigade commander.

The movement of node centers and remote radio access units (RAUs) forward to cover the movement to contact zone is an important and extremely difficult operation. Commanders and staff rely more heavily on MSE communications. It is a critical asset, especially during planning phases. Like MSE, MCS enhances command and control during stationary planning phases or in operations where CPs are set for extended periods. But a long-distance rapid movement must still be controlled primarily by FM radio.

The most important lesson learned during the CFX was the difficulty of the brigade main CP and brigade TAC in keeping up with the battle as it progresses over long distances. New command and control schemes are being devised at all levels in order for command posts to accomplish their required function of providing critical intelligence information and combat multiplier synchronization.

During previous NTC rotations and field exercises, the brigade CPs performed extremely well and had no trouble staying in the battle. Battle hand off between CPs was smooth and jump times (time needed for relocation of a CP) were fast. Communications (SINCGARS, MSE, MCS and retransmission operations) generally worked well at the NTC with one of the brigade CPs always in control of the battle. Therefore, prior to the CFX, it was thought that we just needed to fine-tune a few things concerning CP operations to be as well trained as we could ever hope to be. With this in mind, the brigade planned and executed the November CPX in the Saudi desert.

One of our main training objectives on the November desert CPX had been to critically analyze CP load plans and decide what actually would be carried from the life-support areas into battle. Streamlining was the goal, and one we thought we had already achieved. However, we discovered that our CPs were still traveling too heavily loaded. As important as certain items of equipment may seem in stationary planning situations, they can severely limit movement speed and operations on the move.

The TAC operations (S3) M577 must be configured to facilitate operations on the move as part of the brigade wedge. This is difficult due to the large map boards required for brigade-level desert offensive operations and the amount of food, water, personal equipment, camouflage nets and other supplies that must be carried on the same vehicle. Inside the M577, a map board covers the entire right side from ceiling to floor. The left side of the track is filled with four SINCGARS radios and the MCS computer. There is no storage space inside the track, so load plans have been revised, leaving out such items as tables, chairs, briefing boards, external map boards and any other "luxury" items that were formerly set up in accordance with the Standard Integrated Command Post System.

Two battle captains (one each from the brigade S3 and S2 sections) sit on a coffin seat inside the track and monitor four nets—brigade and division command nets and brigade and division operations and intelligence (O&I) nets. They are in position to update the map board and can coordinate with each other via the internal intercom through their CVCs (combat vehicle crewman helmets). Being effective at this while moving over rough terrain at 15 kps requires a well-trained crew. If the operations M577 is disabled, the two battle captains can immediately jump to the equally equipped S2 section's M577, which follows as part of the TAC.

The only other vehicles with the TAC are the two highly mobility multipurpose wheeled vehicles (HMMWVs) that belong to the brigade commander and the brigade fire support coordinator (FSCOORD). The brigade commander, FSCOORD and Air Force liaison officer (ALO) are forward in the command group, traveling in two M113A3s. This TAC configuration allows the TAC to operate on the move and keep up with the wedge. It assists the brigade commander in fighting the battle and feeds him information from the brigade and division O&I nets.

It would be ideal to have the brigade main CP stationary while the TAC is moving within the brigade wedge. It always had been brigade SOP for one of the CPs to be set and in control of the battle while the other displaces forward. This is a sensible procedure and should be practiced when distances allow. The brigade main CP, with its five M577s, extensive communications capabilities and large staff is a tremendous asset in fighting the current battle and planning for the next one. It is limited, however, by the fact that it must be stationary and located within communications range of the brigade command group, TAC, maneuver TFs and artillery. However, in a scenario where the brigade travels 60 kilometers in 4 hours on a movement to contact, bounding the main CP and TAC, with one always set, will not work. They cannot keep up.

It appears that the best solution is for the main CP to cross the line of departure (LD) behind the brigade wedge and move at the same time as the TAC. The brigade main CP continues to move behind the brigade wedge until contact appears likely. It would then go to ground (set up) at a distance of 9 to 15 kilometers from the likely point of contact (or when expected contact occurs). With one FM retransmission station dropped off at the appropriate location by the TAC, the main CP could stretch its internal control forward to a range of approximately 33 kilometers. The main CP must also execute a retransmission scheme as it moves forward, dropping retransmission elements at locations that best facilitate communications back to the division main CP. Once the brigade main CP is set, MCS, MSE and AM radio assets can be more fully integrated. The brigade TAC would continue to move forward to around 3 to 5 kilometers from enemy contact and control the direct fire battle. The command group moves to the critical point on the battlefield and the brigade commander commands from there. If contact does not develop, movement of the two CPs continues.

At the division level, where CPs are larger, the same kind of command and control problems exist in long movements to contact. For instance, the division main CP's expandable vans will be difficult to move across this type of terrain. The division TAC is as big as the brigade main CP and will have the same kind of problems. The division forward command group has to be as far forward as possible, but is still tied to the assets controlled through the TAC or main CPs. This is a formidable problem that still requires workable solutions.

The brigade rear CP moves forward with the FSB (forward support battalion) main body. Doctrinally, one of the missions of the brigade rear CP is to assume control of the battle if both the main CP and TAC lose control. This is perhaps an unrealistic expectation in this situation. The rear CP is too far behind to assume effective control of the current battle. This mission could be better accomplished by a designated TF commander and his TOC.

The establishment of the forward link with the brigade, while maintaining the rearward link with DISCOM (division support command), is a difficult but critical mission. The FSB moves slowly and has an extremely difficult time linking up after a long attack, due to the preponderance of conventional trucks that are "road bound" and unable to traverse desert terrain. They are a hindrance in a movement to contact and can jeopardize the operation. Routes must be meticulously planned to facilitate responsive support.

Experienced leaders must accompany support truck movements. Although the requirement is real, it is doubtful if HEMTTs organic to maneuver TFs can make two round trips a day from the BSA or FAST at these attack distances. Similar to the CP problem, the BSA must not become entrenched at its last location. The BSA must be able to move forward on short notice. The lack of secure nets compounds command and control problems in the brigade rear areas. Routine maintenance or administrative/logistics traffic can compromise an entire brigade's operation.

The use of the [brigade wedge] turned out to be the most important command and control asset and combat multiplier of the war for 2d Brigade. It facilitated rapid movement over great distances, instant and easily executed responses to fragmentary orders issued on the move, and the precise placement of combat power at the critical time and place. The brigade made extensive use of the wedge, moving hundreds of kilometers in a variety of combat operations.

The brigade wedge was used for the first time by the entire brigade battle TF in January when the brigade moved north to occupy border defensive positions. The brigade TF, in the wedge formation, moved 65 kilometers in 4 hours in what turned out to be the final practice of this formation before its use in combat. It worked extremely well in this move, just as it had in the December CFX.

With the aid of GPS navigational devices, the wedge was able to change directions several times after only one radio transmission from the brigade commander to the lead TF commander. Everyone on the command net acknowledged the change; those not on the command net simply continued to guide on the lead TF. There was no problem with individual or groups of vehicles separating from the formation. Every vehicle crewman knew the formation diagram and understood the spatial relationship of his platoon, company and TF.

The brigade wedge was used in attacks up the Wadi AL Batin as part of the theater deception plan, and on the long flanking movement west and exploitation deep into Iraq. The attack formation wedge was able to maintain its intended nine by seven kilometer dimension expanding and contracting as necessary, while moving hundreds of kilometers at 20 kilometers per hour. Throughout these operations, everyone was extremely confident that this formation was the SOP solution to the command and control challenges of the requirements to move brigade and division combat formations extremely long distances on little or no notice. It simplified operations to the point where reactions to unexpected situations and response to fragmentary orders from the brigade commander were automatic.

During the attack and exploitation against the Republican Guards in Iraq, objectives often shifted by as much as 40 to 50 kilometers. These changes were often received while the brigade was on the move toward a previously defined objective. Because of the flexibility of the wedge formation and the brigade's training and confidence in using it, these shifts in direction were deftly accomplished. One radio transmission from the brigade commander and the entire brigade battle TF executed changes on the move.

The possibility of fratricide was greatly diminished by moving and fighting from the wedge. When the brigade arrived at one of its later objectives, the division had run up directly behind (within 1 kilometer) another division that was engaged in a fight with the Medinah Division of the Republican Guard Forces Command. Spot reports of activity to the brigade's front were pouring into CPs at all levels. Disciplined, well-trained soldiers and units were immediately informed and control was maintained by a completely intact C2 system, after a 300 kilometer, extremely rapid attack. The tight control in the brigade wedge formation was a key ingredient in preventing fratricide.

The wedge also provided a readily formed defensive formation when movement stopped. Navigation was enhanced considerably. Breaking maneuver elements out of the wedge to execute a series of well rehearsed plays in an attack or in reaction to enemy fire was a key component in the use of this formation. After executing these maneuvers from the wedge, reassembling and continuing movement in the wedge was accomplished almost effortlessly. In hindsight, no better formation could have been used in accomplishing the myriad of combat missions over the distances and terrain encountered in Desert Storm.

This article is condensed from the November 1991 issue of *Military Review.*

RAPID PREPARATION AND DISTRIBUTION OF BATTLEFIELD INFORMATION

Timothy J. Gibson

The latest advances in computer communications technology were put to their first wartime test last spring during Operation Desert Storm. The Army Central Forces (ARCENT) Command and Control Information System (AC2IS) provided Army level staff officers with a secure means to quickly pass electronic messages and transfer data files long distances.[1] The system combined special computer networking equipment with existing automation and communications equipment to connect users. AC2IS users in Saudi Arabia regularly communicated with other users in Saudi Arabia, the United States, and Germany. As the United States' involvement in the mid-East winds down, the equipment is being moved to the continental United States for use. In fact, the system has been selected as the Army's prototype Standard Theater Army Command and Control System (STACCS).

Historically, during war, commanders communicated by simply speaking or writing to each other. To pass information from one major command to another, a report was typically written and sent by courier to its destination. As telephones and radios were added to the military inventory, the soldiers and commanders could talk to each other more quickly over longer distances. Times have again changed, and technological advances now touch every aspect of military communications. Even the information passed has been shaped by technology. At the higher levels of command, enemy formations and strengths are tracked and analyzed with computers, courses of action are war-gamed with programs using artificial intelligence, and logistical and personnel information is compiled and tracked on computer spreadsheets. Once this information is analyzed and compiled by computers, the same machines can be used to pass the information between commanders and staff organizations.

Background

In today's Army, theater level staff work, such as reports, briefings, information papers, and operations plans, is accomplished with personal computers. In Saudi Arabia, staff officers regularly used spreadsheets and databases to track the arrival and location of units and supplies. Briefing charts, with operational information for senior commanders, were changed and distributed daily to other headquarters. There was a need to send large amounts of information securely over long distances.

For example, let us look at the case of the theater's daily logistics report. This report was prepared at 22d Support Command Headquarters in Dhahran in eastern Saudi Arabia. This report was a medium sized (approximately fifty kilobytes) Lotus 1-2-3 spreadsheet that was compiled with data from both the Dhahran area and from King Khalid Military City (KKMC) which is 380 miles north-west of Dhahran. Once officers at the 22d Support Command Headquarters compiled and briefed the report to their commander, they sent the report to the Army Headquarters in Riyadh, 350 miles to the southwest. The Army headquarters staff made any changes necessary for their purposes, presented it to their commander, and then forwarded it 8000 miles to the rear Army headquarters in the United States.

To be of any practical use, this report had to be distributed quickly. Air courier was provided throughout the theater but it was too unreliable for daily communications. A ground courier was too slow. Sending the report by facsimile (FAX) machine was slow and introduced errors when clerks manually transcribed the report into their spreadsheet. Reading the changes over the telephone was time consuming and produced similar errors.

The best way to distribute reports quickly and accurately was electronically over a secure system. AC2IS was more accurate and could transfer the file to any other station on the network, including stations in the United States or Germany, in less time than it took to make a connection on a secure FAX machine. It was possible to transfer the file between two personal computers equipped with modems, a communications package, and a secure telephone if you had two trained operators to coordinate the file transfer. However, using modems was too time consuming when more than two or three files were regularly sent. Two of our local area networks regularly shared over 100 files (averaging 40 kilobytes) a day. A dedicated secure data transfer system like AC2IS provided a better method for handling this amount of traffic; it provides for a more efficient use of time and of communications lines.

The AC2IS software was a simple menu driven program. Within an hour, users could normally be trained at their workplace on their personal computers to prepare and send messages, and to transfer MS-DOS files to another user. During this training, they also became familiar with the software's other features.[2]

A dedicated data system like AC2IS also reduces the load on the tactical switching system. Messages and charts sent over FAX machines or personal computer data links overload the local switch and trunk groups during peak usage periods. AC2IS uses a store and forward messaging system and has a packet switch to route messages over multiple trunk lines to prevent overloads. Before the AC2IS system was installed between Dhahran and KKMC in December 1990, the 22d Support Command relied on FAX machines for data transfers and the utilization rate for the supporting tactical switch (an AN/TTC-39A Tri-Tac switch) at Dhahran was over 90 percent. After AC2IS was installed and the command encouraged users to switch from the FAX machines to AC2IS terminals, the switch's utilization rate fell to near 65 percent and stayed there for the remainder of Deseret Shield and Desert Storm.

In summary, AC2IS allowed the user to make a memo, chart, or spreadsheet on his or her own computer then transmit it to a remote destination error free at the push of a button. Users preferred it to the FAX. It also provided better use of the telephone assets by reducing the attendant risk of overloading the switch during peak periods.

Equipment and Architecture

The basic AC2IS building block was the local area network (LAN). A LAN server acted as a mail host for the attached user terminals. The AC2IS LAN server was a Hewlett Packard 9000/350 computer. The first LAN servers installed in Saudi Arabia were standard commercial models, while later LAN servers were ruggedized Hewlett Packard equipment bought under the Army's Common Hardware / Software program. The LAN server software, which was written by the TRW Corporation, ran under the Hewlett Packard Unix Operating System and provided access to the operating system itself, as well as administrative, electronic mail, file transfer, and MS-DOS co-processor capabilities for the LAN.

The LAN server acted as a mail host for up to eight active users using personal computers equipped with commercial Ethernet cards (Figure 1). Users logged onto the system through these personal computers, and when not logged on these same

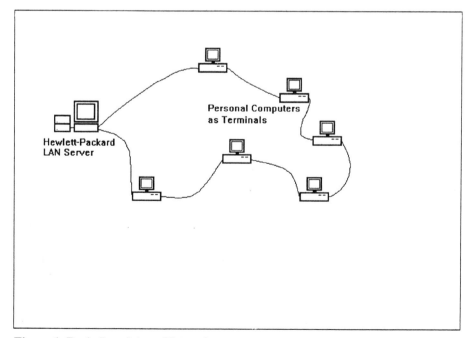

Figure 1. Basic Local Area Network

personal computers could be used for normal applications.

The basic LAN could be varied by adding more Hewlett Packard mail hosts to the LAN. These "analyst consoles" used the same Hewlett Packard equipment and software as the LAN server but were configured as mail hosts for eight additional users rather than to control the LAN (Figure 2). Furthermore, the analyst consoles could still be used to transmit messages or transfer files. Adding these analyst consoles allowed for more users in a large headquarters. A LAN with a LAN server and two analyst consoles could serve as many as twenty-four user terminals.

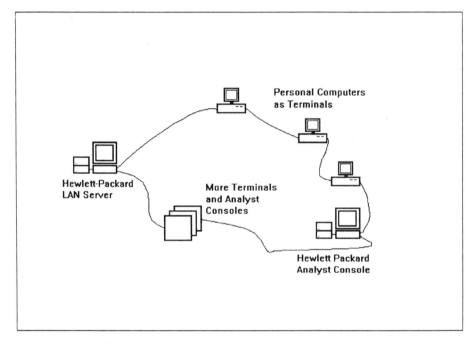

Figure 2. LAN with analyst console

Individual LANs have a very limited use. For the system to be a useful military command and control system, several LANs must be connected to allow information to be exchanged throughout the theater. The AC2IS LAN server was connected to other LAN servers through a Wide Area Network (WAN). The WAN was based on an AC2IS packet switch network which used tactical 16 kilo-bit digital communications lines.[3] Each packet switch can be connected to a maximum of six LANs and three communications lines (Figure 3). The packet switches used the X.25 communications protocol; therefore, each LAN required a gateway to convert data from the LAN's Ethernet protocol to the packet switch's X.25 protocol.

The AC2IS network in Saudi Arabia used four packet switches and six inter-switch trunk lines, with each packet switch directly connected to each of the others (Figure 4). At first this inter-connectivity seemed to be an unnecessary redundancy, however, the 49.45 percent operational rate for the AC2IS tactical communications lines at times made this redundancy seem inadequate.

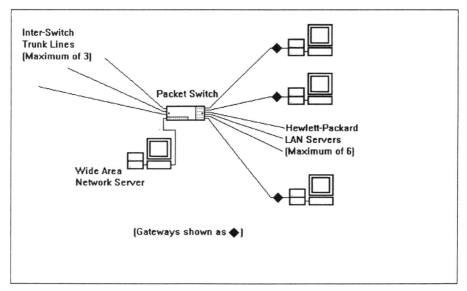

Figure 3. Packet switch complex

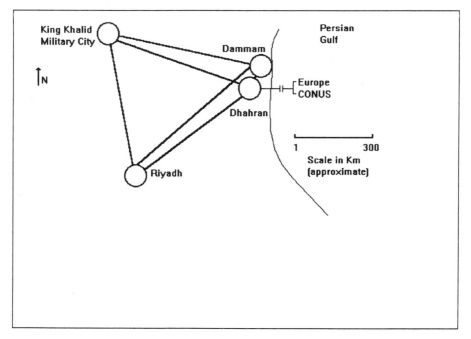

Figure 4. Packet switch network

Each packet switch site needed a Hewlett Packard computer to act as a WAN server. Because a WAN server can be both a LAN server and a mail host in addition to being a WAN server, shortages of equipment were overcome by installing a packet switch with a WAN server and then running a local network directly off the WAN server. The original installation at 22d Support Command in Dhahran consisted of one WAN/LAN server, with two analyst consoles, and thirteen terminals. This configuration was administered by three soldiers.

Security

AC2IS provided a "secure" means of transmission and was certified to pass Secret level data. This allowed it to handle nearly all information that normally passed at the Theater Army level. Physical security for the WAN and LAN server, and the terminals was accomplished by maintaining physical control over the equipment and the area. Security past the LAN server was accomplished by encrypting the data after it left the LAN with a standard KG-84A Cryptographic Key Generator. A KG-84A was needed at each end of the line to encrypt and decrypt every communications circuit (Figure 5). This resulted in AC2IS using a great number of KG-84As. For example, the Dammam WAN packet switch node had seven KG-84As in use at all times: four to the subordinate LAN servers, and three more on the trunk lines.

A single message passed through many way points on its trip from one PC terminal to another. At a minimum, a message travelling from Dhahran to KKMC was routed through all the devices shown in Figure 6. The sender composed the message on his or her PC and then submitted the message to the LAN Server for transmission. The LAN Server passed the message to the gateway where the message address was changed from Ethernet to X.25 protocol. The gateway then passed the message to a KG-84A which encrypted the message and passed it over a communications medium (anything from wire to satellite) to another KG-84A on the other end of the circuit. This second KG-84A decrypted the message from the gateway and passed it to the packet switch. The packet switch then chose the best available path to the message's destination and sent the message out over that path through another KG-84A. The process was then reversed at the other packet switch or switches.

Packet Switching

AC2IS was designed to use existing tactical communications systems. The AC2IS communications backbone in Saudi Arabia was the Echelons Above Corps (EAC) digital voice communications network without any modification. The supporting communications equipment all belonged to the Tri-Tac family of equipment. The transmission mediums ran the gamut from short line-of-sight microwave and tropospheric-scatter radio to communications satellites. The switches were all AN/TTC-39A's. The AN/TTC-39A is a digital, computerized switch which provides service for both digital and analog subscribers and was designed in the mid-1970's. The actual communications network is shown in Figure 7 with the switches shown by their "number." By no means is this the entire EAC switching or communications network, Figure 7 depicts only the small portion of the network used by AC2IS.

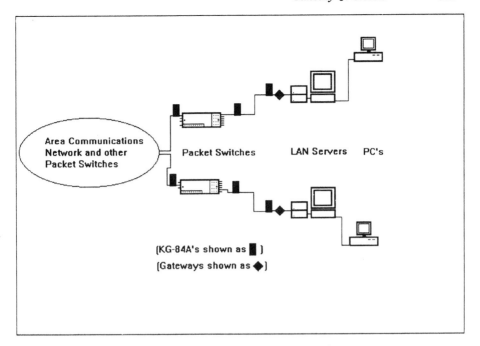

Figure 5. Packet switch complex with cryptographic equipment

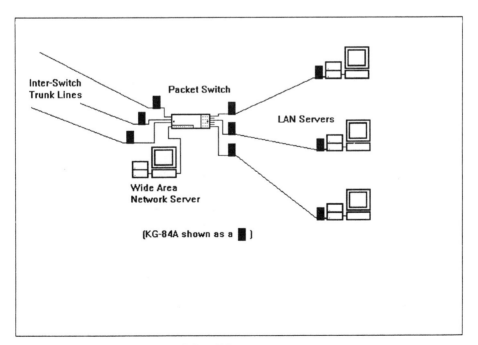

Figure 6. Message route from PC to PC

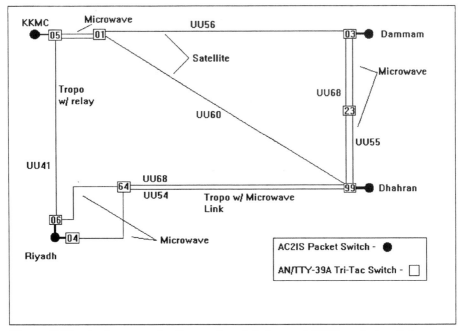

Figure 7. Physical communications network between AC2IS packet switches

There were six AC2IS inter-switch trunk communications lines in Saudi Arabia. The first of these inter-switch trunks was established from Dhahran to KKMC (circuit number UU60). This circuit operated on its own for several weeks before the remainder of the system became operational. Table 1 shows the circuits by name and type as they became available.

The operational rates of the tactical communications circuits supporting AC2IS were at times poor. It was common for the AC2IS circuits to drift back and forth between operational and non-operational many times an hour with a obvious impact on their operational rates. These low operational rates were generally caused by the signalling equipment being pushed past its designed specifications and the shortage of maintenance spares. We were able to overcome these problems by working closely with the supporting U. S. Army Signal units and by providing ourselves communications redundancy with our packet switches.

The packet switches used by AC2IS, which were produced by BBN, were rugged and reliable and allowed AC2IS to get information through even when the communications circuits were poor. While all data is sent by packets, the AC2IS packet switching system differed from most Army equipment because of the way these packets of data were routed.

When data is sent over communications lines it is broken up into packets and sent over a circuit. Most Army equipment uses the "virtual circuit" method for sending these packets. A connection, much like a voice telephone connection, is made. When the devices on both ends of the connection are ready, the data is sent.

Packet switches do not send every packet over the same route; rather, they send each packet over the best route available when that particular packet is being sent. For example, a message sent from Dammam to Riyadh might have some packets go directly to Riyadh while others would be routed through Dhahran or KKMC. The packet switch in Dammam picks the path depending on the traffic. Due to the difference in transmission times, some of the data packets arrive in the wrong order at Riyadh; therefore, the packet switch appends header information to each data packet to enable the packet switches on the other end to put the message back together in the proper order.

The finest feature of the packet switch method was that the switches themselves "talked" to each other and they "knew" which lines were up. If there was any possible path which would allow the data to arrive at its destination, even if a message from Dammam to Riyadh had to go through Dhahran and KKMC, the packet switch network found it.[4]

Circuit	From	To	Available	Type
UU60	Dhahran	KKMC	24 Jan 1991	Satellite
UU54	Riyadh	Dhahran	8 Feb 1991	Mixed (Note 1)
UU55	Dhahran	Dammam	9 Feb 1991	Microwave
UU41	Riyadh	KKMC	14 Feb 1991	Tropo (Note 2)
UU56	Dammam	KKMC	17 Feb 1991	Satellite
UU68	Riyadh	Dammam	21 Feb 1991	Mixed (Note 1)

Note 1: This communications path from went through several types of transmitters. These consisted of two tropospheric scatter radio links with a microwave shot connecting them.

Note 2: UU41 was actually operational in late January 1991. However, it initially connected the Riyadh node as a LAN from the KKMC packet switch. UU41 became operational as an inter-switch trunk on 14 February 1991.

Table 1

Initial Fielding

AC2IS was initially fielded in Saudi Arabia by a four-man team from Germany. The AC2IS was based on a system in use in Europe and the Army forces in Saudi Arabia had no personnel trained on the system. From November 1990 to late January 1991, the team conducted briefings for commanders, installed one circuit and two packet switches, and conducted user's training. This initial installation put AC2IS "on the map." The first of the two packet switches were at the 22d Support Command in Dhahran. This location had a combined WAN/LAN server with a packet switch, two analyst consoles, and thirteen user terminals.

The second WAN/LAN server, with five user terminals, was at the 22d Support Command (Forward) at KKMC, approximately 400 miles away. The 22d Support Command used the system to track incoming supplies and equipment, which arrived daily at the port in Dammam, and to coordinate the shipment of needed material to the logistics bases at KKMC.

Expanding the System

In late January 1991, the decision was made to expand the network as more network equipment and personnel became available for AC2IS. The first LAN in Riyadh was added to the network at the Army Headquarters. This original Riyadh node was a LAN in the Army war-room which was connected to the KKMC packet switch. However, with the arrival of operators and equipment and the addition of another trunk line, we were able to add a packet switch and WAN server to the Riyadh area. The final configuration in Riyadh had a WAN/LAN server providing service to (1) the Army Headquarter's Logistics section; (2) the original LAN in the war-room, now configured off the Riyadh packet switch; and (3) another LAN at Riyadh's Personnel Command.

The Army Headquarter's Mobile Command Post at KKMC was added to the network in early February, with the equipment installation and user training being completed just before the start of the ground war. The Mobile Command Post used AC2IS extensively to coordinate with the main Army headquarters regarding operations orders and unit movements during the ground war.

While the Mobile Command Post was being added in western Saudi Arabia, a very ambitious plan was initiated to add another packet switch with four LAN's in and around the eastern port of Dammam. These four LANs eventually provided service to the 11th Signal Brigade, the 593d Area Support Group, the 7th Transportation Group, and the 321st Material Management Center. These LANs and the servicing packet switch were installed during February and early March after a major effort.

The last major changes in the system took place at the 22d Support Command in Dhahran, where the AC2IS had gotten its start. The 22d Support Command site in Dhahran had grown to eighteen users on one WAN/LAN server and two analyst consoles.

Although the system could theoretically serve twenty-four users, the eighteen users in Dhahran were experiencing unacceptable delays when trying to transmit messages during peak periods. Additionally, with the end of the war and the subsequent redeployment of troops back to the United States and Europe, the 22d Support Command was expanding its operations and needed more terminals. To support these changes, we brought in another Hewlett Packard LAN server and three gateways and changed the system from one WAN/LAN server with two analyst consoles to a WAN server with three LAN's. Reconfiguring the machines was simplified because during this time we were also replacing the commercial Hewlett Packard equipment with the ruggedized Hewlett Packard components.

Conclusions

Numerous commentators have documented the vital role of high technology equipment in the Allied Coalition's victory over Iraq. Computer equipment played a major part in that victory, whether in the form of a tank's fire control computer or a personal computer on a staff officer's desk. AC2IS was not so critical to theater Army command, control, and logistics that its absence would have cost us the victory. However, the need for a system like AC2IS exists at the Theater Army level. Within three months, AC2IS grew from two WAN/LAN servers with eighteen users to four WAN/LAN servers, twelve LAN servers, and over eighty users. In addition, AC2IS provided an inexpensive (the entire Riyadh complex cost less than $200,000) means to securely pass volumes of information on the battlefield. The system greatly improved information exchange and coordination between headquarters by making message and data transmissions quick, simple, and error free. While the success of AC2IS during Desert Storm is surely proof of our ability to establish new high technology systems, it also shows the need for an established Theater Army command and control system. In Saudi Arabia, we had the luxury of time, and were able to develop this system as we went along. In the next conflict, this may not be possible.

Endnotes

[1] AC2IS is a derivation of the USAREUR (U. S. Army Europe) Tactical Command and Control System (UTACCS). UTACCS has been under development by the Army since the mid-1980's and provides database applications in addition to the basic communications functions of AC2IS.

[2] Authors note: We found that it was better to give users basic training on the features everyone used and make ourselves available for more advanced training. This prevented us from "scaring off" users with long training sessions which detailed all of the system's capabilities.

[3] Actually, the communications lines can be any speed. The Tri-Tac switching equipment had both 16 and 32 kilo-bit digital trunk groups. We chose to use 16 kilo-bit trunk lines because they were easier to gain access to. The transmission medium, whether it was by satellite, tropospheric scatter radio, microwave, or 4 wire digital telephone line, was transparent to the system.

[4] Having packet switch capabilities does not come without a price. First, the packet switches required dedicated, not dial-up lines. Furthermore, on the AC2IS inter-switch trunk lines, the packet switches always needed 10-15% of the 16 kilo-bit digital lines for "housekeeping."

An abbreviated version of this article appeared in the March 1992 issue of *SIGNAL*.

THE FIRST SPACE WAR:
The Contribution of Satellites to the Gulf War

"We could see, hear and talk all through the war. After a few hours, he (Saddam Hussein) could not." [1]

Sir Peter Anson and Dennis Cummings

This article examines the contribution to the coalition forces' success in military and civil space systems, communications, surveillance, earth observation, navigation and public news reporting roles. The Gulf was the first occasion in which a full range of military space systems was used in anger. Approximately 60 Western military satellites were directly involved. It was the first real test under war conditions of the $200 billion U.S. space machine, and the first justification in combat of the $1 billion French and British investments in military space.

Space added a fourth dimension to the war. It influenced the general direction of the conflict and saved lives. Space enabled a fully secure and effective trunk and tactical communications network, large enough to support a 400,000-strong army, to be established in-theater in a few weeks. It provided detailed images of Iraqi forces and the damage inflicted by allied air attacks. It gave early warning of Scud missile launches. Space provided a navigation system of stunning accuracy that touched upon the performance of every combat soldier, and on missiles, tanks, aircraft and ships.

Commercial space communications and observation systems were also used by the coalition forces, in addition to carrying the first real-time television battle pictures to the world public. The Gulf conflict can fairly be described as the first space war.

Communications

A seasoned military communicator said afterward, about the role of satellite communications:..."The Gulf conflict taught us no new lessons—just a reminder of their brilliant flexibility." In fact, this intended compliment is an understatement on two counts. First, it fails to convey the enormity of the communications task and the competence with which it was fulfilled. Perhaps more importantly, it overlooks a new and disturbing phenomenon of the space age—the ability of the media to bring the live action of the war into the homes of ordinary people on both sides, as well as the forces taking part and their political and military leaders.

Communications satellites carried the majority of the military trunk traffic (secure speech, data, facsimile, telegraph) into and out of the theater. They provided tactical links within theater and bridges for other terrestrial VHF/UHF radio systems whose line-of-sight limitations prevented them from spanning the desert reaches. They provided total communications to ships at sea, to troops on the move and even to military aircraft. They carried home-television into coalition troops and television news reports out to a world public. They brought the coalition supreme commander within a telephone call of the White House, Downing Street and the Elysée Palace. And when military satellites became overloaded, civil space circuits were leased and pressed into service.

When, on August 2, 1990, Saddam Hussein announced the invasion of Kuwait to a shocked world, the United States had a single administrative unit in Bahrain and two training missions in Saudi Arabia, served by satellite communications. The United Kingdom and France also had some support echelons in the area, but no military satellite links. However, overhead in their 35,000 km geostationary orbit waited some 15 individual U.S., French, and British military communications satellites whose terrestrial footprints covered the Gulf area.

The Iraqis, in contrast, had no military space assets, although they did enjoy access to civil international networks, Intelsat and Inmarsat, plus a share in Arabsat which operates two regional telecommunications satellites covering the area. However, the Arabsat earth station in Baghdad was claimed to be an early victim of the bombing campaign.

The detailed work-up of the U.S., U.K. and French operational space and ground segments in support of the combat forces during Desert Shield exemplified the inherent capabilities of space communications. These include rapid deployment, high quality, security, reliability, power, and flexibility. It also demonstrated the growing military dependence on satellite communication in all services and at every level of command. Nevertheless, considerable ingenuity was needed to reconfigure the space segment and to manufacture, extend, patch, adapt, and modify ground systems to bring them up to operational scratch over the five months of grace afforded by Desert Shield.

U.S. Satellite Communications Systems

The flexibility of space communications was brilliantly demonstrated by U.S. authorities in a reconfiguration of their space segment to match traffic demands. Prior to hostilities, the U.S. space communications workhorse, the SHF Defense Satellite Communications System (DSCS) provided the telecommunications cover of the area through its Eastern Atlantic (EA) and Indian Ocean (IO) satellites. The total DOD traffic throughput over these two satellites was about 4.5 Mb/s— equivalent to around 70 commercial voice circuits. A little more than 1 month later, with the first U.S. forces in theater, 48 tactical terminals had been deployed; the traffic throughput had risen to 38 Mb/s (600 voice channels); and DSCS IO was saturated. Traffic demands were still building.

By mid-September, DSCS 9E was reconfigured (in a novel realignment of its high gain and multibeam antennas) to increase its Gulf traffic capacity. At the same time, under longstanding agreements, the United Kingdom provided U.S. forces with capacity on its Skynet 4B satellite positioned at 53° E.

In the meantime, the U.S. tactical terminal population had risen to 53. It was at this time that President George Bush announced the deployment of 200,000 more U.S. troops to the Gulf. The decision was then made to boost the Gulf traffic capability by relocating the DSCS Reserve West Pacific (WP) satellite from its 180° geostationary parking slot to 65°E. Shortly after DSCS WP began operation, traffic had risen to 44 Mb/s (710 voice circuits), 60 U.S. earth stations were operating in theater and the United Kingdom's Skynet 4A at 30° E was providing additional reserve capacity.

By the time traffic to U.S. forces in the Gulf had peaked, yet another SHF satellite, DSCS Indian Ocean Reserve, was available, the throughput had risen to 68 Mb/s (1,100 voice circuits), and the earth station population was 110.

In addition to DSCS SHF services, U.S. forces in the Gulf were also served by UHF geostationary satellites, the Fltsatcom/AFsatcom and Leasat/Syncom families. A fleet of 9 spacecraft in all, those located at 15° W, 73° E, and 71.5° E, provided cover of the Gulf area. Primarily intended for the command and control of U.S. nuclear forces worldwide, this UHF network is reported as serving more than 2,000 ships, submarines, aircraft, and army/marine units overseas.

U.S. interests both in mini-satellites and in polar communications were exercised by the use of two experimental multiple access communications satellite (MACSAT) spacecraft, which were launched on a Scout rocket shortly before the Kuwait invasion. These small (150 pound) UHF satellites employ store-and-forward techniques, in this operation picking up logistics information while over-flying Saudi Arabia and dumping in over the United States and vice versa.

U.K. Satellite Communications Systems

For the United Kingdom, the flexibility of space communications was demonstrated both in a relocation of satellites and in a substantial enhancement of its Skynet ground segment resource within the space of a few weeks. The ingenuity of engineers at the U.K. research establishments, RAE and RSRE, was stretched to achieve hurried modifications of new and untried mobile ground terminals to maximize their technical capabilities before they could be shipped to the Gulf.

Prior to the conflict, the British Army could call on only 6 aging and small (1.7m antenna) transportable terminals, each configured for a single 2.4 Kb/s channel of multiplexed voice and telegraph. The U.K. MOD also possessed a small number of personal manpack terminals. Six months later at the outset of Operation Desert Storm, U.K. forces were operating 26 land mobile/transportable terminals in the theater, with a combined throughput of more than 23 Mb/s. In user terms, the capability of these U.K. ground terminals rose over the period of the conflict from a mere handful to more than 300 commercial voice channels.

In space, the United Kingdom's complement of Skynet 4 satellites with their UHF and SHF payloads had been auspiciously completed with the launch of the third spacecraft, Skynet 4C, in August 1990. Equally auspiciously, the British Army's VSC 501 Land Rover terminal production line was just opening up. Its 12-month production program was telescoped into 6 months. Terminals and support facilities were rushed into service, but not before they had been quickly modified to meet an unforeseen and expanded operational requirement.

The VSC 501s had been designed principally to meet a requirement to provide a national link to commanders in the NATO Central region for which a single low-speed multiplexed speech, data, and telegraph channel was ideal. In the Gulf, the VSC 501s were needed to carry multichannel speech and operational and logistic data and to interface with a wide range of civil and military bearers. Greater multichannel speech capability was achieved through the incorporation of a QPSK modem, which had been designed for large fixed anchor stations. The newly adapted terminals passed their acceptance and climatization trials in live desert action.

For more than 10 years prior to Desert Storm, the British Army had been pondering an operational need for a satellite communications 'adaptor' for elements of its backbone Ptarmigan combat radio network. The role of the adaptor was to provide beyond line-of-sight anchors into other trunk networks and to act as a bridge in the event of network battle damage.

The deployment of U.K. land forces to the Gulf raised an immediate requirement on the part of the Ptarmigan community for interconnectivity between their headquarters and the United Kingdom, and between dispersed forces in-theater. These Ptarmigan bridges were achieved by the loan from the United States of TSC-100 and TSC-93 earth stations which were hastily modified to British standards and deployed in the United Kingdom and the Gulf.

The U.K. experience served again to demonstrate the inherent flexibility of satellite communications and its capability of meeting strategic and tactical requirements in a single, fully integrated, dynamic network. As a result, a reliable and secure battlefield communications architecture was rapidly established in a few week in an area almost totally devoid of usable communications infrastructure (Figure 1).

Naval Communications

Many of the naval ships supporting the operations either in the Gulf or elsewhere also enjoyed communications via satellite, which allowed direct links with other allied vessels and with local and national headquarters. One may well ask why it is that so little needs to be said about naval use of space communications. The answer is that the Navy's peacetime use of communications is very similar to the wartime set-up. Far less energy was required to be devoted to making special arrangements.

The U.S. Navy has since criticized its continued dependence on the UHF satellite band, which is subject to congestion, interference, and limiting capacity. It was reported that more than 30 percent of the U.S. naval traffic was carried over commercial satellite networks. This may be linked to UHF deficiencies. The U.K.'s Royal Navy, on the other hand, has set a world standard in its use of SHF satellite communications. The SCOT ship borne terminal is now standard fit on all Royal Navy vessels of frigate class and above, providing reliable, jam resistant links of high capacity potential.

Nevertheless, Royal Navy ships had to be specially fitted with additional terminals to allow them to communicate with other user systems in the Gulf. UHF terminals were installed to allow them to talk with the U.S. Navy fleet in the area, and commercial Inmarsat terminals were fitted to provide contacts with merchant ships as part of their task of enforcing the United Nations' embargo.

Use of Civil Communications

In view of these immense military satellite communications resources deployed in support of the coalition forces, it is surprising that very extensive use had also to be made of the international commercial networks, Intelsat and Inmarsat.

Inmarsat reported a 50 percent growth in Gulf traffic between January and March 1991, a period when commercial shipping would have been expected to give the area a wide berth. Intelsat has also reported substantial traffic increases over Desert

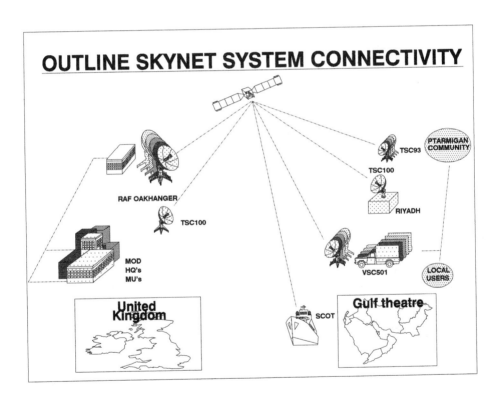

Figure 1. Skynet Connectivity

Shield/Storm, although the bulk of this growth was attributable to television traffic. Intelsat reported that full-time television channel usage increased from 2 to 22 channels, while short-slot bookings peaked at more than 400 channels during one day in January. Intelsat also reported that 65 temporary television and telecommunications earth stations were licensed to operate in the area.

In this period of intense global television activity, Cable News Network took to the space waves and became a worldwide household name. The vivid real-time pictures of life in Baghdad under bombing would not have been remotely possible without satellite relay. Peter Arnett of CNN claimed that he could set up and operate his Inmarsat attache-case terminal and report to the world within 3 minutes. One effect of this real-time reporting astonished the military authorities as much as public viewers when a live television broadcast of a Scud attack on Tel Aviv reportedly gave Baghdad the information to re-target its next salvo. Although the tiny Inmarsat portable terminal was designed specifically for a telephone link and lacked the power for television transmission, Arnett and his fellow reporters were able to transmit still-photographs of exceptional quality over Inmarsat using the output of digital cameras.

Satellite news reporting brought a new and disturbing dimension to international conflict because of its unique ability to carry the war into living rooms of billions worldwide. The war was fought in the full glare of media coverage. It was seen that world opinion could be shaped by a single broadcast. It was also clear that, whereas democracies are vulnerable to such free news reporting, totalitarian regimes are not. The daily pressures on coalition leaders were intensified by this unique public insight into the military campaign and tactics. The television broadcasts also reached the waiting armies on both sides.

Today, the smallest news gathering satellite earth station weighs around 35 kg— perhaps 45 kg with digital camera and other accessories. The notion that war reporters will one day possess a capability to reach the world public through a terminal that might be carried in a coat pocket is a very chilling thought.

Navigation

The proud motto of Royal Air Force navigators is "Man is not lost." But it is a motto couched more in hope than reality. Land forces and light combat aircraft are particularly vulnerable to navigation errors, and the featureless deserts of Kuwait and Iraq were expected to present a stern test of the navigation skills of coalition air and land forces.

Fortunately, coalition man was never lost. He was able to move with confidence over difficult desert terrain, avoiding enemy defenses, assured of re-supply, and able to pin/point and target enemy arms and installations with remarkable precision, thanks to the technological "discoveries" of the war—the global positioning system (GPS).

The U.S. Navstar GPS has been around since 1978, when the first satellites in the system were launched. One explanation of why the combat potential of GPS was not appreciated until now is the delay in deploying the full space system. The fully operational GPS, consisting of 21 satellites (plus 3 on-orbit spares) in 6 orbital planes at 20,000 km, is not due to be completed until 1993.

This constellation will ensure that a user anywhere on the Earth will be able to view a minimum of 4 satellites simultaneously. Each satellite transmits at L-Band (1.2 GHz) precise (P) encrypted signals for military users and coarse acquisition (C/A) signals for other users. The P signal enables military receivers to compute position down to 15 meters accuracy. The C/A facility offers a basic 30 meter accuracy but, in contingency situations such as that presented by the Gulf, the satellite coding is degradable to 100 meters under the control of the systems' U.S. Air Force authorities. However, it is reported that this facility was not exercised in Desert Storm as the Iraqis did not possess GPS receivers in any quantity. Fixes in position require signals from 3 satellites; fixes in position plus altitude require 4 satellites.

At the start of Desert Shield, the space segment consisted of 13 satellites, with a further spacecraft rushed into orbit in August 1990. This complement of satellites provided two-dimensional positioning service in the Gulf area for up to 22 hours per day, with three-dimensional cover for around 16 hours per day.

It was not until after the first troops had arrived in Saudi Arabia that the vital need for GPS receivers in the desert conflict was fully appreciated. At the time, small lightweight military GPS receivers, (SLGRs—affectionately known to the troops as sluggers) had been selected and ordered by 11 NATO countries. The U.S. Department of Defense was also in the process of evaluating portable commercial receivers. But the immediate experience of the coalition troops on the ground literally blew the top off pedestrian defense procurement processes. By February, one manufacturer, Trimble Navigation, had supplied more than 3,000 commercial receivers and was rushing through orders for a further 6,000 units. Magellan Systems Corporation, another leading supplier, had delivered around 2,500 hand-held receivers. All in all, well over 12,000 personal receivers are likely to have been used by coalition forces in the Gulf.

The commercial hand-held models, priced at around $3,000, are remarkably rugged and compact and well suited to battlefield conditions. They are the size of a car radio and can be powered by torch batteries. Such was their immediate attraction that some U.S. troops even had their relatives purchase commercial units for them at home and post them to Saudi Arabia.

Magellan GPS receivers could also be found in UH1H (Huey) and Cobra helicopters, in F-111s and B52s, in British Tornados and French Jaguars, as part of the air crews' survival kit, which enabled remarkable rescues. They also could be found on ships and landing craft, on tanks and armoured vehicles, and in forward observation posts directing air and ground artillery strikes.

Using a hand-held GPS receiver, a ground soldier could locate his position. Using a laser range finder he was able to obtain the range and bearing of the target for relay to an air control officer to provide precise target information for ground support aircraft. These, in turn, using their own GPS equipment, were able to offset their bombing instruments and attack with devastating surprise and lethal precision. Thus the effectiveness and safety of an $18 million aircraft could be enormously enhanced with a $3,000 hand-held instrument.

GPS receivers are now credited as making possibly the single most important contribution to the success of the conflict. They certainly saved many coalition lives and casualties, and significantly enhanced the effectiveness of most teeth arms. For troops on the ground, they also provided a great boost to morale.

Some sluggers were developed on commercial designs and funding, clear evidence of technology cutting across the conventional division of civil and military equipments and markets. This was to be a recurring feature of space equipment employed by the coalition forces.

The increasing popularity of GPS in widespread commercial and military applications, together with their decreasing size and costs (a Japanese company has now weighed in with a $1,000 version) make it easy to believe that GPS receivers will in future become a standard item in every soldier's battle kit. The only surprise is that this near perfect navigation system, which was initiated with launches in 1978, has taken so long to come of age.

Surveillance

The French Minister of Defense, Pierre Joxe, said afterward that the allied victory was due in large part to the U.S. fleet of spy satellites. It was, perhaps, a tacit acknowledgment of the availability of this U.S. intelligence to coalition partners, although Minister Joxe was actually making a case for an independent European capability. The U.S. defense experts in turn applauded the contribution of the French SPOT Earth observation satellites. Nevertheless, Minister Joxe was acknowledging the supremacy of the U.S. space surveillance machine with its range of missile early warning, ocean surveillance, photographic and radar reconnaissance, electronics eavesdropping and weather satellites. They provide a virtually total and global capability, which is starkly exemplified in a facility for photographing images below 25 cm resolution anywhere in the world from orbits of 200 km and more out in space. This multipurpose space armada, with its massive supporting processing and communications chain, is one of the most technologically advanced sectors of the U.S. arsenal and represents a significant slice of the $18 billion DOD annual space budget.

Key surveillance support to Gulf forces was also provided by the fleets of civil and commercial Earth observation and weather satellites, together with some from undisclosed then-Soviet space sources. It is calculated that coalition forces derived intelligence from more than 30 Western military and commercial surveillance spacecraft (Figure 2). The figure could, in fact, be considerably higher. Detailed data on the numbers and capabilities of military satellites are well guarded. Whatever the actual number, allied superiority in the space surveillance field was as overwhelming as it was in communications, with the exception that the Iraqis were likely to have obtained valuable weather data from the several civil meterological satellites. These included the European Meteosat and U.S. geostationary operational environmental satellites (GOES) which probably continued their international services uninterrupted throughout the conflict.

Spy Satellites

Arms control experts claim that space imaging sensors require resolutions of around 5 meters to detect military ground units and less than 1 meter to identify individual tanks and artillery pieces.

Although the U.S. government does not divulge the capabilities or numbers of its spy satellites, it is widely publicized that the most powerful spacecraft in its space inventory are the KH 11/12 series, which carry multispectral optical sensors. These shuttle-launched 16-ton leviathans provide imaging resolutions reportedly below 25 cm in daylight and clear weather from their 300 km polar orbits. A related U.S. military spacecraft, Lacrosse, offered Gulf forces the advantages of all weather day/night radar surveillance with resolutions reported as low as 1.5 meters. It has been suggested that Lacrosse may also carry optical sensors and a radio eavesdropping electronics intelligence payload.

The KH and Lacrosse spacecraft are flagships of the U.S. space surveillance fleet, which also includes a number of dedicated Elint satellites that have been launched in low Earth orbit (LEO) and geostationary Earth orbit (GEO) orbits since the 1960s. But with the almost total destruction of the Iraqi command, control, and communications nervous system by coalition attacks in the first 24 hours of the war, these Elint satellites may have been left with little to do.

The provision by the surveillance satellites of detailed battle damage images marked another significant advance in military operations. Complementing the more accurate photographic reconnaissance by day with night radar images, interpretation staff were able to assess the discrete damage caused by precise smart weapons, a facility that would otherwise have required reconnaissance aircraft overflights.

This capability also highlights another unique feature of space communications, which is that of collecting and distributing intelligence from a variety of space, land, ship, and airborne sensors on a single, transparent communications system. Moreover, the employment of satellite data links for this task also enables the image processing and interpretation to be undertaken in centers safely and conveniently remote from the battlefield.

Early Warning

The launching of modified Scud missiles against Saudi Arabia and Israel had an important psychological impact, despite the aging (1950s) technology employed by the missile. The success of the U.S. Patriot anti-missile missiles in countering this threat was gripping news on world television screens at the time. The role of the U.S. Defense Support Program (DSP) satellites in providing early warning of Scud launches to Patriot crews is less well known. These third generation spacecraft, designed to provide early warning of Soviet intercontinental missiles, were apparently successful earlier in monitoring Iranian Scud launches against Iraq in 1986. It is believed that the United States had as many as 4-5 DSP satellites in orbit during the Gulf crisis.

The DSP satellite monitors missile launches from its 35,000 km geostationary perch by means of a scanning infrared (IR) telescope, capable of 3 km resolution. The satellite relayed the Scud missile's IR plume signature to a ground controller who undertook target discrimination, a process occupying some 2 minutes of the Scud's 7 minute flight profile. The missile's timing and trajectory were then relayed via communications satellite to alert Patriot batteries in Saudi Arabia and Israel. Another element of the U.S. space-based early warning systems, the White Cloud ocean surveillance satellites could also have provided information on Iraqi combat aircraft movements, limited as those were. Last year, a White Cloud equipped with IR sensors was reported as detecting U.S. fighter jet exhaust signatures, perhaps a first step toward a space-based air defense network.

SURVEILLANCE/EARTH OBSERVATION SATELLITES AVAILABLE TO COALITION FORCES

SATELLITE	FUNCTION	ORBIT	OPERATOR	RESOLUTION	No. OF SATELLITES IN SERIES/ GULF OPS	LAUNCHES
MILITARY						
LACROSSE	Radar Surveillance (+ optical and sigint?)	LEO <700km	US DoD	metre-class	1/1	DEC 88 1991? 1992?
KH 11	Imaging reconnaissance (optical/IR/radar)	LEO <500km	US DoD	<25cm	8/1	#8-1987
KH 12	Advanced Imaging reconnaissance (optical/sigint)	LEO <450km	US DoD	?	?/?	#1-1990
WHITE CLOUD	Ocean Surveillance	LEO 100km inclined	US DoD	?	10+/?	#10-1987
MAGNUM	Electronic/signal intelligence	GEO	US NSA	-	?	#2-1989
VORTEX (CHALET)	Radar surveillance Elint	?	US DoD	1.5m?	?	?
DEFENCE SUPPORT PROGRAMME (DSP)	Early Warning (Thermal IR)	GEO	US DoD	3km	22/5?	2nd generation -1987 3rd generation -1989
Defence Meteoro-Logical Satellite Programme (DMSP)	Weather observation (microwave/visible/ IR sensors)	LEO 800km	USAF	-	30/3-5	1960-1990
RORSAT	Radar ocean reconnaissance	LEO 250km	USSR	?	?	1987-2
EORSAT	Elint ocean reconnaissance	LEO 450km	USSR	?	?	1987-2
USSR Reconnaissance	Photographic reconnaissance	LEO 200km+	USSR	<25cm	?	1962-1990
ALMAZ	Radar reconnaissance (3 GHz SAR)	LEO 270km	USSR	15-30cm	2/1	1987-1989
CIVIL						
SPOT	Earth observation (visible imagers)	LEO 800km	SPOT Image (France)	10m HRV 20m pan-chromatic	2/2	1986 1990
LANDSAT	Earth observation (visible imagers)	LEO 700km	EOSAT (US)	20m	5/2	#4-1982 #5-1984
GOES	Meteorology (visible/IR)	GEO	NOAA (US)	1km	7/2	#7-1987
NOAA	Metorology (visible/microwave radiometers)	LEO 850km	NOAA (US)	-	11/?	#10-1986 #11-1988
METEOR	Meteorology (visible/IR radiometer)	LEO 800-1200km	USSR	>2km	?/2	#3-02 1988 #3-03 1989
OKEAN	Oceanography (radar/visible/IR)	LEO 600km	USSR	>1.5km radar	?/2	# 1983-87 #1-1988 #2-1990
RESURS-F	Earth observation (photo reconnaissance)	LEO 300km	USSR	5-8m	13/?	1987-1989 (14-30 day missions)
RESURS-O	Earth observation (visible/thermal IR)	LEO 600km	USSR	170-600m	5?/	#5-1988
DATA RELAY						
TRACKING AND DATA RELAY SATELLITE (TDRSS)	Data relay for LEO earth observatory surveillance satellites	GEO	NASA/ Spacecom (US)	-	4/3	#3-1988 #4-1989

Courtesy : Interavia Space Directory & international press sources

Figure 2. List of Surveillance Satellites

Meteorological Satellites

It is now possible to buy on the open commercial market, at a cost of around $7,000, receivers capable of recording information from a barrage of national and international civil weather satellites in GEO and LEO polar orbit. These include the Commonwealth of Independent States (CIS) Meteros and Okean satellites, the U.S. GOES and National Oceanographic Atmospheric Administration series and the European Meteosat spacecraft. Thus both coalition and Iraqi forces will have equally enjoyed the full range of weather reports and images from the international World Weather Watch. The U.S. forces will also have had access to more precise specialized information from their defense meteorological satellite program (DMSP) spacecraft, more than 30 of which have been launched since the 1960s to serve the very specialized needs of the U.S. space and missile programs.

Yet another example of the commercial market coming to the aid of military users was seen when the latter found its militarized weather stations too cumbersome for combat conditions and turned to the German company Wraase to provide more than 100 commercial terminals which were rushed to the Gulf and carried into battle.

These actual and detailed weather reports from space were vital for ground, sea and air forces. The advent of laser guided weapons and smart munitions and the need for clear weather conditions places new emphasis on accurate and current weather reports. (Although these new weapons accounted for only 10 percent of coalition munition arsenals, they offer potential accuracy in excess of 90 percent against 25 percent or less for conventional weapons). The additional hazards of sandstorms and smoke from burning oil wells also placed a high premium on space weather reports.

Commercial Earth Observation

The U.S. DOD has reported that civil remote sensing satellites played a key role in the Gulf war in providing up-to-date, wide area information in the theater. Surveillance satellites, military or commercial, are obliged to tradeoff resolution against the area of instantaneous cover. It therefore appears likely that the U.S. Landsat and French SPOT satellites were used to provide wide-area surveillance to complement the fine-resolution, spotlight searches undertaken by the U.S. KH and Lacrosse satellites and their Russian equivalents.

Although existing commercial Earth observation satellites lack the resolution for many military tasks, (SPOT offers the best performance at 10 meters), it was reported that the Pentagon spent up to $6 million on Landsat and SPOT data during the war, for tasks that included quick response map-making, flight planning and images showing the location and description of large infrastructure items.

These instruments provide 185 km square images. Landsat 4 & 5 also carry intersatellite link payloads for communication with the DOD tracking and data relay (TDRSS), which provides access to near-global cover from the U.S. mainland.

The SPOT satellites also carry optical sensors that provide multispectral images at 20 meters resolution or panchromatic (black and white) at 10 meter resolution. SPOT 1 and 2 each carry two optical imagers capable of recording a combined instantaneous Earth picture covering a swatch 120 km wide. The normal Earth location revisit period is 26 days. By tilting the optics, off-nadir viewing allows any site to be observed up to nearly 1,000 km either side of the satellite's track, reducing the revisit period to two days and permitting stereo imaging. This latter facility was employed with considerable success in the Gulf in producing stereoscopic image videos of flight routes and targets for preflight briefing of pilots. A remarkable new facility.

Since current SPOT satellites do not have a capability for intersatellite relay, the spacecraft's imaging data are transmitted to a global network of ground receiving stations. The local SPOT data processing center was located at Riyadh in Saudi Arabia.

Lessons for Europe

Despite the crucial importance of the role of commercial satellites such as the French SPOT and its supporting image interpretation centers, the space surveillance war was unquestionably dominated by the superior U.S. military reconnaissance fleet. As a consequence, the war rekindled interest in a Western European space surveillance agency and satellites. The French-led Helios, Europe's first military surveillance satellite, reportedly will offer the image resolutions required by the military intelligence community when it is launched in 1994. After the Gulf war, Europe launched its first radar satellite, the European Space Agency's ERS-1 but, at 30 meters, its resolution may again offer only limited military intelligence. Europe's military surveillance torch is carried by the Western European Union, which has undertaken to set up a satellite image interpretation center in 1992 and has proposed an ambitious collaborative European program of optical and radar observation satellites.

A Time of Change

Military experts generally agree that satellites helped to win the political battle, sustained command and control, shortened the war, and saved lives. Without space communications and navigation, it is difficult to imagine that the war could have been other than even more costly, protracted, and bloody. Without the confidence provided by space communications and surveillance, it is not inconceivable that the allies might have concluded at the outset that they lacked the means to counter Saddam Hussein's aggression at acceptable cost.

Without high quality space imagery, Saddam Hussein might have gotten away with his mission, given the undisturbed time to buildup his missile, chemical, biological, and nuclear capability.

The war has also taught the space community some sharp lessons. It has shown that the inherent flexibility of satellite communications cannot be brought to fruition unless the ground segment is designed and equipped to exploit it. We may not always be afforded the grace of Desert Shield. The war also proved the true and remarkable importance of GPS after 14 years of muted operation. The war showed that high technology has blurred the distinction between civil and military systems—it demonstrated the military potential of commercial communications and Earth observation systems and narrowed the gap between the military and commercial space ground equipment. In some cases the commercial variant was even proved to be superior. The conflict demonstrated the vulnerability of democracies to the public glare of worldwide space television news reporting. Space has given the media a freedom that may be difficult ever to withdraw.

When politicians and treasury officials call for more for less, it is wise to guard against the possibility that our military forces do not end up getting less for more. Space is expensive, and, with the end of the Cold War, it is likely to be an attractive target for budget cuts. The rapid shifts in the focus of Western security, which has veered from Cold War through conventional disarmament to the Gulf emergency in less than 2 years, emphasizes the seemingly impossible task of predicting the nature and location of the next war. The success of space in the Gulf serves to emphasize that its highly effective, economic, and flexible capabilities will be needed even more in the increasingly volatile world of the future. For Europe, one first priority should be careful consideration of a comprehensive military space surveillance program.

It has not been the purpose of this paper to compare the contribution of space systems with their terrestrial navigation, communications, and surveillance counterparts, nor to suggest that space will ever entirely supplant the latter. While in some cases, space offers a unique service, in most others it provides an essentially complementary facility. Nevertheless, the story of the Gulf space battle, taken as a whole, draws the conclusion that its impact was so powerful as to suggest that to exploit military space to the full, its activities must be governed as a single coordinated resource. Space has become the fourth element of military power.

Experts may continue to debate whether or not the Gulf conflict should enjoy the sobriquet of the first space war. A British defense chief raised more important issues when he said "The Gulf taught us that space has changed the whole nature of warfare."

This paper was presented at the 12th AFCEA Europe Symposium.

[1] Martin Faga, Assistant Secretary for Space.

SILENT SPACE WARRIORS

Alan D. Campen

The Gulf War is the first instance where combat forces largely were deployed, sustained, commanded, and controlled through satellite communications. The role played by communications satellites has been overshadowed by the weapons and tactics that depended on assured, high data-rate communications for their well-publicized successes.

Those satellite systems that complemented each other so well in the Persian Gulf must now compete with each other and with the military strategic tactical and relay satellites, or Milstar, for resources in what may be an even tougher fight for survival in the 1990s. Investment strategies revealed by the future year defense program, now known as FYDP, do not adequately underwrite the myriad of communications satellite systems fielded over the past two decades.

Information Warfare

The weapons that devastated Iraq's infrastructure and war machine were based in and around the Persian Gulf. The support systems that allowed this array of sophisticated weaponry to be applied with precision were spread around the globe, many based in space and all netted together by space-based communications. These included the sensors that tracked tanks, artillery, and Scuds; the intelligence centers that correlated and fused these data; and the command centers that adjusted war plans based on this near real-time information. Of this, the public—and perhaps many in the military—knows little.

Desert Storm was an information war. As former AFCEA Chairman of the Board Dr. Ralph W. Shrader says, "Never before has the demand for instant transfer of information been so strong and so well answered."

Combat forces from many nations were knitted together by a communications network of scope and complexity unknown in military history. At some point in the journey, virtually all of that information flowed over U.S. and allied communications satellites, some of which have urgent needs for replenishment or modernization that must be looked after from an already oversubscribed defense budget.

Military satellite communications formed the backbone for command and control and for support in this short but intense war. Intra-theater links were used for command and control, early warning, navigation, and dissemination of intelligence information. Inter-theater links provided connectivity for the Central Command back to its home base in Florida and to the supporting U.S. European Command in Germany. The early deploying 82nd Airborne Division coordinated its supply efforts over satellites, and troops used the defense satellite communications system, known as DSCS, for morale calls home. When the war began, DSCS satellites were even used in one instance for near real-time transfer of pilot reports through a tactical air control center to engaged combat forces in the field.

DSCS, which is the backbone of defense satellite communications, entered and ended the Gulf conflict on technically wobbly legs. None of the defense satellite communications system spacecraft that played a primary role in Desert Storm was fully operational when the Gulf War ended.

Spacecraft to complete the modernization of the defense satellite communications system have been built but, because of the *Challenger* accident, most still sit in storage. It might take 10 years to loft them all into orbit assuming everything goes well with new launch vehicles and strategies. As a minimum, it will take four successful launches of these DSCS-III satellites before the constellation is considered healthy. Further, much of the ground segment of the defense satellite communications system is 15 years old and also needs refurbishment.

As one expert warns, "We were very lucky this time." While that comment may be true, innovation and a cooperative and effective management structure among many defense and service agencies ensured that, as the director of the Defense Communications Agency (Since renamed the Defense Information Systems Agency—or DISA) was briefed, "The DSCS met the surge and ground mobile force requirements with no preemption of service."

That was no easy job considering the almost total lack of an infrastructure for communications in the Gulf area.

Predicting Need

No one knew what demands for communications would arise during the Gulf buildup because older and proved methods of relating voice circuit needs to troop population have become obsolete in the computer age.

Experts say that communicators will not be able to determine how much capacity actually is needed until the user has to pay the bill or until someone discovers how to equate communications service to the effectiveness of military force. While the Gulf War demonstrated the effect of automation on communications, military communicators have reconciled themselves to the fact that demands for service always rise to exceed system capacity and that funds for improving communications usually run last in a race for money with weapons systems.

Communications

Impressive as the logistics infrastructure in the Gulf was in terms of air bases and seaport facilities, the U.S. defense communications system that had once transited this area of the world was no longer in place. All that remained of U.S. defense communications in the Gulf area, where high frequency radio systems once hopped among such countries as Libya, Ethiopia, and Saudi Arabia, were one shipborne and three tactical satellite terminals, installed in support of the Air Force and Navy.

Two defense satellite communications system spacecraft initially were involved in the buildup: the Indian Ocean satellite, an aging second generation spacecraft netted into Landstuhl, Germany, and the Eastern Atlantic satellite, a modern and more capable DSCS-III unit, netted into Croughton, England, and Fort Meade, Maryland.

LTGen. James S. Cassity, Jr., USAF (Ret.), former director, command, control, communications and computer systems, Joint Staff, explains that "in August [1990], we had the barest of a communications infrastructure in the Persian Gulf area. Except for embassy communications, our military communications consisted of little more than the command ship, the *LaSalle*, and an administrative support unit in Bahrain."

By September 3, 1990, the population of super high frequency earth terminals had grown from 4 to 48. At this point, the Indian Ocean satellite was nearing saturation, as then configured. Requests for more satellite access were pouring in, and something had to be done quickly to increase system capacity.

DISA reconfigured the Eastern Atlantic defense satellite communications system spacecraft to provide better support to the commander-in-chief, Central Forces, by adding more throughput between Saudi Arabia and the United States. The agency accomplished this by swapping antennas normally used for tactical customers with those intended for strategic purposes.

The high gain gimbaled dish antenna was repointed to the East Coast of the United States; the multibeam receive antenna was configured to provide maximum gain to the Gulf region; and the multibeam transmit antenna also was aimed to the East Coast. The agency adjusted the Indian Ocean satellite to increase capacity on that path and reassigned terminals between the two satellites. This increased capacity to about 603 voice circuits, but earth terminal population had grown to 53. The United Kingdom offered capacity from its Skynet IVB communications satellite system, which seemed to stabilize the requirements.

President Bush then announced the deployment of another 200,000 troops, who again would increase the communication capacity requirements. To meet the new needs, one of the West Pacific satellites—an aging DSCS-II spacecraft being held in reserve—had to be moved to 65 degrees east longitude. How soon it could support Desert Shield depended on the laws of physics and management decisions on satellite drift rates that involve many agencies sharing responsibility for inextricably interrelated space vehicles, payloads, earth terminals, and the networks.

The Air Force—with its hand on the throttle and eye on the fuel gauge—brought the satellite into position on December 19, 1990, where it was discovered that one of the traveling wave tubes had failed. This required an unplanned switching and test period. Meanwhile, the earth terminal population had grown to 59.

By December 28, the terminals numbered 69. The United Kingdom again offered more capacity from its system, but the loan was not accepted because the capacity was not needed, and a control terminal was not available to provide network control.

When the West Pacific satellite finally checked out on January 15, 1991 the total throughput in the defense satellite communications system was about 1,057 voice circuits, and the terminal population had reached 110. That much circuitry would cost about $16.6 million per month if commercially leased.

Two DSCS II satellites with identical beacons now were located within 5 degrees of each other, and earth terminal operators were finding it hard to tell them apart. DISA controllers explain that the beacon on one satellite was shifted to the opposite end of the baseband from the normal position, enabling the operators to determine from the spectrum analyzer if they were locking onto the assigned satellite.

By the end of the war, the defense satellite communications system was providing 75 percent of the inter- and intra-theater multichannel trunking. Before it was over, demands from the Gulf area for circuitry on the super high frequency system to Europe and the United States were more than 1,000 voice circuits, or a channel for every 500 troops.

Desert Storm involved 25 percent of the Air Force and Navy, 50 percent of the Army, and 66 percent of the Marine Corps. The demands for data, ranging from logistics to administration to intelligence, consumed the bandwidth of virtually 100 percent of the military UHF and SHF communications satellites that could be scraped together by the U.S. Defense Department and its allies.

Intelligence Support

Missile warning reports from satellites went nearly around the world, enabling Patriot batteries in the Gulf and Israel to make spectacular intercepts that had significant political if not military implications.

Timely and accurate battle damage assessment is required if the outcome of war depends on highly accurate delivery of relatively few smart weapons. Such assessment relies on pictures and on reports from experts who have examined photographs and other forms of imagery. Even the substantial capacity of the DSCS was hard-pressed to keep up with the flow of images to the combat units from processing centers located in the United States and other fusion and correlation centers located far from the combat theater.

Officials say that, of all military communications satellite systems, only the defense satellite communications system is optimized for that volume of data throughput. UHF systems, such as the Navy fleet satellite system, can handle images but at slower speeds and with much less granularity. EHF systems have an enormous potential information capacity but only if the bandwidth has been optimized for that purpose during design. The Milstar EHF communications satellite system now is undergoing a redesign to lower costs and to shift its focus away from thin-line nuclear war continuity (high survivability and low throughput) to something more useful to conventional war fighting. To what extent Milstar will be able to support growing needs for battlefield intelligence is still an open question among experts. Modified Milstar satellites will not be launched until the late 1990s.[2]

UHF/EHF Satellites

Up to 2,000 UHF terminals in the combat theater accessed 98 channels on a six-satellite tactical constellation. The Navy sent traffic to the fleet through the international maritime satellite organization, called INMARSAT, available to military forces in this instance because of the United Nations involvement in the war. The Marines used four 10-minute periods each day to pass traffic back to the

United States through the store-and-forward capability of an experimental lightweight satellite, called Macsat. Even the precursor to Milstar—an experimental extremely high frequency transponder that is hitch-hiking on the Navy's fleet satellite communication spacecraft—was pressed into service to ensure instant communications between Chairman of the Joint Chiefs of Staff Gen. Colin L. Powell, USA, and then Commander-in-Chief, Central Command, Gen. H. Norman Schwarzkopf, USA.

Although television networks had leased much commercial satellite capacity (22 channels), traffic flow estimates by the Defense Department show that commercial leases carried more than 22 percent of military wideband traffic between the Gulf area and the United States. As in previous wars, civil communications carriers again have proved themselves able and responsive when and where needed.

Improvisation

The gulf conflict employed communication satellite systems in ways uncharted in service communications doctrine, taxing the ingenuity of customers, satellite network planners in Washington, D.C., and communications technicians at the earth terminals.

There was neither time nor airlift available to deploy the terrestrial switching and trunking systems that normally wire the battlefield together, so the military used satellite trunking for local distribution in the tactical area, in some instances to cross runways or to reach a location only a few miles away. The war was in its final stages before installation of the more conventional area distribution systems, such as high frequency, microwave, fiber optics, and troposcatter, was begun.

Army, Navy, and Air Force units freely exchanged earth terminals to support needs that either had not been foreseen or could not be met in the rapid buildup. At the war's end, the Navy was beginning to install Air Force tactical terminals on amphibious and command ships. The Air Force was endeavoring to regain terminals that had been loaned to integrate British forces into the tightly knit and data-hungry command and control structure orchestrated by the commander-in-chief, Central Command.

The strategic DSCS, which normally provides backbone, global voice, and data trunking and extends from the United States down to the combat theater, displayed capabilities once sought only in tactical UHF and EHF systems. Before Desert Storm, a relatively clean distinction existed between strategic and tactical communication satellite systems. That differentiation was forged into policy, doctrine, organization, procedures, and the budget. Experts agree that the defense satellite communications system was high in capacity, low in mobility, moderate in antijam capability, and expensive. Tactical systems traded-off capacity for maneuverability, lower cost, and greater quantity.

Fast moving combat forces could not function effectively if severed from high data-rate umbilicals, and UHF systems were not up to that job.

The DSCS was the only satellite network that could support rates at which critical intelligence information must flow if wars are to be prosecuted on such a scale of speed, precision, and complexity as Desert Storm demanded and new AirLand Battle doctrine prescribes.

The war showed that strategic satellite terminals could provide direct support to rapidly moving ground forces. These units, which are called ground mobile force (GMF) terminals, normally are found at corps level, not at battalion, brigade, or regiment level. Nevertheless, they accompanied combat forces deep into Iraq, ensconced on flat-bed trucks, rolling in the middle of 40-mile-per-hour tank columns.

Petroleum farms—set up to fuel the rolling armor—became communications parks as well, as technicians switched between 20-foot and 8-foot antennas to meet rapidly changing operating conditions. A defense official reported to an AFCEA conference that ground mobile force terminals relocated more than 100 times during the 100-hour ground war.

Deck space on the six aircraft carriers was not available for SHF satellite terminals, although belated efforts were made to install them on some of the amphibious ships in the battle groups. Throughout the air war, the daily consolidated air operations order (the ATO) was delivered to the fleet by helicopter, and imagery had to be curtailed to fit the bandwidth limits of UHF satellites or else had to be couriered.

The new unified U.S. Space Command and its military component commands came into their own in the Gulf War, often scrambling to discover what functions they could and should perform. Space system management was forged in a chain that ran from the joint forces commander in Saudi Arabia, where priorities were set; through the Joint Staff, where any conflicts were adjudicated; to the many technical agencies that move satellites, point antennas, calculate power budgets, and set switches in space; to the technicians who tend the earth terminals. This complex communications satellite management structure was almost entirely new and untested.

Lessons for Today, Tomorrow

Military authorities caution that extreme care must be exercised in drawing conclusions from what was a very unusual conflict. Little evidence exists of any effort to impede either space-based or terrestrial telecommunications.[1] Other than severe interference from solar flares, which reached an 11-year peak of intensity on February 1, 1991, and severely degraded satellite communications for six days over a period from 6 p.m. to midnight each day, the technical performance of communications systems was as it should have been in a benign environment.

Nonetheless, officials point to certain events that are of interest for communication system planners in the short term and historians in the long term.

• In the Gulf War, any enemy electronic system that had the potential to jam communications was either destroyed by the allies or switched off by Iraqi technicians. As Air Vice Marshall Bill Wratten, RAF, says, "Any anti-radiation missile, whether it gets a hard kill or whether it enforces switch-off, has achieved its aim." The use or even threat of anti-radiation missiles establishes the hard kill dimension of electronic combat and hints that electronic technicians might not have to fight a wizard war alone. This could impact the design of electronic warfare capabilities in tactical-level communications systems.

• Interoperability is not an insurmountable technical problem—once the cultural and bureaucratic barriers come down, as Raymond J. Hufnagle, Jr., contended in his article on non-technical barriers to interoperability (*SIGNAL,* March 1987, page 79). Problems can be solved quickly when they must, because, at the bottom line, interoperability is a management problem.

• The DSCS had to deploy much farther down the echelon of command and into the combat zone than its designers had planned, because UHF did not have the throughput that a non-linear and fast moving AirLand battle doctrine apparently requires.

• Management of the space segment of satellite communications is a complex and lengthy process. It must be done by network management experts who can view in real time the entire global network, most of which is not based in space. [Elsewhere in this book, Sir Peter Anson and Dennis Cummings conclude that "to exploit military space to the full, its activities must be governed as a single coordinated resource,"]

• Demands for real time movement of intelligence products from interpretation centers to very low level combat units may be abhorred but cannot be ignored. Future tactical systems must either be upgraded or provisions made that will allow these combat units to have direct access to wide-band satellite systems.

More than a decade ago, a naval studies board pronounced that "space is both a threat and an opportunity...". In the light of Desert Storm and the declining budget over the coming years, that might well be appended to state that space is both *threat* and *opportunity*, and the choice is a policy decision. Depending on the outcome of difficult budget and program decisions that the Defense Department and Congress must make, future historians might note that Desert Storm was the first and last one controlled from space.

Endnotes

[1] Not all observers are sanguine about the threat to space-based systems. Francois Gere, of the Paris-based Foundation for the Study of National Defense is reported to have commented on transformation of space into the next battleground: "The next Saddam Hussein may go after U.S. satellites," he warned. *Defense News,* 4-10 May 1992.

[2] The initial MILSTAR satellites will still contain the antinuclear design and will be low data rate systems. Six revised satellites are now under contract. The first of these is to be launched in December 1997 and five more at intervals through December 2002. The later satellites will have the medium data rate capability.

The following is one example of the extraordinary uses of satellite communications: "We took a Zenith 286 laptop computer and a portable satellite dish and gave them to a parts clerk in the middle of the Saudi desert. He was able to get his requisition back to us in only two minutes and 50 seconds. So we saved about 14 days, and each day in the pipeline was costing $20-million a day...I want to put it into the contingency corps, the XVIII Airborne Corps." From interview with General Jimmy D. Ross, Commander U.S. Army Materiel Command, as reported in May 1992 issue of *Armed Forces Journal*, p. 52.

Edited and updated from an article that originally appeared in the August 1991 issue of *SIGNAL.*

INTEGRATING TACTICAL AND STRATEGIC SWITCHING

Jean M. Slupik

A viable information systems architecture requires the total integration of commercial and military communications systems, including the planning, implementation, and management.

Communications systems employment and doctrine contributed as much to the superbly stunning success of Operation Desert Shield/Storm as did the much-publicized high technology weapons. Never before in the history of modern warfare has an information architecture been established so quickly in a theater so devoid of a usable infrastructure.

Once deployed, this contingency architecture successfully supported a large-scale conflict. It withstood the demands of today's modern weapons systems, information management networks, and intelligence dissemination tools by integrating the commercial, strategic, and tactical communications systems into a cohesive network.

The Defense Information Systems Agency (DISA) with responsibility for providing the theater commander with sufficient and reliable strategic communications support had, within the first 48 hours, deployed an Area Communications Operations Center team to assist the CENTCOM J-6. That team had supported CENTCOM on numerous exercises and was trained and prepared to deal with the strategic communications requirements. Initial efforts concentrated on:

• developing satellite scenarios to meet the myriad deployment and employment options;

• tracking and mapping the flow of tactical communications assets into the theater;

• estimating the configuration and size of voice, message, and other network requirements; and

• evaluating strategic communications interfaces.

Strategic Network Systems

Operation Desert Shield/Storm clearly demonstrated our growing dependence upon satellite communications resources at almost every level of command. Connectivity among widely separated units would have been impossible were it not for satellites.

The DISA team aided CENTCOM in designing a network by integrating commercial, long-haul, and tactical military communications. In less than a week after hostilities began, CENTCOM was operating a bare-bone, long-haul network with satellite communications nodes at Riyadh, Dhahran, and Al Jubayl in Saudi Arabia and at Thumrait, Oman.

The Defense Satellite Communications System (DSCS) functioned as the primary, long-haul system providing support to in-theater forces as well as providing strategic connectivity to the United States, Europe, and the Pacific.

Maximum utilization of DSCS capabilities required frequent network reconfiguration and close operational management. Proper allocation of bandwidth and satellite power were critical factors. With over 90 percent of the links supporting mobile tactical subscribers, the satellite controllers were continuously monitoring the system to ensure adherence to procedures and that subscribers remained within allocated operating parameters.

By late September, however, with the heavy ground components just beginning to arrive in theater, DISA was already concerned about overloading the system. By the start of the air campaign, DISA was supervising the operation and control of over 100 tactical satellite terminals in the largest tactical satellite network ever constructed.

Commercial, high-volume, transmission systems, or T-1s, also were extended into theater over the INTELSAT networks. These T-1s significantly enhanced throughput, and enabled components to extend switched and dedicated voice and message trunks to many locations. Extension of strategic circuits over T-1s allowed the component commands to turn their tactical satellite terminals back to direct support of combat operations.

Voice Switching

From the beginning, the Defense Switched Network (DSN) required a concentrated effort from the commercial, strategic military and tactical communications system planners. Flexibility was crucial, as the initial handful of strategic voice circuits quickly grew into a robust network with over 300 trunks. In its final configuration, the network provided worldwide access through eight DSN gateway switches. These DSN trunks were terminated in 25 tactical switchboards extending service directly to CENTCOM headquarters and the service components. These extensions had been rehearsed in contingency exercises, and all personnel were familiar with activation procedures. The huge pipes of the T-1 systems quickly proved their reliability and soon the majority of DSN trunks had been shifted to commercial systems.

Two significant interoperability issues emerged during this operation. The first dealt with interface problems between the DSN network and the tactical TRI-TAC network. The second concerned the tactical area codes (NYX codes) programmed to support the CENTCOM network.

Initial DSN connectivity was extended over seven trunks from a TTC-39 in Riyadh, over a tactical ground mobile forces satellite terminal to one of the CONUS switching centers. Although all trunks had a high reliability rate from the theater to CONUS, they worked only intermittently in the reverse direction. By November, this reliability had degraded to 20 to 30 percent call completion rate. As an interim solution, the trunks were directionalized, providing only one-way service out of the theater.

A team was quickly assembled from DISA's Joint Interoperability Test Center, its Defense Communications Engineering Center, AT&T (owners of the CONUS DSN switch) and GTE (builder of the tactical TRI-TAC switches). Over the next three months they completed an extensive troubleshooting/fault isolation effort that found all equipment operating within acceptable specifications. Nonetheless, the call completion rates were still unsatisfactory. The problem was finally isolated and corrected when AT&T was asked to lower the transmit levels of signalling tones from the #5ESS. The TRI-TAC switch could now properly recognize that the signals and trunks were quickly placed back into service.

The numbering problem called for a software solution. Each unified command had been assigned a block of tactical area codes (NYX) for use during contingencies. These codes enabled the DSN network to route calls from the strategic to a tactical network. CENTCOM had been assigned NYX code 300 for the first DSN switch into the theater. However, the Desert Shield network grew so rapidly that, by mid-August, CENTCOM had nine NYX codes routing through eight DSN switches. This was unacceptable, and CENTCOM asked DISA for a single NYX code for the theater.

Code NYX 318 was programmed into all eight DSN switches, enabling them to now search through multiple routing paths for access into the theater, and call completion rates significantly increased.

This fix sufficed until the combat force was doubled and a new generation of tactical trunking and switching systems were introduced into the theater. The Army had only just completed fielding its Mobile Subscriber Equipment (MSE) in the CONUS III Corps and was introducing it into the European-based VII Corps when both of these units were ordered into the AOR.

VII Corps had built its TRI-TAC network using a fixed directory numbering plan—called FDUL/FDSL—which requires separate routing plans and NYX codes to process inter- and intra-theater calls. NYX codes 309, 409, and 709 were programmed into the DSN switches, and new customer access instructions were issued. This satisfied the requirements for MSE units and VII Corps.

Message Switching

In early August the only strategic message switching centers in the theater consisted of two 300-baud, point-to-point AUTODIN circuits to Riyadh and Dhahran, Saudi Arabia. There, two small communications centers continued to process large volumes of message—that is, record—traffic in an effort to support the influx of forces into the AOR. Although quickly upgraded to 1200 baud, no suitable message switching capability would exist until the TRI-TAC TYC-39 switches began to arrive.

The next critical situation occurred outside the theater, at the Naval Communications Area Master Stations in Europe and the western Pacific. These became saturated with AUTODIN message traffic destined for the carrier and battle groups transiting to and from the theater. The situation was crucial enough for the Joint Staff to impose MINIMIZE on all message traffic into Europe. This action quickly alleviated the on-queue message status at two of the European AUTODIN switching centers. The backlog in the Pacific forced the Navy to implement a message review board process whereby experts review each message to determine if it was to be delivered or destroyed.

DISA personnel, in close coordination with CENTCOM, maintained strict discipline over all message switch actions, circuit requests, circuit outages, and alternate routing actions. The network slowly matured as additional forces arrived in theater and established connectivity into the TYC-39 network.

By the end of November, the AUTODIN network was operating within established message processing parameters, with only minor service disruptions. The network remained stable until January 15, at the start of the air campaign. Over the next 24 hours, the 15 AUTODIN switching centers were flooded with traffic, and two came very close to saturation. DISA again requested the Joint Staff to impose MINIMIZE, this time not only on traffic inbound to the AOR but on a worldwide basis as well. This control became effective on January 18, and the drop in traffic was dramatic.

A snapshot of the worldwide on-queue message traffic at the switching centers is shown in Figure 1 and reflects a drop from 150,000 message on January 18 to 50,000 messages on January 22. By February 2, the average on-queue message count was under 20,000.

It took a while longer to achieve the same effect on the theater's 26 AUTODIN circuits. As shown in Figure 2, the on-queue count on January 18 was 14,500 messages. A significant decrease did not occur until January 31, when the count dropped to 7,400, and this decrease continued as the war progressed.

Data Switching

The Defense Data Network (DDN) also provided support to forces in theater. The DDN became a major contributor when, for the first time, the common-user, packet-switched network was used in support of combat operations.

Initially, the Army component (ARCENT) took the lead in providing this service within the theater, and DISA provided connectivity with CONUS DDN nodes. The first in-theater link was operational less than a month after the invasion of Kuwait. From this modest beginning emerged a high-use network with six gateways and hundreds of computer hosts and terminals supporting theater forces.

As of February 22, 1991, there were 1,690 kilopackets of data per day being sent into the MILNET from the Army's communication system in the AOR.

Although DDN experienced an enormous growth in traffic volume as depicted in Figure 3, the system was able to absorb it without problems or significant stress. DDN supported many facets of the operation, and several areas deserve recognition. Specifically, it supported over 1,500 electronic mail systems, the Navy's Cruise Missile Program Office, the Air Force's Airborne Warning and Control System, and

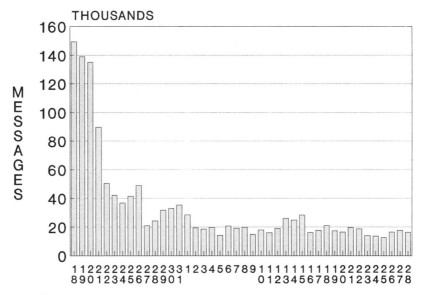

180001Z JAN: WORLDWIDE MINIMIZE

Figure 1. AUTODIN Worldwide Traffic 18 Jan-28 Feb 1991

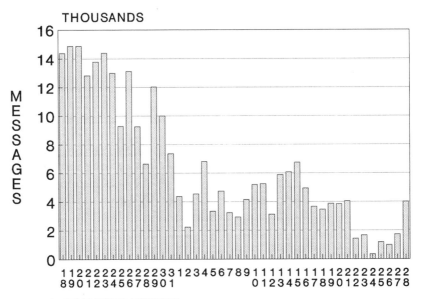

180001Z JAN: WORLDWIDE MINIMIZE

Figure 2. AUTODIN AOR Circuit Traffic 18 Jan-28 Feb 1991

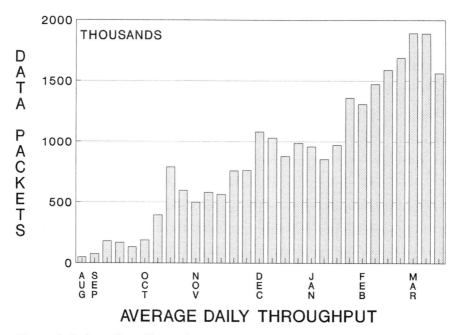

Figure 3. Defense Data Network

the personnel accounting systems for all four services. This experience has driven home just how much the military services depend on their data systems and reliable interconnecting communications links.

The DISA Role

Operation Desert Shield/Storm underscored the pivotal role that DISA plays in providing sufficient and reliable strategic communications connectivity to war zones. DISA and CENTCOM learned a valuable lesson: A viable information systems architecture requires the total integration of commercial and military communications systems, including the planning, implementation, and management. CENTCOM's enormous demand for strategic connectivity between the theater, CONUS, Europe, and the Pacific constantly challenged DISA in its ability to extend DSN, AUTODIN, and DDN access. DISA met the challenge by providing CINCENT with a dynamic, robust strategic network in support of a quick, decisive victory.

Edited and updated from an article that originally appeared in the January 1992 issue of *IEEE Communications Magazine.*

ESTABLISHED ARCHITECTURE KEYS MARINE DATA

Merrill L. Pierce, Jr.

The success of the U.S. Marine Corps' automated data processing efforts in operations Desert Shield and Desert Storm reflects homework done long before the Iraqi invasion of Kuwait. By the time the Marines began deploying to the Gulf, they had in place a viable automated data processing architecture, and they developed all software applications to run in that environment.

Throughout its data processing development, the Corps also kept in tune with contracting regulations and state-of-the-art equipment, established standards and adhered to and trained within those standards. This provided a full service automated data processing support structure to the entire Marine Corps worldwide.

In addition, the Corps was able to overcome the problem of voluminous air tasking orders by using standard local area networks. Similarly, it developed the ability to access maintenance and supply information from the front lines.

Using the data processing system drove home four points that support past policy and highlight future trends: an in-place standard architecture and support framework save time and money; flexible, dynamic and active planning provide field data services without changes in user activities; local area network and wide area network technology is an effective means of battlefield communication; and tactical and administrative systems are merging.

Some concerns, however, cause further reflection on the way Marines provide automated data processing as a combat service support function. Decreasing funding levels, the reduction of active forces and the implementation of the Defense Department's corporate information management initiative each will have an effect on the flexibility and sustainment of the present support architecture. The Corps may find it difficult to continue to exploit current successes within this new framework and to focus on providing continuously improving support.

Gulf Overview

Organic computers in the Kuwaiti theater of operations were reliable and responsive. Commanders quickly realized that data processing and data communications systems were available, usable and essential to resolving problems typical of tactical command and control.

The standard Marine Corps data processing architecture provides a framework in which networks of micro- and main frame computers serve users throughout the Corps. This architecture was extended to encompass users in Southwest Asia through the use of local area network and wide area network technology, ruggedized and commercial microcomputers and commercial main frame computers mounted in portable shelters. As a result, Marines in Southwest Asia received services identical to those provided to Marines elsewhere in the world.

Historically, the Marine Corps has focused on the automated data processing support philosophy of centralized technical direction, policy formulation, acquisition and oversight at Headquarters Marine Corps. Execution of processing operations is decentralized.

This fosters uniformity in the design, development and operation of data processing support throughout the Marine Corps by standardizing hardware and system and application software as much as possible. At the same time, this framework fosters responsive support. All functional areas are supported by common user hardware and system software whether the processing is done in garrison, while deployed or in a combat environment.

The operational concept is to provide data processing support through the established command structure and a hierarchy of regional automated services centers. Large-scale computers at sites in the continental United States and Japan provide processing support to their respective geographic regions. Commands within those regions gain support through remote job entry facilities. These activities are interconnected by the Marine Corps data network, a common-user data communications network that provides terminal-to-computer and computer-to-computer communications capability. All terminals connected to the network can access any host computer in the network in an on-line, interactive mode.

When an operational area is not within an established region, a new region is created around a force automated services center. This was done in Jubail, Saudi Arabia, where the deployment of the 1st Force automated services center created a support facility for the region defined as the Kuwaiti theater of operations.

A force automated center is a deployable Fleet Marine Force asset normally deployed when the logistics buildup exceeds the capability of the AN/UYK-83 and AN/UYK-85 microcomputer equipment to handle essential personnel, supply and maintenance functions. Units within the combat service support area can be hard-wired via local area networks or individual terminal work stations for direct access to the center's computer.

Local area networks connect individual microcomputers that also provide the platform for electronic mail between Marine Corps commands. They also have the ability to access the main frame computers at the regional service centers.

Within this support framework, Marines expedited automated data processing support to the units employed in Southwest Asia. While doing so, Marines found that accomplishing their mission was a rapidly moving target.

Architecture Advantages

When it became apparent that the buildup rapidly would exceed the support capability of microcomputers, the decision was made to place a main frame in Saudi Arabia. The dilemma of providing what was considered to be administrative computer support in the tactical environment was met by teams from the Marine Corps Combat Development Center, the Marine Corps Research, Development and Acquisition Command and the C[4] division of Marine Headquarters.

Once the requirement was validated by the combat development center, the research, development and acquisition command began to create a tactical platform. The platform processed the administrative applications that were developed to function in the C[4] standard architecture. The result was the force automated services center.

From August 2 to October 5, 1990, the team was able to take the automated services center from the drawing board to full operation at Jubail. Procuring commercial equipment, mounting equipment in an international standards organization shelter, loading and testing system and application software, training personnel, and providing transportation, installation and equipment setup were accomplished quickly. This was because of familiarity with the equipment required to perform the mission.

No software modifications were required because all Marine Corps applications are portable across this architecture. The systems operated the same in Jubail as they did in Camp Pendleton, California, or in Camp Lejeune, North Carolina. Data processing support personnel, operators and users continued to operate as if they had never left their home base. Having systems that operate over the spectrum of garrison-based and deployable equipment allowed the Corps to train the way it fights.

When it was determined that a second Marine expeditionary force was to deploy, the team again was able to implement a solution—this time with the lessons learned from the first implementation. Only 59 days elapsed from the day the decision was made to build an improved version of the force automated services center to the day it was fully operational in Jubail.

Flexibility for a Change

The principal advantage of having main frame processing power in the theater is that it reduces the dependence on scarce data communication resources (paths and equipment) to process large-scale applications typically done in the United States. Simultaneously, additional benefits are gained when essential data communications with the mainland are managed more effectively by channeling them through main frame gateways.

The amount of staff action, exercises conducted or discussions held on system sizing and concepts of operation did not matter. The actual composition of the automated data processing package for combat service support became as dynamic as the size of the supported Marine air-ground task force, its mission and the characteristics of its area of operations.

After hundreds of hours of staff work, planners were convinced that the task force commander should deploy a force automated services center with only two large-scale software applications to support Marine expeditionary force logistics functions within about 60 days after deployment. Reality was radically different from the plan. By February, three service centers were in the theater providing processing and remote job entry functions for 17 major applications covering logistics, manpower and aviation. Additionally, logisticians noted that availability of an automated services center five days after deployment would have made their tasks much easier.

Planners had to absorb the difficulties of change to avoid forcing the user to bear any of this burden, a key to a successful operation. Fortunately, the architecture offered a building block approach to provide the appropriate magnitude of support. As the scope and the mission of the undertaking increased, all that was needed was to add processing power and storage factors to meet sizing requirements.

Local, Wide Area Networks

This first use of microcomputer and local area network technology on the battlefield highlighted the applications of data communications between higher, lower and adjacent units and the strategic role played by this technology. Local and wide area networks became an essential part of tactical and administrative communications for Marines in Southwest Asia, augmenting voice and record traffic.

Users attached to local area networks through wide area networks obtained connectivity that allowed units at the Kuwaiti border to access force automated services centers for in-theater processing—or regional automated services centers for continental United States processing, when necessary.

Equally important was the ability to pass large packages of data and to disseminate information in relatively short periods of time to support the command and control function. Information typically was passed from source to user in less than one hour. All local area networks were encrypted using Marine Corps standard communication security equipment, which ensured meeting operational security requirements.

Each major subordinate command had developed applications for use on its microcomputers. Having microcomputers down to the battalion and squadron level enabled the Marine expeditionary force to connect the various level command elements easily to local or wide area networks to distribute information rapidly. This network environment enabled exploiting applications such as automated delivery of air tasking orders, joint target lists, requests for fire missions and validation of intelligence target lists.

The information flow using local and wide area networks followed doctrinal lines and unit standard operating procedures. Units would generate their requests for air missions and forward them to the division air officer, where the requests were compiled and then sent to the air tasking officer. Once validated, requests were sent to Central Command, where they were put in the air tasking order.

The air tasking order, sometimes 300 to 500 pages long, often arrived at the Marine squadron much later than the time required to launch the sorties. This problem occurred with much of the bulk data sent as general service traffic. To alleviate the problem, the Marine expeditionary force command element would arrange a file transfer from Riyadh, Saudi Arabia, and then distribute data to Marine units via local area networks.

A standard format allowed units to receive the file, then extract information or insert it into their own data base applications for history files or subsequent mission assignments. By using the local area network, the expeditionary force could distribute the air tasking order and confirm its receipt within the hour.

While fleet Marine forces units long had been experimenting with local area network technology in support of command and control, the network's extent and robustness only were theorized. A clearer scale of its usefulness was established when, during the first 36 hours of the ground war, Marine Corps local area networks processed 1.3 million electronic mail messages. No difficulty arose in processing that volume of traffic, nor were any outages or system degradation experienced.

Supply and maintenance information, long considered by logisticians and tacticians as administrative data, soon came to be seen as critical to the success of the operation. Although systems supplying these data originally were relegated to back lots and warehouses, commanders soon found that access to these data had to be as close to front lines as possible.

Personnel operating within bunkers along the border of Kuwait generated supply and maintenance transactions. While these systems did not exploit the enemy, detect its presence or deny it freedom of the battlefield, they had to operate in the same environment as the systems that did perform those functions.

This article originally appeared in the August 1991 issue of *SIGNAL.*

SPECTRUM MANAGEMENT

Earl S. Takeguchi and William J. Wooley

"Today we are fielding multi-million dollar systems even before we have determined their spectrum impacts."[1]

An information war is fought as much in the *airwaves* as it is on land, sea, air and space. Information management, including distributing and transferring information, while simultaneously employing electronic combat and radars, has become an essential centerpiece in U.S. military command, control and communications strategy. Our warriors must learn how to manage the three primary means of transmitting and distributing processed data or information on the battlefield—cable, courier and the radio frequency spectrum. The use and management of the radio frequency spectrum becomes even more critical as mobility, command and control requirements increase from emerging technology and more needs arise for real-time information.

Information warfare cannot be waged by a military force unless it can effectively and efficiently control the electromagnetic spectrum. Our armed forces may be unprepared to manage the competing demands for thousands of radio frequencies needed to fight this new kind of war.

The pressing need to achieve order in the spectrum is always overlooked in the rush to gird for war and, once recognized and provided, is just as quickly forgotten.

Marconi's Problem—The Laws of Physics

The U.S. Army's expert on radio frequency management has commented that "spectrum management started when Marconi made his third radio set." It is immutable physics that no two entities can occupy the same space at the same time. This fact is every bit as true of electrons as it is of aircraft and automobiles, if not as well recognized. The consequences of failure to predict and deconflict in the electromagnetic spectrum are pretty much the same as they are with vehicles—confusion at least, collision at best, chaos at worst.

A state of confusion exists when someone usurps "your" radio frequency. Collision results in interference and jamming. Confusion becomes chaos when frequencies are not provided to operating forces in a timely manner, discipline breaks down and users begin to "bootleg" radio frequencies. This is what happened in the very early days of Desert Shield when combat forces had to deploy without authorized radio frequencies consistent with a frequency plan.

The lack of an authorized frequency is no deterrent to the use of radio or frequency-dependent equipment. The mission must come first for the operator, and does. However, that initiative to satisfy mission requirements could result in a breakdown in discipline in the use of the RF spectrum as equipment density increases. *Operator initiative* becomes much more than a nuisance when weapons and force control depend so absolutely upon order in the RF realm.

War in the Ether

Radio frequency management is a sovereign responsibility, but our host, the Kingdom of Saudi Arabia, eventually delegated national prerogatives to the U.S. Central Command. However, U.S. combat forces arrived in Saudi Arabia in August 1990 without the proper tools to jointly allocate, monitor and control that precious, finite resource. It took several anxious months to settle turf battles, develop an allotment process and find the talent and tools to clear a path for thousands of radio nets that would soon saturate the ether over Saudi Arabia, Kuwait and Iraq.

Fortunately USCENTCOM was able to improvise a suitable management system before Desert Shield became Desert Storm and before a major annoyance grew into disaster.

Centralized Control Fails

Techniques for managing the radio spectrum are not all that different from those used to control airspace: one either has the tools that allow dynamic, precise, real-time control or, lacking those, one apportions blocks of airspace by time or by volume. Airspace managers used the "reservation" technique in Vietnam. It was effective, but terribly inefficient and wasteful of a precious resource. By the time Desert Shield rolled around, the military services had the tools and techniques to maintain centralized, real-time control of airspace, but not *airwaves*. CENTCOM's radio frequency managers tried to maintain centralized control over the spectrum, but, lacking both tools and theater-level experience, quickly fell behind the pace of force buildup.

Centralized assignment control and management, whereby every assignment is centrally made, is an accepted way of doing business for many frequency managers and had been successfully used before by CENTCOM for small, well-coordinated exercises.

The concept is embedded in peacetime permanent frequency procedures that presume an inclusive and accurate data base. The centralized concept proved to be ill-suited for maneuver warfare in the Gulf because the database was seriously flawed: It was virtually useless because of massive changes in force structure and rapidly maneuvering units.

Centralized frequency assignment assumes the technical characteristics and geographic location of a given radio transmitter are known and that the radio won't move about too much. From this, experts can approximate how far and in which direction every signal will propagate. All of these static characteristics are then aggregated into a plan to keep the many radios separated in space and in radio frequency so they won't interfere too much with each other. Powerful computers do the analysis and deconfliction is performed—unless the assumptions change.

Independently developed mechanisms for spectrum control, which each military service brought to the theater of operations, were not compatible and could not interoperate. The notion of centralized assignment of frequencies at theater level could not bridge this gap.

In-theater experts had little experience beyond that of allocating frequencies in joint exercises such as Bright Star. The volume of requests—which were actually being transhipped to the United States—soon swamped a highly centralized system. The "system" itself was actually little more than an administrative process based in Annapolis, Maryland[2] to collect and catalogue requests for fixed facilities. It could not begin to service thousands of constantly moving emitters or with similar transmitters operating in close proximity. For a time this vital function was based at MacDill Air Force Base, Florida, and later shifted to Buzzards Point, Washington, DC.[3]

The Air Force, which employs many emitters for air operations and base support, favors the centralized approach. However, its network posture (airfields) is static and predictable, lending itself to highly centralized control procedures. Further, pilots don't like to change radio frequencies and call signs very often, because that adds another variable and a chance for fatal error in an unfriendly environment.

Centralized spectrum control works for Navy battlegroups as well and for much the same reason. However, the dynamics of operation, shifting geometry on the battlefield and sheer numbers of radios involved in Army and Marine operations mandate some other method.

"Jointness" and a single solution to RF management is hard to achieve because there are so many differences in the ways that radios and frequency-dependent equipments are used to support warriors on land, sea and air.

Bootlegging For Mission Accomplishment

That there soon would be serious problems in allocating and controlling the radio frequency spectrum became known almost as soon as the first aircraft arrived bearing the XVIII Airborne Corps.

The XVIII Airborne Corps submitted its initial radio frequency request to Central Command on August 7, 1990. The CENTCOM FMO (frequency management office) consisted of one individual (later two) who acted as a mailbox and conduit back to JFMOCENT REAR in the United States. As of October 1, the request from the XVIII had still not been fully approved. The Corps, out of necessity, began assigning and managing non-approved frequencies in their area of operation and distributing a list of the "unauthorized frequencies that it was using."[4]

"So how did you get assignments to meet the immediate radio frequency requirements? Or, to be more precise, why were you accused of bootlegging?" That question was put to a sergeant in the XVIII Corps.[5] "Commanders don't like to be restricted," he said, "much less held up because of a frequency assigned for command and control radio nets. I kept two frequency assignment records—those authorized by CENTCOM and those that we had to use to satisfy the mission but were not authorized by CENTCOM. Picking and using random unauthorized frequencies, that's what they call bootlegging. I had things under control, and we were lucky. Next time if we run into a more sophisticated enemy, we may not be so successful."

A sergeant from the 5th Signal Command added: "Part of the problem was not fully understanding how everyone fit into a multi-nation, all Services' operation. In the heat of battle, there was a lot of competition between the Services for frequency assignments. Each Service was trying to secure frequencies to meet its battlefield needs, unaware of the communications mission and the frequency requirements of the other Services. There was a total lack of coordination, cooperation, and communication from the CINC level all the way down to the lowest Army-fighting echelon."[6]

CENTCOM had tried to forestall just such a situation, but its centralized approach was peacetime oriented and had been inundated and overwhelmed in this fluid environment. The CENTCOM Frequency Record System data base registered assignments by location. "...[Their] theater frequency assignment process, centrally controlled at JFMOCENT REAR,...was completely inadequate for a joint tactical operation of this magnitude...paper intensive, and structured [to] collecting data on fixed location communication systems."[7]

The 35th Signal Brigade, XVIII Corps, was making frequency assignments to their radio relay networks by the "stubby pencil" method—after all, there was no space or room in their backpack for a computer.

Some operating units were only marginally better, initially, to manage the use of assigned frequencies. The 11th and 3rd Signal Brigades were the only U.S. Army units that brought their automated frequency engineering capability to the field. Given the use of entire frequency bands by each the different foreign military units (Saudi, British, French and other coalition forces) numerous interferences were being reported in the 220-404 MHz, 1350-1850 MHz and 4.4-5.0 GHz bands.

Circuit quality was continually degraded and outages common until the 11th Signal Brigade, working directly with the 35th Signal Brigade and other units, began using the AFES (Army Frequency Engineering System) to reassign microwave and tropo systems.

The XVIII Corps Signal Battalions had no automated communications engineering or frequency engineering tools, and this became a very technical problem when they were asked to "get legal" and use only their authorized allotment of frequencies in a high-use, spectrum-dense, small geographic area.[8]

Allotment and Decentralization

Interim measures were quickly adopted: tactical allotment of frequency blocks by CENTCOM and decentralized control within those blocks by the operating units. This allowed the corps and divisions to operate autonomously, yet "managed" at the theater level.

Priority was given to the UHF Band I (220-404 MHz)—the most congested band and the one plagued with interference problems. This band provides for tactical satellite, air/ground/air, data links and multichannel systems. Despite the urgency, it required almost two weeks to gain concurrence from all military services in the area.

This action required changes to some operational frequency assignments, and no one likes to do that. The Band I allotment plan was approved by CENTCOM and assignment authority transferred to service components.

The allotment plan concept was extremely difficult to implement in the SHF (4.4-5.0 GHz) band. Frequency assignments were scattered throughout the band for high powered Tropo and low powered microwave systems, and the requirements in this band were projected to increase. Installed links carried vital circuits, and transitioning to an allotment plan could be devastating. Shutting down these systems to implement an allotment plan was operationally touchy and very difficult.

A viable option was to use an SHF frequency engineering and assignment capability to make compatible assignments to the large number of high powered tactical Tropo and microwave radio systems deployed in a relatively small geographic area. The 11th Signal Brigade—having the greater number of radio systems and the only capability to quickly assign compatible frequencies and perform cosite interference analysis—was assigned theater-wide responsibility for this SHF band.[9]

Matters were under far better control by the time the VII Corps appeared on the scene in December. The implementation of allotment plans for tactical frequency bands and the decentralization of assignment authority eliminated the excessive administrative coordination that had been levied on the XVIII Corps. Requirements for the VII Corps were identified and coordinated well before its arrival.[10]

Joint Restricted Frequency List

The lack of spectrum management also had an adverse impact on electronic warfare—the key to success of the air operation. *SIGNAL* Magazine quotes[11] the vice director of the Joint Electronic Warfare Center, Kelly Air Force Base, Texas, as follows: "The center used planning cells to develop the joint restricted frequency list, which defines frequencies off limits for electronic warfare. Col. Dickson describes the list as the equivalent of a no-fire zone for electronic warfare. Commanders develop this list as part of their battle plan, and the list is the responsibility of communications-electronics officers, the Joint Staff and J-6...Because a good spectrum management system within the joint arena—as well as in the coalition warfare arena—is lacking, developing this list is difficult...commanders basically do not have a good idea of who is operating on which frequency at a specific time. Neither do they have an automated way of managing this situation that is compatible with other services, compatible with allies and able to handle data on a timely basis...As a result, the joint restricted frequency list during the Gulf conflict got out of hand at times...leading to many cases of frequency fratricide. This lack of control over spectrum management remains a serious electronic warfare problem..."

Some Principles

These Principles of Tactical Frequency Management are used by the Army for large-scale tactical operations:

• Frequency management is performed at all echelons of command, but *frequency control* is performed by the *individual operator*. As the Army notes, a radio will be operated whether or not there is an authorized frequency.

• Frequency management must be shared at all echelons. The more echelons deployed, the greater the need for decentralized frequency management.

• Frequency management offices should be manned by qualified personnel who understand requirements of assigned units within their echelon.

• Ninety percent of all frequency coordination should be completed prior to deployment. The remainder should be deconflicted, on the spot, but without additional administrative procedures.

• When different equipment types operate in the same spectrum and are deployed in the same geographic area, the frequency band should be proportionally allotted by type of requirement, e.g., air-ground-air, TACSAT, radio relay, etc.

• Allocation of frequency resources should be aligned with the CINC's priorities.

• The frequency spectrum should be managed to optimize reuse and sharing.

• Frequency managers should anticipate requirements and plan accordingly. Proactive frequency management requires knowledge of operational contingencies and battlefield planning.

• Accurate technical and deployment data are needed to perform electromagnetic compatibility engineering and interference analysis. On the dynamic battlefield, this information is available only at the lowest echelons of command.

Focus For The Future

For the moment at least, the search for lasting solutions to the recurring problem of RF management is on the front burner in the defense department. The challenge is to keep attention focused on technical training, contingency spectrum planning and people until computer technology can produce the tools to convert a manual, logistic monster into a totally automated and electronically coupled capability to manage the electromagnetic spectrum.

Endnotes

[1] Army briefing to the Senior Level Spectrum Management Conference, Annapolis, Maryland, January 22, 1992.
[2] ECAC, or Electromagnetic Compatibility Analysis Center, is a DoD contract operation in Annapolis, Maryland.
[3] Buzzards Point is the location of the Air Force Frequency Management Agency, which, for a time, became the location of the Central Command Joint Frequency Management Office (Rear), or, JFMOCENT REAR.
[4] After Action Report, Operation Desert Shield Frequency Management (September 30-December 5, 1990), [Department of Army.]
[5] Army Spectrum Management-1992 Conference, Fort Gordon, Georgia.
[6] Ibid.
[7] After Action Report. See 4, above.
[8] Ibid.
[9] Ibid.
[10] Ibid.
[11] Robert K. Ackerman, "Electronic Warfare Explodes As Threats Spawn Diversity," *SIGNAL*, March 1992, p. 35.

THE JOINT CEOI

Donald L. Jones and Richard C. Randt

An information war is fought in the airwaves. Competition for radio frequencies is intense and can be disruptive unless there are firm controls over allocation and use of the spectrum. Further, while U.S. forces now encipher a high percentage of radio transmissions, an adversary can still glean useful information from unencrypted transmissions and thus be better able to establish our order of battle or to interfere with transmissions. A *directory* of users and nets—Communications-Electronics Operation Instructions (CEOI) or Signal Operation Instructions (SOI)—is a prime means to minimize this vulnerability.[1] However, producing this document for the Persian Gulf War was a major undertaking and the experience now guides planning on the Joint Staff.

This directory is called a Joint CEOI (JCEOI) in the multiservice and/or multinational environment and it gives frequencies, call signs, call words and suffixes that change randomly on a periodic basis. An analogy may be drawn between the JCEOI and a common-user telephone network. A telephone network without a "phone book" is limited in utility to the numbers one can retain in memory or otherwise jot down in personal notes. Possession of the book opens virtually limitless communications possibilities. The CEOI is the sine qua non of single channel tactical radio communications, serving two fundamental purposes: first as a *directory* and also as a measure of *transmission security* (TRANSEC).

As a TRANSEC measure the CEOI can, through the random generation and daily change of call signs, call words, suffixes and frequencies, impair the effectiveness of an enemy's effort to collect signals intelligence. Hostile DF and jamming operations are made more difficult to execute when frequencies change often.

The emphasis on TRANSEC has decreased because of vast increases in use of secure voice equipment at the tactical level. Frequency hopping radios such as SINCGARS and other Low Probability of Detection techniques have lessened the need for changing frequencies. However, joint warfare doctrine has increased the need for the JCEOI as a directory. Any lingering doubts about this were erased by the glaring lack of communcations interoperability in the Grenada operation and documented by the XVIII Airborne Corps.[2]

Shortly thereafter, the joint commands, beginning with CINCLANT, began to require JCEOIs. CINCLANT's approach was the "all-inclusive" style of CEOI, wherein every possible unit under CINCLANT control was put into the book. As you will see, that approach raises problems when the operation grows beyond a small contingency and particularly so when other nations are involved.

NSA Role

The National Security Agency (NSA) designed and produced the CINCLANT JCEOI and it passed muster in several major exercises. However, exercises impose restraints that limit full use of a JCEOI. At the outset of the Gulf War, CINCLANT units deployed to the CINCCENT area of responsibility and quickly found that their contingency JCEOI would not function because frequency assignments were not compatible with other U.S. and Allied tactical units, host country requirements and other unforeseen restrictions.

NSA was again called upon to produce the JCEOI for Desert Shield and Desert Storm. It was a monumental undertaking. [Editor's note: Over a dozen editions were published consisting of over half a million pages and weighing in at 85 tons.]

Stacked on pallets and trucked from Fort Meade, Maryland to Dover Air Force Base, Delaware, the classified directories were couriered to Saudi Arabia on chartered aircraft and distributed directly from the aircraft to using organizations. Even NSA's prodigious production plant was stressed by this effort.

The first decision dealt with style of the JCEOI. Should it follow the pattern of the CINCLANT document and cover everyone down to platoon level or should it be limited to the top command levels, leaving combat units to separately generate their own CEOIs and SOIs? Despite clearly foreseen logistical problems, the all-inclusive alternative was selected.[3] This alternative was chosen because many CINCLANT units were earmarked to deploy and their databases were complete and ready to use. Secondly, the frequencies that would be allocated for a CINCCENT JCEOI were initially unknown and early indications were that they would not be in abundance. Maximum control and optimal utilization of frequencies could best be achieved in a single, consolidated JCEOI. Also, too many units would have to completely redesign their existing SOIs/CEOIs to make them suitable for the Gulf area. The consolidated approach was the quickest way to get a usable product in the hands of the user.

While the process of planning and designing the CINCCENT JCEOI was ongoing, units had already arrived in the theater. What they used for a CEOI varied widely. Some units took their garrison CEOIs, while others attempted to use their wartime CEOIs, many of which were earmarked for contingency deployment to Europe.[4] [Editor's note: See article on Spectrum Management for more details on this work-around.]

Unfortunately, a single generation JCEOI is very sensitive to changes in force structure. In fact, that difficulty did arise. Despite canned contingency plans and pre-planned troop lists, last minute deletions and substitutions caused a number of supposedly final designs to the the Desert Shield/Desert Storm JCEOI to be radically revised, some before and some after printing.

Soft Copy and Electrical Distribution

At the outset of the Gulf War, CINCCENT, its supporting forces and NSA, became enmeshed in the production of a JCEOI and supporting force SOI/CEOI, which would be implemented in paper format. The media for JCEOI/CEOI/SOI has traditionally been a printed booklet, produced by conventional publication methods. There have been developments over the past ten years to give fighting forces the ability to produce their own and in the field, independently of any centralized agency. The key benefit of self-production is flexibility: the field commander can tailor forces to a situation and instantly update the communications directory. Long logistic tails and 120-day turn around times are eliminated.[5] But nothing like this was available to support a deployment the size of Desert Shield.

About a year prior to the Gulf War, a formal working group (WG) was established under the auspices of the Joint Staff to set standards for a Joint CEOI and select a hardware/software package that would permit decentralized generation, printing and distribution. The JCEOI WG realized that before it would be possible to give everyone a decentralized electronic capability, it needed to establish a viable contingency capability to preclude the need for another scramble over JCEOI in the future. This requirement was expressed thusly by Joint Chiefs of Staff Chairman General Colin Powell, "I want to be able to go to war within three days." An on-the-shelf, paper-based JCEOI was needed for each CINC, as well as on-the-shelf contingency SOIs and CEOIs for each major supporting force that might be be called to any area of the world.

The working group determined that the Army-sponsored Revised Battlefield Electronic CEOI System (RBECS) provided the most capability and greatest potential for fulfilling the future needs of all services and other joint users. The SOI/CEOI/JCEOI and the TRANSEC variable are generated by RBECS and stored in the NSA-developed Data Transfer Device (DTD) for physical distribution. DTD will securely hold crypto keys, the SINCGARS TRANSEC variable, and the entire SOI/CEOI/JCEOI that applies to a major network of tactical radios.

Preassigned Frequencies

The final solution for a paper-based system was driven by available frequencies. If frequencies are not pre-assigned, the immediate drill on entry into the theater of operations is obtaining and assigning frequencies and establishing tactical radio nets. Paper CEOIs would be "fill-in-the-blank" style, hardly conducive to a smooth, error-free, quick-strike operation.

The compelling need to make some assumptions about available frequencies gave rise to the concept of a single contingency SOI/CEOI that would be good anywhere in the world. This would involve using a set of frequencies, adequate in number to preclude communications fratricide, usable in any locale, and not subject to future restrictions. That is a tall order. But, without assumed frequencies, SOIs/CEOIs could not be printed in advance. A unit might very well arrive in the war zone in three days, but without approved frequencies. [Editor's note: This is precisely what happened with the initial deployments of XVIII Airborne Corps in Desert Shield]

The JCEOI WG took a pragmatic approach. In a contingency, U.S. forces will either enter sovereign territory by invitation—in which case frequency requests would likely be approved—or will be attacking—in which case the question of approval is moot.

Based on this rationale, the WG surveyed the band with the most usage—the VHF-FM band—for frequencies critical to safety of life and limb, or otherwise restricted by international treaty. Such frequencies that could be the source of an "international incident" were discarded. This world-wide survey yielded 603 VHF frequencies, for use with a 50 kHz bandwidth, that are believed to universally lack explicit national protection.

This seemingly heavy-handed approach to national sovereignty is simply a best estimate of what is reasonably expected to work and one that will cause the least interference with local national systems. It is well-recognized that international treaties and diplomatic agreements must be respected and that U.S. forces must diligently avoid provocation and incident. This approach provides an initial negotiating position.

Frequency Reuse

Having defined the available set of VHF-FM frequencies, it was then necessary to devise an allocation scheme to accommodate the various users, with minimal mutual interference. As we learned in the Desert Shield/Desert Storm JCEOI, the frequency reuse ratio goes up dramatically among common users as more discrete frequencies are earmarked. There were no discrete frequencies specifically assigned to Army divisions, yet there were enough frequencies to go around. In many cases the reuse ratio was one to one.

The Marine Corps and the Army have agreed to an integrated frequency utilization scheme that overlays eight different frequency plans on the 603 contingency frequencies for the VHF-FM band. This provides a reasonable allocation of discrete and common use frequencies for each Army division, separate brigade, armored cavalry regiment and the Marine Expeditionary Force. The block of common use frequencies is sufficient to minimize both the unit reuse ratio and the internal interference. The design of the eight plans is such that any of the Army or Marine units can operate side-by-side, with minimal frequency interference, if deployed to any of their designated primary or secondary areas of responsibility.

Simplifying Interoperability

Unlike the public telephone system, there are communities of interest in military operations that can markedly simplify interoperability. These communities of interest are generally along organizational lines; that is, divisions, corps headquarters, Marine Expeditionary Forces, separate brigades, etc. Most communications takes place within these communities. Inter-organizational communications is generally limited to doctrinally-defined interfaces, such as command nets. Above division level, inter-organizational communications in the VHF-FM band is minimal due to the physical distances involved and the availability of other means such as multi-channel telephone systems, SATCOM, etc. The point is that there is a manageable number of places where it is necessary to cross an interface and employ more than one CEOI.

Each war fighting CINC and all their supporting force organizations then become individually responsible for devising, designing and updating their own contingency JCEOI/CEOI/SOI. Further, loss or compromise of one portion of one unit's SOI does not put the rest at risk.

Summary

The foregoing recapped how the Gulf War forces were provided with a JCEOI and what went wrong. The JCEOI WG sees a three-step corrective process:

• Ensure that all CINCs and their designated supporting forces are equipped with a paper-based contingency system able to take any force structure into any contingency area within three days, with a minimum of on-the-ground deconfliction, and sustain those forces for 90 days.

• Decentralized generation of JCEOIs, SOIs, and CEOIs by means of the RBECS software. Distribution, at lower levels will be by DTD, floppy disk, locally produced paper, or whatever methods are appropriate.

• In the interim transitional period, RBECS software and RDGs will be available. Systems can be generated and can be distributed by file transfer, and physical provision of floppy disks. Provision of systems to the actual operator level will still require some local printing. However, with the proliferation of PCs and printers in the services, especially at higher echelons, this is not seen as a major obstacle.

This article was excerpted from an unpublished, internal working paper on actions of the Joint Working Group on CEOIs.

Endnotes

[1] [Editor note: A typical soldier might carry one to three (ten-day) packages of assignments into the field in a packet designed to fit into the pocket of combat fatigues. A larger package could be carried, but these are easily misplaced, lost or captured. Should that happen—and it did in the Persian Gulf War—the information has been compromised and the whole job must be done over again.]

[2] Capt. Marilyn M. McAllister, "Needed for rapid deployment: a joint contingency CEOI", *Army Communicator,* Fall, 1987, p. 11.

[3] The alternative—although initially discarded at the outset of the Gulf War—has subsequently resurfaced as the right approach in the future. Called the *Umbrella JCEOI/Supporting Force Concept* and endorsed by the Joint Staff, it will be tested and perfected as the contingency JCEOI/SOI/CEOI scheme to be employed in advance of more sophisticated electronic/computer techniques.

[4] Prior to the Gulf War, the only formal contingency SOI system was that earmarked for use by the Army in Europe. Frequencies allocated to those SOI systems were cleared only for use in the Federal Republic of Germany and some selected NATO areas.

[5] A prime developer of such a decentralized capability has been the U.S. Army Project Manager for the Single Channel Ground and Airborne Radio System (PM-SINCGARS), with substantial input from NSA and the DoD Electromagnetic Compatibility and Analysis Center. The culmination of this effort will be the Revised Battlefield Electronic CEOI System (BECS) (RBECS). Although begun as an Army development, it became apparent that each service had a requirement for something like RBECS and that many joint applications were awaiting its availability. The original BECS program was based on an HP-111 laptop machine that rapidly became obsolete in the computer technology explosion. The RBECS software is IBM/MS-DOS compatible and is virtually hardware independent, requiring a 286 or better machine. Another difference is that RBECS software is unclassified. The random generation process is based on a Random Data Generator (RDG) designed to attach externally at the RS-232 port. The RDG is a small, relatively inexpensive device that is a Controlled Cryptographic Item

JOINT STARS IN DESERT STORM

Thomas S. Swalm

The 1991 Gulf War was a proving ground for post cold war concepts, and Joint STARS dramatically illustrated the effect of timely intelligence and precision targeting on employment of high technology weapons in conventional warfare.

The Joint STARS emanated from converging U.S. Air Force and U.S. Army doctrine on how to execute the AirLand battle. Years before Desert Storm, planners at the Army's Training and Doctrine Command at Fort Monroe, Virginia and the U.S. Air Force's Tactical Air Command at nearby Langley Air Force Base, Virginia were hard at work trying to define systems and concepts to meet the challenges of the modern battlefield. Joint assumptions were that the tenets of the AirLand battle would include depth, agility, initiative, synchronization and that the classical tactical air roles of counter air, interdiction, close air support and reconnaissance would be upgraded to fit this concept. These same planners had concluded that to win in modern battle, friendly forces would have to perform all weather, around the clock operations with high technology weapons to provide:
- precision, control and intelligence
- dynamic fluid, non-linear operations
- integrated combined arms battle
- operations against reinforcing echelons
- deep operations.

All Light All Weather Attack

The Joint STARS represented an effort dating from the May 22, 1984 Army-Air Force Memorandum of Agreement to field an integrated radar and attack control system designed to locate and attack stationary and mobile targets in the first and second echelon under all light and weather conditions. As such, Joint STARS was designed to be to the ground battle what the Airborne Warning and Control System (AWACS) was to the air battle.

The system is composed of a platform—a modified Boeing 707 (designated E-8A)—which carries a multi-mode radar sensor for detection and tracking of enemy forces, processing equipment, mission crew work stations, and command and control interfaces. Data collected on board were then fed to six ground station modules that received, in real-time, the radar data processed in the aircraft. Ground commanders, in turn, analyzed the data for application to the battlefield. The importance of this real-time process was dramatically demonstrated at the Battle of Khafji (which is discussed later).

Key To AirLand Operation

As conceived, Joint STARS was a key to the Joint Air Force-Army AirLand Battle concept. Utilizing this strategy, the E-8A was flown by a composite crew of Air Force Systems Command, Tactical Air Command (TAC), Army and contractor personnel. It was linked with the Army ground station module, and provided Central Command forces with a revolutionary new battlefield capability. It is important to emphasize that this system was not expected to reach initial operational capability until the mid-1990s.

The Joint STARS aircraft employed its special radar modes (moving target indicator and synthetic aperture radar [SAR]) to track and target tanks, artillery, and other ground forces, providing ground commanders with a picture of enemy movements as they occurred, as far distant as 155 miles. Once enemy forces were detected, Joint STARS would relay the targeting information to tactical aircraft, standoff missiles, or Army artillery for precise, real-time attacks that would not only control the enemy forces' rate of entry into the battle, but also prevent breakthrough of allied positions.

Going To War

An initial request was made in August 1990 to send the E-8A Joint STARS aircraft to the Middle East. However, the system was still in development testing and more than three years from an initial production decision. The Air Force—having the executive service responsibilities—was naturally concerned about sending a complex developmental system into potential combat.

However, during a European operational field demonstration in September and October 1990, more than forty general officers flew in the aircraft and were impressed with the limited but successful demonstration. There was strong Army advocacy for Joint STARS use among senior officers of the VII Corps—then deployed to Saudi Arabia. General Schwarzkopf was so impressed by the E-8A's potential to locate Iraqi tanks that, shortly after Operation Desert Storm began, he requested the new system.

Once the decision was made to deploy the two Joint STARS aircraft, TAC headquarters responded on December 26, 1991 by sending an advance team to prepare for the aircraft. The 4411th Joint STARS squadron deployed with sixty Air Force, five Army and sixty-eight contractor personnel. Joint STARS operational Detachment 1, composed of forty-two Army and seven contractor personnel, operated and maintained the ground station modules that were deployed to U.S. Army Central Command, the Tactical Air Control Center, Marine Central Command, VII Corps and XVIII Airborne Corps.

Flying commended two days later. After being declared operational, one of the two aircraft flew every day. Many missions averaged thirteen hours of flight time and covered the entire Kuwaiti theater of operations in one orbit.

90 Percent On First Pass

Proof of value was demonstrated by the fact that aircraft directed by Joint STARS had a 90 percent success rate in finding targets on the first pass. In one incident, according to Colonel Muellner, two A-10s and an AC-130 directed by Joint STARS destroyed fifty-eight of sixty-one vehicles in a single convoy. On another occasion a unit forming to attack VII Corps was 80 percent disabled before it could get into action. As mentioned earlier, when the Iraqis attacked the little Saudi town of Khafji during the early days of the war, Joint STARS informed the coalition leaders that the attack consisted only of a small Iraqi force. Joint STARS also helped to pinpoint Scud missile sites, passing the information to Army Tactical Missile System sites, multiple-launch rocket system batteries, and U.S. Air Force strike aircraft.

Altogether, the two E-8A aircraft flew forty-nine missions (logging a total of 535 hours) and supported 100 percent of their mission assignments. Joint STARS operators successfully detected over one thousand targets (such as Scud storage areas and missiles, tanks, armored personnel carriers, convoys, artillery pieces, bridge assembly areas, and POL storage sites) and controlled 750 fighters.

Needless to say, all parties concerned were well pleased with the performance of this developmental system. According to Colonel Muellner[1], once Joint STARS was in the theater locating targets, the fighter-bombers consistently ran out of ammunition before they ran low on fuel.

Surveillance Becomes Control

As had been the case in early operations with AWACS, Joint STARS was originally planned to operate only in the surveillance role during the Gulf War. This policy lasted a mere two days, after which a weapons allocation officer was assigned aboard the E-8 to control his own F-15Es, particularly against tactical ballistic missile sites. From there the system went on to assume a complete C^3I role operating in an interlinked network (including AWACS, Rivet Joint, ABCCC and various Army and Air Force command and intelligence centers). The system quickly proved its worth in tactical surveillance and precision targeting as well as "reducing the fog of war" for theater commanders. Examples of various Joint STARS operations include:

• linked with AWACS to provide a complete picture of enemy tactical movement over the battlefield

• located mobile Scud launchers and provided precision control of strike assets

• located a convoy comprising FROG artillery rockets that was destroyed by F-16s armed with cluster bombs

• operated around the clock in the worst weather in the Middle East in several decades

• detected a Republican Guard unit planning to counter attack during the liberation of Kuwait that was targeted from a Joint STARS ground station and destroyed by Army Apache helicopters

- supplied real-time information to the VII Corps about an Iraqi SA-8 site, which was targeted and destroyed by ATACMS
- direct intervention of the Joint STARS mission commander prevented fratricide by U.S. Marine Corps forces on the right flank of the British armored thrust during the early stages of the ground war
- operated as an airborne intelligence correlation center for data dissemination through the tactical command network
- detected and targeted the nighttime Iraqi retreat from Kuwait and directed multiple air strikes against these targets
- provided on-scene damage assessment of interdiction targets (using SAR) to enable real-time re-attacks.

The U.S. Air Force has programmed 20 Joint STARS and the Air Force Chief of Staff General Merrill McPeak said: "We will never again want to fight a war without a Joint STARS kind of system."

Endnote

[1] Colonel George K. Muellner, (now Brig. Gen.) USAF, was the senior Air Force officer in charge of the Joint STARS deployment. "Excerpted from Proceedings, AFCEA Europe Madrid Symposium, April 28 - 30, 1992."

References:

Reaching Globally, Reaching Powerfully: The USAF in the Gulf War, A Report, September 1991.

Hales, Grant M., *Air Power in Desert Shield/Desert Storm Part II. The Tactical Air Command Operation Desert Storm: A Case Study of Tactical Aircraft Employment.*

Couluris, Paul J., *Joint STARS: A Terrestrial AWACS*, Defense and Technologies International, December 1991.

Turnley, Peter, "The Day Bush Stopped the War," *NewsWeek* (International Edition), January 20, 1992. A special report.

IRAQI COMMAND AND CONTROL: The Information Differential

Alan D. Campen

M ost of the world's fourth largest military force did not fight long, hard or well during the Gulf War and those who sift the sands of Kuwait and Iraq for lessons for the future are confounded with ambiguities, uncertainties and conflicting data. At best it was an implausible conflict, where most—but certainly not all—coalition forces and weapons experienced less stress in combat than they might have encountered in a field training exercise.

Despite exhaustive and often critical analysis, we may never know whether Iraqi forces were overwhelmed by vastly superior firepower, or outmaneuvered by an opponent who "owned the desert and the darkness," or were paralyzed by loss of command and control, or intimidated by unerringly accurate missiles and bombs that descended without warning, or befuddled by B-52's that, every 3 hours around and by the clock, shook the earth, numbing brains and rupturing eardrums.

Myriad coalition capabilities were aggregated and brought to bear instantly, constantly and were so thoroughly integrated that post-war discrimination is a near-impossible chore.

Brinkmanship and inept leadership[1] certainly were consequential factors in this brief and one-sided war. However, the massive attack in the opening minutes of the air operation destroyed much of Iraq's control and communications infrastructure and it is not clear that Saddam Hussein or any successor could have successfully passed instructions, had they any to send.

James W. Pardue, Jr. writes[2] of Iraqi C2 & Intelligence: "...entirely inadequate for the type of war mounted against them...incapable of keeping up with the pace of the battle..inability to read battlefield and react to coalition operations caused uncoordinated fire support, fragmented committment of reserves, sluggish reaction throughout theater...corps could not synchronize an adequate reaction, even with more capable Republican Guards."

An Iraqi prisoner was later to report that "Iraqi intelligence officers were using Radio Saudi Arabia, Radio Monte Carlo, and the Voice Of America as sources to brief commanders."

Low morale was hinted when the Iraqi air force fled to Iran and confirmed by massive defections of troops during the early hours of the ground offensive. Apparently having foresaken zealotry in Iran, the weakened and front line divisions of this bloodied and once-vaunted army had little stomach for this kind of brutal war that descended upon them from above. But, allied intelligence did not know this then and cannot fully explain it now.

Although exhorted to do so, intelligence—particulary that garnered by remote and technical methods—has never been able to distinguish enemy's capability from its intentions. Pre-war intelligence produced an Enemy Order of Battle (EOB) list that accurately counted and named all division-sized units, but could not devine that only the Republican Guards divisions held back in reserve were manned at levels much above 50 percent.

But, having said all that, some facts from the war are incontrovertible and the conclusions they support have much to say about future conflicts in the Third World.

The Information Differential

Military history is replete with evidence that not even the soundest of strategy, brilliance of leadership or most innovative of tactics on the field of battle can overcome the disaster that awaits the commander who loses control. Iraq's command and control structure (its command post, headquarters, electrical power and telephone centers) was the first target on January 17,1991, and that hapless nation may have been the first in history to fall victim to what our defense department now aptly calls the *differential* in information warfare[3].

Iraq was left blind, deaf, dumb and deceived; its impressive military strength fatally weakened in the opening minutes of the war by a precisely planned and skillfully executed campaign to destroy the means of force control[4].

Iraq began its incursion into Kuwait with an extensive air defense system built with equipment from such diverse sources as West Germany, France and the Soviet Union. According to William A. Burhans, writing in the *Journal of Electronic Defense*[5], major targets were protected by Soviet-produced SA-2, SA-6 "Kvadrat" and SA-8 "Osa" missiles, while troop units were defended by the SZU-23-4 "Shilka," SA-13 "Strela-10" and portable SA-14 "Strela-3" missiles.

Air superiority—the essential first step in AirLand battle—was gained almost as soon as the curtain raised on the war and it was sustained throughout the air operation by repeated attacks—some say *over-kill* due to faulty bomb damage assessment reports (BDA)—throughout the war. In the first moments, helicopters, closely followed by aircraft, fired clouds of anti-radiation weapons and systematically took down the thick and layered Iraqi air defense network before it could take its expected toll on coalition aircraft.

Airman/journalist James P. Coyne asks why the Iraqi air defenses failed and concludes: "Most important, the Iraqi air defenses, built along the Soviet model, depended heavily—almost 100 percent—on centralized control. Saddam's central command and control facilities and networks were severely damaged in the opening hours of the air war, and he was never able to rebuild them. Most SAM and AAA batteries were forced to operate autonomously, with little coordination or central direction. There was no early warning of incoming coalition attackers. The result was the dense barrage fire Americns saw on television. Most attackers were able to avoid it[6]."

Some Tomahawk cruise missiles dispensed ribbons of carbon fibers over Iraqi electrical power switching systems, causing short circuits, temporary disruptions and massive shutdowns in the power systems[7].

Soviet military officers who participated in a round-table discussion on the Persian Gulf war are reported by Mr. Burhans as reasoning that the failure by Iraq to employ its extensive air defense system can be attributed to two factors. First, the "almost unopposed bombardment of Iraqi positions from medium altitudes" (meaning out-of-range for some systems) and, secondly, the use of 1950s/1970s technology that the "[A]mericans had studied these weapons well during the Arab wars and found an 'antidode' for them..."

The Soviet officers are reported to have concluded that the duration of such an intensive air operation is, in itself, evidence of a robust Iraqi air defense system, but one that was eventually overwhelmed through superior countermeasures and electronic warfare tactics.

"Approximately three support aircraft were required for each strike aircraft. If chaff dispensers aboard the aircraft failed to operate, the pilot was obliged to return to base[8]."

There is some evidence that Iraqi forces did monitor the radio channels used by allied airborne forward controllers to vector attack aircraft into "killing boxes." As was the case in Vietnam, the air forces were reluctant to change calls signs and frequencies and one official believes the Iraqis capitalized on "these lapses." In one reported example, the commander of a mobile Scud was heard by coalition monitors to radio his superior that he was pulling units because the "F-16s are coming after me[9]."

Counter C[3]

On the heels of the lightening blow against air defense came repeated missile and air strikes against the electrical power and telecommunications centers, disabling a highly centralized control network tying Iraqi forces deployed in Kuwait to the ultimate authority-source in Baghdad.

It is ironic that the Soviet Union—Iraq's prime mentor—was the first to advance the belief that the balance in war might be tipped by attacking the opponent's control structure. Drawing from the rich legacy of the Great Patriotic War, the Soviets developed a theory of information warfare, calling it Radio Electronic Combat. The objective of this doctrine was to degrade the enemy's control structure by at least 50 percent through combinations of physical destruction, electronic interference (jamming) and deception.

Coalition air forces easily met that goal and in some instances raised it to nearly 100 percent while adding a new factor: intimidation. Some Iraqi prisoners reported their fear of anti-radiation missiles was so great they refused to turn on electronic equipment, some reportedly convinced that even receiving equipment would act as a magnet for instant death[10].

While soldiers and airmen of the former Soviet Union are as deeply divided as are U.S. military experts over the decisiveness of air power versus ground operations in war, they do seem agreed that Iraq either lacked the tools or was unwilling or unable to use them to blunt the air attack. "Iraq's poor showing could be traced to its failure to procure [or employ] electronic counter-measures (ECM) and automated operational-strategic command-and-control gear[11]."

In assessing Iraqi air defenses, one Soviet military specialist is reported[12] to have written: "With raid sizes of tens, or even hundreds, it is impossible to allocate targets between divisions without automation...Absence of an automated control system alone reduced the Iraqi ADF firing capabilities by approximately forty percent."

Tower of Babel

Colonel Sepp Ramsperger was communications officer for the 2nd Marine Division when it overran Iraqi positions in Kuwait. He interviewed Iraqi officers and retrieved items of equipment and documents which help us to understand the abject failure of Iraqi forces to communicate.

Iraqi battalions brought 14 different kinds of radios to the battle and none of these could interoperate with one another. "One Iraqi battalion would have a British system, while an adjoining battalion would have a Russian system." Colonel Ramsperger concludes from his battlefield observations that the idea of a common radio frequency is alien to the Iraqi army. He opines that—following the Soviet model—they are not supposed to talk to one another.

Col. Ramsperger unrolled the chart he had liberated in Kuwait, showing the communications plan for the Iraqi 14th Infantry Battalion. This communications net diagram was a classic star net with eleven pairs of radios, but, operating on *eleven different radio frequencies*. The Colonel contrasted this network to the configuration employed by a comparable U.S. Marine Corps unit, where commanders share the same frequency and communications can flow up, down and laterally. He said it revealed the difference between a dictatorship and a team.

Pointing to an Iraqi unit on the flank in the signals diagram, Col. Ramsperger noted that only the battalion commander would know of an attack on that unit. He said this isolation was confirmed to him during an interview with an Iraqi brigade commander who said he was "surprised at the speed with which we arrived. He had no idea we were coming, even though the unit right adjacent to him had been attacked two hours before."

Why would the Iraqis employ so perverse a system? The reason is obvious to Col. Ramsparger: "It allows the commander to control information, which means he can control the panic button."

When briefed on this incident, Chicago Tribune military affairs writer David Evans saw "the severe control over vital information in the Iraqi army is a metaphor for the regime in Baghdad. Saddam Hussein's power is based on control of the panic button too."

EMCON Suicide

A senior Iraqi officer in charge of communications at division level confirmed that rigid controls were placed on the sending of any message traffic. U.S. troops refer to this kind of administrative shackle over communications as EMCON (emission control), leading one soldier to wryly comment that the "enemy committed EMCON suicide."

Iraqi EMCON was effective, so much so that the coalition's tactical signals collectors—normally a highly valued source of intelligence at the brigade/battalion level— found little of interest as they searched vainly through the airwaves for signs of enemy activity.

But here as well, the scenario of Desert Shield clouds that picture too because considerations for operational security (OPSEC) held U.S. and allied forces—along with their tactical collectors—well back (up to 60 kilometers) from the border, thus lessening the chance they would hear low-power emissions from Iraqi front line organizations.

Deterrent to Jamming

But why did Iraq not at least employ the principals of Soviet REC doctrine against our highly vulnerable UHF satellite systems? U.S. commanders readily concede that lack of alternative modes made it necessary to rely so heavily on UHF satellite communications as to almost saturate that system. The Navy FLTSATCOM and its piggy-backed Air Force SATCOM system could have been severely disrupted, if not silenced, through simple and inexpensive technology known to be in the hands of Iraqi forces. Intelligence sources report discovering four Soviet-made UHF jammers that could generate from 1 to 2.5 kW—more than enough to close down the links that carried, for example, 95 percent of wartime traffic to and from the U.S. Navy.

A senior official on the Joint Staff suggests that the jamming threat to satellites may have been overstated in the past and he notes that the Soviet Union withheld a similar ability to disrupt U.S. strategic communications satellites during the Vietnam War. Further, he continues, there have been many instances since when the Soviet Union (or any nation or individual with a technically simple jammer) might have thwarted or severely disrupted U.S. military expeditions with a low-risk, even surreptitious, electronic attack on the up-links to our unprotected satellites.

Airpower advocates have long belittled the threat of tactical jamming, contending that enemy emitters will be quickly and easily silenced by direct attack. Desert Storm provided the opportunity for them to make their point. Iraqi forces quickly learned the near-instant and lethal consequences of switching on high power emitters in the face of an enemy swarming overhead with anti-radiation missiles. It is now possible to drape such a thick blanket of silent and unseeable anti-radiation cruise missiles over the battlefield that any emitter can be silenced before it can perform a useful function.

Perhaps satellite communications may not be as vulnerable to intentional interference as they might have been before electronic warfare came of age and before most international intercourse came to be conducted through space-based systems: each a powerful deterrent.

The Gulf War convinced DoD officials that there is at least a strategic role in warfare for commercial communications satellite systems and post-war planning now includes mobile earth terminals that will enable U.S. military forces to access both commercial and military satellites in the K_u and C bands.

Buried Channels

Iraq was well aware of the hazards of electronic warfare and—using the Soviet model as a guide—they had trenched telephone cables and fiber optics down to at least division level.

While buried cables are hard to locate and even more difficult to interdict by aerial bombardment, they also are inflexible, useful for a static defense and not much else. Coalition forces hoped that the relentless aerial attacks would force Iraqi ground units out of their holes and into the open, forcing them to resort to radio systems to maintain troop control. That did not happen. They remained fixed and Iraq was reported still able to maintain limited connectivity through buried telephone cables and fiber optics, although U.S. armored forces reported instances where their rapidly moving tracked vehicles had cut Iraqi telephone and other signal lines to front line forces.

Electronic and Stealth Warfare Proven

Israel provided what should have been a forewarning of the devastating power of electronic warfare when they eliminated the Syrian air force in the Bakka Valley. Electronic warfare—or electronic *combat* as the U.S. Air Force prefers—came of age in the Persian Gulf, but is already fighting a new battle for survival in the fierce struggle over declining defense budgets.

The U.S. Air Force has reportedly rethought its pre-war decision to eliminate the F-4G Wild Weasel, a mainstay in its electronic warfare arsenal, although Senator Nunn now asks why the U.S. Navy cannot perform that function for all.

Some analysts are disappointed that the final report from the defense department to the congress provided no conclusive evidence as to the effectiveness of stealth technology versus active countermeasures: These two expensive technologies go head-to-head in every budget battle. Whatever the mixture of hard and soft kills employed—and the very mixture frustrates hard conclusions—the effectivenss of counter-C^3 should no longer be debatable.

There can be no doubt that the suppression and destruction of a large and sophisticated air defense system purchased early air superiority. That, in turn, enabled the sustained aerial bombardment that "prepared (an airman said *destroyed*) the battlefield" for the coalition ground forces, demoralized the Iraqi army and enabled the ground operation to advance its timetable and attain quick victory.

Endnotes

[1] Gen. Lt. A. I. Malyukov, Chief of Staff of the Soviet Air Forces, "blamed Iraq's defeat directly on Saddam's inability to conceptualize warfare in terms other than his Iran-Iraq War experience, where airpower had minimal impact on ground operations." Gen. Lt. Sergei Bogdanov cited "the passivity and indecision of the top Iraqi leadership and the poor training of the command personnel" as decisive factors. For details of Soviet reaction to the Persian Gulf War see "Soviet View of the Storm," by Capt. Brian Collins, USAF, *Air Force Magazine*, July 1992.

[2] "Iraqi Army's Defeat in Kuwait," James W. Pardew, Jr., *Parameters*, Winter 1991/92.

[3] Joint Warfare of the US Armed Forces, Joint Pub 1, 11 November 1991, p. 57.

[4] Iraqi Air Defenses—Initial Soviet Post—Mortem, William A. Burhans (Russ-Eng Translations), *Journal of Electronic Defense*, October 1991.

[5] Of the 35 first-day targets in Baghdad, 29 were command centers, headquarters complexes and telephone and electrical switching centers. See page 9, *Airpower in the Gulf*, James P. Coyne, pub. Air Force Association, 1992.

[6] Ibid.

[7] "Secret Carbon-Fiber Warheads Blinded Iraqi Air Defenses," David A. Fulghum, *Aviation Week & Space Technology*, April 27, 1992.

[8] Ibid. and Falichev, O., "'Shilka' versus the B-52," *Krasnaya zvezda [Red Star]*, April 3, 1991. Interviews with allied pilots confirm that the availability of defense suppression was often a "go/no go" decision. The actual mix of strike and electronic warfare assets and how they were employed on a typical naval air mission are described in *The Electronic Sanctuary*, P. 47..

[9] U.S. Searches for Electronic Equipment Used by Iraqis to Foil Allied Attacks, *Aviation Week & Space Technology*, March 18, 1991.

[10] Interview with Col. S. D. Ramsperger, USMC, II Marine Expeditionary Force.

[11] "Soviet View of the Storm," Capt. Brian Collins, USAF, *Air Force Magazine*, July 1992.

[12] Ibid.

Readers are referred to the article entitled "Ears of the Storm," (p. 65) for additional information on Iraqi electronic capabilities and counterair tactics.

EPILOGUE

"When large bodies of armed men are assembled and expected to act in concert, the part played by communications cannot be overestimated." [1]

Reasonable people will differ over the future mission, size and structure of U.S. armed forces, but there should be no disagreement about the need to equip any force with the most modern information systems. Whether the mission is pursuing drugs, or waging peace in a disorderly new world or fighting another war of "calculated and discriminating violence," [2] armed forces of the United States will confront opponents outfitted with the best information technology available in the international marketplace. What Dr. Tom Rona wrote in 1976 is every bit as true today and into the future: "...dependence on technology inevitably creates vulnerabilities that an intelligent enemy will not be slow to exploit. The opportunities for doing so, moreover, increase rather than diminish with the complexity of the technology in use."

What matters most now is that we seek out and correctly interpret the key factors that enabled the remarkable and unprecedented military operations in the Persian Gulf and determine their relevance to other missions, places, times and circumstances.

Experts caution that Desert Storm is no "blueprint" for future wars. Perhaps, but that should not obscure the fact that between August 1990 and February 1991 highly skilled information specialists diagnosed and solved multifarious technical problems, bringing together many dissimilar information systems in joint operations. To examine the challenges they faced and the solutions they found is to gain invaluable insights into future requirements.

The search will not be easy. Desert Storm yields no simple, incontestable answers. Incontrovertible explanations for the swift victory range from use of overwhelming force, to sophisticated technology, to low morale, incompetency, and loss of troop control by Iraqi leadership. Partisan politics and the intense competition for diminishing defense resources further cloud the quest. Yet, *answers* abound and they are already driving irrevocable decisions, at home and abroad.

Information—The Defining Factor

The superior management of information should stand high in every list of enabling factors. Without the *information differential*, little else would have mattered. U.S. forces were endowed with both the *time* and the *talent* to construct an information structure that enabled almost flawless execution of its war plan. But time and talent are precious and ephemeral commodities: the one a unique function of circumstance, the other too quickly enervated by shortsighted decisions over resource allocation[3].

A few vivid vignettes from the Gulf War may provide useful beacons and warnings to those who are planning the next generation of information system:

• *Skilled troops and sophisticated weapons—otherwise combat-ready—idled at ports and airstrips, awaiting arrival of heavy and bulky communications vans that, when assembled, could scarce keep up with the fast-moving commanders.*

• *Communications networks humming at near-perfection and yet failing to meet many of the customer's inflated—but now essential—expectations, because they were geared for the voice and message world and could not transport imagery data.*

• *Warriors impatiently waiting in command posts for images or firing solutions that had been readily provided them during peacetime exercises, but were now missing, delayed or lacking in requisite precision.*

• *Targets missed or attacked unnecessarily because the cycle for battle damage assessment (BDA) functioned at a different tempo from the cycles for weapons targeting and execution: too fast for some, too slow for others.*

• *Vital intelligence garnered, fuzed and correlated through sophisticated technology, but belatedly delivered—often in leather pouches—because electronic packets were unavailable.*

Fight on Arrival.

DoD's information systems chief, Paul Strassmann, believes that the defense enterprise cannot succeed unless combat forces arrive on the battlefield prepared to fight. Joint Chief's Chairman General Colin Powell has reportedly given the troops 3 days to muster for the next conflict.

Future warriors must arrive in their area of responsibility (AOR) with a "basic load" of communications as well as munitions. This is no longer an unreasonable challenge. The technical means will soon exist to blanket any combat theater in the world with an information system that integrates the disparate, dedicated networks now separately supporting intelligence, decision-making, command and control, fire support, strike planning and execution.

This incipient information environment already has a name: Vice Admiral Mackey christened it the *Infosphere*[4]. The U.S. Navy has termed it *interlocking information grids*[5]. The Infosphere will bear no resemblence to the information systems seen in Desert Shield/Storm. The terrestrial segments (if there are any) will be limited to equipments carried on the person, in the kit, or, at least, within the command vehicles. No more frantic scrambling over the battlefield, dragging bulky components in fruitless pursuit of more agile customers.

The global, integrated, multi-media, demand-assigned information network will be air- and space-based: repeaters, translators and buffers lofted—but no higher than necessary—by remotely piloted vehicles, high-flying gliders, and low Earth orbit and geo-synchronous satellites.

There will be a small, dedicated segment from military development, but commercial equipment will dominate, because it is cheaper, more capable, and it will be available. Further, civil technology will satisfy most needs because globe-hopping executives will demand no less responsiveness from their information systems than do their military counterparts.

Unity of Management

Unity of command is essential to military operations and *unity of management* will be no less vital to assure smooth operations of the Infosphere. Networks to provide users with global, high-quality, end-to-end, terminal-to-terminal connectivity will necessarily be composed of an unpredictable, constantly shifting agglomerate of commercial, foreign military and U.S. government systems that must be integrated and managed as one system. That is unfit work for amateurs or for parochial interests having visibility over only limited segments of those networks.

This prime management role must be shared between the joint commander's J-6 and the Defense Information Systems Agency, both of whom absolutely depend upon the uniformed military services for people with technical expertise and operational experience. However, military information systems specialists could quickly become an extinct species if their role is misunderstood and unprotected.

Inflated Expectations

Customers expect too much from their communications and intelligence services in war. Their inflated expectations are understandable: users have been duped, misled by near-perfect support routinely delivered during training and exercises. They are not the first to be so deceived.[6]

U.S. combat forces have come to believe that such high levels of continuous intelligence and communications services are both necessary and feasible: that somebody—who is not clear—will bring peacetime levels of support to the battlefield.

Technologies are available to gain significant increases in throughput of new information systems, but capacity has historically trailed demands, and that is not likely to change. Unless and until it does, large-scale, real-time simulations during exercises provide the opportunity for commanders to experience and react to the impact of varying levels of communications and intelligence support.

More For Less

Desert Storm revealed how information systems can produce more combat power for less money; a notion that should appeal to Congress but that is strangely absent in the House Armed Services Committee assessment of Persian Gulf War[7].

Air-delivered weapons (helicopters, missiles and aircraft), delivered with astonishing accuracies, accounted for over half of the kills and suggest that the Army term *battlefield preparation* should now be changed to *battlefield destruction*.

Some see this as a harbinger of future; that is, battlefields where tactical missiles and smart bombs will be the primary agent of destruction, leaving ground forces to mop up and occupy territory. The potential impact on future force structure from leveraging of information warrants far more attention than it has received to date.

As one expert writes[8]: "The synergistic effect of the lethality and precision of these weapons and the real-time sensor and information fusion systems employed, indicates another evolution in the air dimension of the battlefield. A lethality system appears to exist that can provide continuous, instant, almost 100 percent probability of kill for anything that moves.

Perhaps the *First Information War* is more of a blueprint than first thought.

Endnotes

[1] Van Creveld, Martin, in *Technology and War*. p. 38.

[2] *From Space and Electronic Warfare: A Navy Policy Paper on a New Warfare Area*, date June 1992.

[3] AFCEA's President General John A. Wickham, Jr., commented that it was all too easy to disassemble a military capability just because its function was not understood.

[4] Vice Admiral Mackey, Director C^4, Joint Staff, remarks at AFCEA International Convention, June 1992.

[5] *Space and Electronic Warfare: A Navy Policy Paper on a New Warfare Area*, June 1992, OP-094.

[6] Barbara Tuchman wrote about similar problems experienced by the Germans in World War I: "This was one of the 'frictions' the German General Staff, misled by the ease of communications in war games, had not planned for." *The Guns of August*, Crown Publishers, 1982.

[7] *Defense for a New Era: Lessons of the Persian Gulf War*, House Armed Services Committee, March 30, 1992. Beyond a brief carping about interoperability—one area where the U.S. military has made significant gains—the report is silent on the role of information systems and the potential impact on force structure.

[8] All-Seeing, All-Killing Air Dimension and Army's Force Projection Dilemma," Lt. Col Thomas R. Rozman, USA, February 1992 issue of *ARMY*. The author further writes, "If the air dimension offers such a precise and invincible destruction system, especially if developed as an integrated AirLand Operations system, then perhaps it is possible that based on such precision, tomorrow's force might be able to reduce the weapons requirement for combat loads and resupply. This reduction might free quantities of another critical part of the AirLand Operations force envisioned, that being strategic and sea transport to 'project' forces....If advances in sensor and information processing, packaging and transmitting, weapon lethality and precision guidance continue to move ahead, even a ten percent improvement over what was achieved in the early months of 1991 probably means a magnitude of destruction that is logarithmically greater."

INDEX

References

"A Look at the Air Tasking Order," John H. Cushman, *Proceedings*, October 1991.

After Action Report—JTF Proven Force Frequency Management, (January 17 - February 19, 1991, March 6, 1991, ECJ6-PF-B.

After Action Report, Operation Desert Shield Frequency Management (Sept 30 - December 5, 1990), Department of Army.

After Action Reviews, series published by the Army Times, 1991-1992.

Airpower in the Gulf, An Air Force Association Book, 1992.

"Army Spectrum Management." Army Briefing to the Senior Level Spectrum Management Conference, Annapolis, MD., January 22, 1992.

"Battle of the Airwaves," Commander William J. Luti, USN, *Proceedings*, January 1992.

"Commercial Communications in Support of Operation Desert Shield," William B. Belford, National Coordinating Center for Telecommunications, National Communications System.

Communications Support for Desert Shield, Desert Storm, Proven Force, and Provide Comfort, August 26, 1991, USEUCOM J-6, draft.

Conduct of the Persian Gulf War: An Interim Report to Congress, Department of Defense, July 1991.

Conduct of the Persian Gulf War: Final Report To Congress, Department of Defense, April 1992

C⁴ Chronology. Desert Shield/Storm Support Office, ODISC4, Department of the Army. July 1991.

DCA Grey Beards Lessons Learned: Desert Shield/Desert Storm, MITRE, August 1991.

Defense For A New Era: Lessons of the Persian Gulf War. U.S. House of Representatives, Committee on Armed Services, Washington D.C., March 30, 1992. U.S. Government Printing Office. (Also known as the Aspin-Dickinson Report).

Desert Shield/Storm, A New Era in Warfare Technology, Ronald D. Elliott, March 10, 1991, INCA Project Office.

Desert Shield/Desert Storm Communications, CENTCOM J-6, a briefing. Not published.

"Desert Storm: A Perspective of Navy Air Contributions," RADM Riley D. Mixon, USN, *The Hook*, Winter 1991.

Desert Storm C⁴I Panel, AFCEA's 45th International Convention, June 4, 1991.

"Desert Storm Ground Force Support System," Dr. Stu Milner, Army Intelligence Agency. A briefing.

"Desert Victory: The War for Kuwait," Norman Friedman, *Naval Institute Press*, 1991.

"Electronic Warfare Played Greater Role In Desert Storm Than Any Conflict," Bruce D. Nordwall, *Aviation Week & Space Technology*, April 22, 1991.

"From Vietnam to Desert Storm," John D. Morrocco, *Air Force Magazine*, January 1992.

HOTLINE, The Air Force C4 Journal, Spring 1991.

IEEE Communications Magazine, January 1992.

"Iraqi Air Defenses—Initial Soviet Post-Mortem," Williams A. Burhans (Russ-Eng Translations, *Journal of Electronic Defense*, October 1991.

"Iraqi Armys Defeat in Kuwait," James W. Pardew, Jr., *Parameters*, Winger 1991-92.

"Iraqi Brass Rendered Troops Deaf During War," David Evans, *Chicago Tribune*. Reprinted in *Daily News*, Jacksonville, North Carolina, July 21, 1991.

Joint Publication 1, *Joint Warfare of the US Armed Forces*, November 11, 1991. National Defense University Press.

"Making Interoperability Work," Lieutenant Dennis Palzkill, USN, *Proceedings*, September 1991.

Operation Desert Storm, The Military Intelligence Story: A View From the G-2, 3d Army, Brig. Gen. John F. Stewart, Jr., U.S. Army, G-2, 3d U.S. Army, April 1991.

Operation Provide Comfort: A Communications Perspective, March 3, 1992, a draft report. Headquarters European Command.

"Soviet View of the Storm," Capt. Brian Collins, USAF, *Air Force Magazine*, July 1992.

Space and Electronic Warfare, A Navy Policy Paper on a New Warfare Area,OP-094), June 1992.

"The Air Campaign," Norman Friedman, *Proceedings*, April 1991.

"The Shield and the Storm: Naval and Marine Corps Aviation in the Gulf War," The Association of Naval Aviation, 1991.

The Ultimate High Ground! Newletter No. 91-3, dated October 1991, Center for Army Lessons Learned (CALL), U.S. Army Combined Arms Command (CAC), Fort Leavenworth, Kansas.

The U.S. Army in Operation Desert Storm: An Overview, June 1991, Association of The United States Army.

I MEF Communications Chronology for Operations Desert Shield and Desert Storm, 15 June 1991. I Marine Expeditionary Force, FMF, Camp Pendleton, California.

2D Marine Division G-6 After Action Report. Not published.

"USAF Officials Explain How War Altered Joint-STARS Requirements," William B. Scott and Beverly Hills, *Aviation Week & Space Technology*, October 14, 1991.

About the Authors

Rear Admiral Sir Peter Anson, Bt., CB., C Eng., FIEE, (Ret), is currently Chairman, Matra Marconi Space UK Limited.

Captain James M. Burin, USN, is currently assigned as Director, Space and Electronic Combat Division, OPNAV. During the Persian Gulf War he was the Air Wing Commander of CVW-5 aboard USS *Midway*. He has over 5,700 hours and 1,400 arrestor landings in the A6 aircraft. He was the mission commander and fired the HARM from an EA-6B in the strike described in the article titled *The Electronic Sanctuary*.

Colonel Alan D. Campen, USAF (Ret.), is Manager of AFCEA International Press. He was Director, Command and Control Policy, Office of the Undersecretary of Defense for Policy from 1982-1985 and Vice President C³I, The BDM Corp.

Major General James R. Clapper Jr., USAF, was Director, Defense Intelligence Agency and former assistant chief of staff, intelligence, headquarters U.S. Air Force.

Group Captain Dennis Cummings, C Eng., FIEE, RAF, (Ret), is currently Company Marketing Manager with Matra Marconi Space UK.

Major Tim Gibson, USA, is assigned at the Joint Command Information Systems with the U.S. Forces-Korea. He collected the information used in this article as the Chief, AC2IS, during Operations Desert Shield and Desert Storm. He holds a B.S. from the U.S. Military Academy and an M.S. in Computer Science from the University of Kansas.

Robert S. Hopkins III is a former Air Force officer who flew Rivet Joint combat missions during Operation Desert Storm. He teaches history at Creighton University, Omaha, Nebraska.

Colonel Randolph W. House, USA, is the commander 2d Brigade, 1st Cavalry Division. A graduate of Texas A&M University, he has served as an infantry company commander; commander, 1st Battalion, 61st Infantry; G3 of the 5th Infantry Division (Mechanized); and executive assistant to the Joint Staff.

Major General John Paul Hyde, USAF (Ret.), was the Deputy Chief of Staff for Communications and Electronics at Headquarters TAC from 1977 to 1980 when CAFMS was born. He is now a Senior Principal at BDM International, Inc.

Captain Gregory L. Johnson, USA, is the S3 plans officer, 2d Brigade, 1st Cavalry Division. A graduate of the U.S. Military Academy, he has served in three mechanized infantry battalions and was a company commander in 1st Battalion, 16th Infantry, 1st Infantry Division (Forward).

Donald L. Jones has been assigned to the Joint Staff (J6K) by the National Security Agency, and he chairs the Joint Working Group on the JCEOI.

Technical Sergeant Toby C. Logan, USAF, has been working with CAFMS since 1987, while assigned to the 727th Tactical Control Squadron-Test and the 1912th Computer Systems Group. He deployed to Saudi Arabia, Spain and Turkey to support CAFMS.

Major General Paul E. Menoher, Jr., USA, is Commanding General, U.S. Army Intelligence Center/Commandant, U.S. Army Intelligence School.

Lieutenant Colonel Johann W. Pfeiffer, USAF (Ret.) was, successively, the Chief of Communications and Computer Operations, Chief of Combat Operations, and Director of Operations for the 507th TACCS from July 1987 to July 1992. He took CAFMS to war in the Gulf from 13 August 1990 to 30 March 1991.

Major Merrill L. Pierce, Jr., USMC, is head, programs unit, information resources management branch, command, control, communications, computers, intelligence and interoperability department, Headquarters, U.S. Marine Corps.

Richard C. Randt is a former Signal Corps officer and is a Principal Technical Advisor at the National Security Agency. He is the NSA representative to the JCEOI Working Group.

Major Jean Marie Slupik, USA, is assigned to the Defense Information Systems Agency. During Desert Shield/Storm she was Chief of the Crisis Action Team at DISA and, in September 1991, deployed to CENTCOM Headquarters in Saudi Arabia as a member of the DISA Forward Deployed Element.

Lieutenant General Harry E. Soyster, USA, is a former director, Defense Intelligence Agency.

Major General Thomas S. Swalm, USAF, (Ret.), is Vice President of Business Development at Grumman Melbourne Systems Division.

Lieutenant Colonel Earl S. Takeguchi, USA, is Deputy Spectrum Manager, Department of the Army. He was Team Leader with ARCENT and the U.S. Central Command in Saudi Arabia, assisting in development of spectrum management policies and procedures.

Joseph S. Toma is chief of the J-6 Special Actions Division of the Joint Staff. He holds a B.Sc. degree in aeronautical engineering and an M.A. degree in international relations. He is a graduate of the Air Command and Staff College and the Naval War College.

Larry K. Wentz is Technical Director of the National Command and Control Systems Division, The MITRE Corporation. He was co-chairman of the DCA "Grey Beard" Team for Desert Shield and Desert Storm.

Major Wayne M. White, USA, was S3 of the 141st Signal Battalion from April 1990 to June 1991 and Assistant Division Signal Officer, 1st Armored Division from September 1989 to March 1990.

William J. Wooley is Chief of the Frequency Management Branch, 5th Signal Command, U.S. Army, Worms, Germany.